# Keeping Our History Alive

## The Old and the New
## of Tucson and Arizona

*Enjoy reading my book*
*Opha R Probasco*

# Keeping Our History Alive

## The Old and the New
## of Tucson and Arizona

**Opha R. Probasco**

Probasco Press          Tucson, Arizona

Prepared for printing by
Ghost River Images
5350 East Fourth Street
Tucson, Arizona  85711
www.ghostriverimages.com

Cover photo by Opha Probasco

Manuscript typed by Kristina Saporito,
with many thanks

ISBN 0-9772561-0-3

Library of Congress Control Number: 2005932683

Printed in the United States of America

First Printing: September, 2005

10 9 8 7 6 5 4 3 2 1

# Contents

I am dedicating this book to my step daughter Sandra Dunaway Wellner and her children Curtis Dunaway and Tammy Dunaway Laursen.

Sandra

Tammy

Curtis

I'd like to acknowledge the following authors of some of the books that I have read on the history of Tucson and Arizona. The history on both is fascinating.

Some of the history I will be telling you about will be from the time I came to Tucson in 1925 when I was six years old and through the year to date, and back into the eighteen hundreds.

Opha R. Probasco

Some of the books and their authors that I have read and used for research are listed below:

| | |
|---|---|
| Jay Wagoner | Arizona Heritage |
| Nell Murbarger | Ghost of the Adobe Walls |
| Thelma Heatwole | Ghost Towns and Historical Haunts in Arizona |
| Charles D. Lauer | Tales of Arizona Territory (Old West) |
| Odie B. Faulk | Arizona (A short history) |
| Marshall Trimble | Roadside History of Arizona (one of many books) |
| C.L. Sonnichsen | Tucson (the life and times of an American city) |
| Bernice Cosulich | Tucson |
| William D. Kalt 3D | Southern Arizona's Tragic Train Wreck of 1903 |
| William B. Barker | The Yaqui Revolt of 1926 |
| Mark E. Miller | Yaquis become American Indians |
| Donald T. Garate | Who named Arizona in the Journal of Arizona |

# INTRODUCTION

In a lot of the old movies it showed men playing poker. This is a myth. In the eighteen hundreds they didn't play poker–they were too illiterate–they played Faro.

History is many times just a rumor we choose to believe or a myth we all agree upon.

When we left Sterling, Colorado in 1925 for Tucson, Arizona we never knew what the town was like how big it was or anything. Some people remarked that they heard that the Indians were still wild and mean. Tucson was a dirty town, it was far from being a city that came much later. The streets had a lot of dirt on them and papers were flying every where, when a dust devil went through. People's eyes were filled with dust particles. The street cleaners were men with push carts, a push broom, and shovel. The paved streets were right in town with alleys and surrounding streets of dirt. There were still some hitching posts in town. We rode the street cars before they shut it down.

The old cemetery on the west side of Stone Avenue down town was still being moved to the Evergreen Cemetery.

When we moved to South Mission Road and Ajo Road in 1926 we lived in a tent with a wood floor and wooden sides that came up about five feet for a year while dad built a house. My younger sister and I had the mumps during that time.

# CIVILIAN CONSERVATION CORPS

The C.C.C. (Civilian Conservation Corps) was a great thing the U.S. Government had during the Depression days Boys from 16 years old and up joined. These young men had a place to eat, sleep, even if it was in tents it was shelter, plus they had medical attention if needed.

There was a C.C.C. Camp in the Madera (White House) Canyon. They worked on the roads, trails, build camps for the public, and many other things to improve the area.

There was also a C.C.C. Camp in the Sabino Canyon area. They built the roads, camp grounds, rest rooms, and many other improvements there also.

A boy that lived in our tourist court with his family named Eldon Baker was in the C.C.C. Camp in Sabino Canyon. Sunday was a rest day and the boys did whatever they wanted to do. There was a pit seven feet deep where they burned all of their trash. Eldon saw a magazine in the pit so jumped down to retrieve it, since he didn't see any flames he thought he was free and clear but he never thought of live coals being there, by the time they got him out of there the hot coals burned his shoes off of his feet and burned his feet pretty bad.

At a later date after his feet had healed up a few of the boys decided to go swimming there in the Sabino Creek, to Eldon's miss fortune he drowned. He was the first person to drown in the Sabino Canyon Creek.

There is no connection between Sabino Canyon and Tanque Verde Falls. The water from the Catalina's runs into the Sabino Canyon and the water in the Tanque Verde Falls come from the Rincon's.

Seems like when you lease expect it an obstacle shows up in your life that hasn't be taken care of. Like after I completely written my book long hand then typed it using the two finger process, I turned it over to Mr. Michael White of Ghost River Images to finalize the rest.

Mr. Michael White tried to scan the typed pages with no success. He called me to let me know that my whole book had to be retyped. What a let down! But, I was so lucky to have such a dear friend Kristina Saporito, who took on the project and retyped the whole book. She's a very bright young lady and a wonderful person to help me make this book a success.

Kristina

14

Giving a talk at the Drexel Heights Fire District awards dinner

# ACKNOWLEGEMENTS

It was in November of 2003 that Maria Hawkes, of the Drexel Heights Fire Department asked me if I would give a talk at their anniversary Award's Dinner. That night came and it was a night to be remembered. The feed back from everyone told me that they enjoyed the talk. Since then Tracy Koslowski every once in awhile would ask me why I don't write a book. I told her I didn't know how. She said all you have to do is to just write. She kept the pressure up and around Christmas time I finally told her that I would. It's been a long hard road, but I got a lot of encouragement from Tracy Koslowski, Lori Dunham, Stacy Contreras and Maria Hawkes. May 12, 2005 I finished writing and called Tracy. She was just as happy as I was being the next day was my birthday the 13th, I thought that was pretty good present. Plus the bunch from the Drexel Heights took me out to lunch for a little celebration. If it wasn't for Tracy this book would have never been written, she is a very fine and smart young lady.

L - R, Maria Hawkes, Tracy Koslowski, Stacy Contreras with the Drexel Heights Fire District

All of the personnel of the Drexel Height's Fire District form Chief Douglas Chappell on down are the finest bunch of professionals you would find anywhere. I am proud to say I know them all.

Patty Pruitt with the Drexel Heights Fire District

Douglas Chappell, Drexel Heights Fire Chief and Tracy
Koslowski, Educational Department

L - R, Abraham Figueroa, Tim Shaw, Captain Hugh
McCrystal and Dave Shafer with the Drexel Heights Fire
District Station #3, Shift A

L - R, Captain Joe Bojarski, Hector Muñoz, Henry Molina
and Mark Cowan–Drexel Heights Fire Fighters and
Paramedics, on duty at the awards dinner

# PARENTS

Our father was born just south of Bloomfield, Iowa on a farm. There were nine boys and three girls in the family. The schools there just had grades through the fourth. Dad went to work for a couple of ladies that taught school at the university in Ottumwa. They were arithmetic teachers and they taught him for two years while he lived there and done all the chores. This helped him in his dealings through out his life.

My dad and his cousin left Iowa when he was sixteen in a spring board wagon. I don't know how many days it took but they wound up in Dead Wood, South Dakota. His cousin, Billy Horn worked for a lumber company and dad worked in a saloon cleaning out the place when it closed. He would sleep in the back storage room and when day light came he started in. He made out pretty good when he cleaned the spit toons, he would use a screen and dumped them all on it. After washing everything on the screen there would be a lot of coins where the men would drop coins and they would land in the spit toons and no one wanted to fish them out.

Dad learned the carpenter trade and after all his traveling he wound up on the plains in northern Colorado. The nearest town was Sterling and that was thirty two miles away. After building a few houses around there Mr. Rinehart asked dad if he would build a house for him that he had made enough money off of his wheat crop to pay for the expense. Dad told him if he had made that kind of money off his wheat crop that he would build his house and it would be the last house he would build for anyone. After that he started farming and built a large two story house with nine rooms.

L-R, Lake Mollohan, Cub Mollohan, Lillie Mollohan and Roy Mollohan, Opha Probasco's aunts and uncles next to Lake's soddie house on her homestead in Northeast Colorado. Homesteaded in 1908

Opha's father on one of his 32 horses in front of our home in 1924 in Washington County, Colorado. Homesteaded in 1908.

My mother, her dad, and family members, there were fourteen in all, went to Colorado on the train and settled in north eastern plains where dad was. There were a few Soddie houses built around that area right after they filed for homestead rights. I have a picture of my aunt's Soddie house they dug down about two feet to the size of their house was going to be, then plow up the sod about four inches thick and built the side out of that. A roof made out of sod was put on the top of the walls.

On Saturday night before mom married dad he would tie his fiddle on the back of his saddle and ride seventeen miles into a small town called Fleming to play at a dance. This is where dad met my mother and they were married in 1912.

Opha Probasco's parents, Roy and Allie Probasco on their
wedding day, November 15, 1912

My oldest sister was born in 1914 her name was Macel,
next was Wyvonna born in 1917, then came my twin

brother Okey and myself. Our youngest sister Bonnie was born in 1921. By the time my brother and I was born dad had already built his home. We had the only house in that area that had indoor plumbing. We had a big furnace in the basement and along the side was a bunch of batteries that went with the Delco light system that was in the house.

L-R,Wyvonna Probasco Mahan, Bonnie Probasco De Vos and Macel Probasco Brothers (children of Roy and Allie Probasco) Picture taken 1993

L-R, Okey and Opha Probasco (twins) in 1993

After working in the fields with all the dust everyday dad came down with Tuberculosis and both lungs were half gone. Doctor Latta told dad to go to Tucson, Arizona and not Phoenix for there was too much humidity there. Just sit out in the sun and see if the dry air will cure the T.B. This is what he done, he went to Tucson given two months to live and he died at the age of 84. We arrived in Tucson in 1925 and stayed in Verch's tourist camp called "Stumble Inn". This was in November and in February dad took us to the second rodeo Tucson had. While we were there dad looked around and bought eighty acres on the southwest corner of Mission and Ajo roads. He tried to buy the corner just north of his but the government wouldn't sell it because it had to be left open for the Indians on the Sell's Reservation to drive their cattle to market.

Grandpa Curtis Mollohan (standing) and Ward Mollohan (his son) on a four horse disk. Picture taken about 1910. Grandpa homesteaded in 1908.

In 1927 two of dad's brothers came out and helped him build some cabins, a store, toilets and a laundry room for the tourist court he was building. After this was done they built our two story home. Instead of using a tank heated by the stove he used a fifty gallon steel drum, painted it black, and fixed a wooden box with cradle inside to set the drum on. He put about eight inches of saw dust in the bottom with glass around the drum. Being air tight the sun heated our water. It was a solar system. A fairly large building was built to enclose showers and the laundry room. The laundry room had a wood stove that a hot water tank was hooked up to, if you wanted hot water for a bath or to do laundry a fire had to be built in the stove. There was a shower and toilet on one side for the women and the same on the other side of the building for the men. The laundry room was in front. It was up to my brother and I to see that there was plenty of wood in the box for the stove to heat the water. Some of the people would wait till they saw smoke coming out of the chimney, then they would get in line to be next.

We had some wood piled up out side of the laundry room to be used for the stove inside. A few people driving by would see the wood and stop and ask dad if they could buy the wood. This gave dad the idea of selling wood. We had a large yard in back that was vacant so dad stopped some of the Indians that were going by on their way to Tucson to sell the wood they had on their wagons.

Probasco's Tourist Court in 1933 at the SW corner of Mission Road and West Ajo Road with cabins in the background

He told them that he would buy all the wood they could bring in. It wasn't long before about every wagon load of wood was going to dad's yard. The wood was all cut into four foot lengths so dad had to find someway to cut the wood. He finally found and old one cylinder stationary engine mounted on the front of a wagon with iron wheels.

Opha Probasco, Dan Gallagher and Okey Probasco next to our old wood saw in 1936

It had a thirty two inch circular saw blade on the back. There was a belt that ran between the engine and the saw blade. He bought this complete unit for a little of nothing. We used this saw unit for a number of years before dad bought another one. We sawed the wood up into different lengths for cook stoves, heater stoves, and fire places. We sold from two thousand to twenty five hundred cords of wood each winter. We did sell a lot of cook stove wood during the summer for that was all a lot of them had to cook with, some had coal-oil stoves. Dad bought a hundred rail road ties from the Southern Pacific Rail Road that had been used under the rails and had to be replaced. These ties were heavy and it was all my brother and I could do to lift some of the heavier ones. We would load twenty five of the ties on the bed of a truck and take them to the yard, then go back for another load. We would saw the ties up into foot lengths. After that we would sit down and chop the cut ties into kindling and sacked them in gunny sacks. We were five mile out of town and it took a long time to load and deliver the wood. My brother and I each had a truck and sometimes it was late getting back home after our deliveries.

Congress Hall Bar where the legislators held their meetings when the capital was in Tucson. After the prohibition in 1933, the name of the bar was changed to the Legal Tender and owned by Eddie Jacobs. This was on West Congress Street.

We bought the wood for $3.60 a cord delivered in the yard by the Indians and we would cut the wood and deliver it for $8.00 a cord. The kindling was 25 cents a sack. We also sacked the wood for the ones that wanted less than a half a cord and the charge for a sack was also $0.25 cents.

Times were tough during the depression and money was real scarce and if anyone had any they didn't want to turn it loose. During the summer us kids would go bare footed all summer and when we did go to town our shoes had holes in them and we wore out a lot of card board that was covering the holes. When school let out till it took up in the fall we (my brother and I) went all summer with out a hair cut. We looked like we needed a shearing job instead of a hair cut.

Dad finally went to town and done some bartering. Since the stores had to use fuel to heat the stores, dad traded wood for clothing at J.C. Penney and the White House department store. Later renamed Meyerson for whom the owners were. We also traded with the Sunshine Barber Shop for hair cuts. The University Cleaners on East Third Street just outside of the U of A gate we traded for cleaning. That sure did help our cause. After going all summer without hair cuts my brother and I looked like hippies and that was before the hippy age.

While the Indians were unloading their wagons the Squaws would sit on the seat of the wagon. After dad paid them, they would take off in a line heading for town. In the evening on West Broadway Street south side of the Plaza Park there was a wide part of the street where the Indians had room to park their wagons. They would wait till there were three or four then they would all take off together heading for the reservation. Sometimes it would be late when they left town and it would get dark and still have five miles to go. This was dangerous for automobiles. Lights on the cars then weren't near as good as they are today. You could be on top of one before you knew it. A friend of ours was killed by running into the rear of a wagon. None of them had lights and there wasn't a law saying they had to have one. One summer evening a thunder storm came up with the wind, blowing a gale and the lighting flashing all around us. It hit a telephone across the street from us twice within a couple of minutes, and they say that the lighting don't strike twice in a row. That's just another myth. It was about eight o'clock maybe nine but it wasn't late when a car pulled into dad's service station telling us that an Indian wagon had been hit by lighting. We went to where the wagon was and the lighting had killed the Indian man and one horse, the other horse was alright. Seems to me that we use to get more rain and thunder storms then we do now.

# POPULATION AND COUNTRY AROUND US

People would ask me what the country was like and how many people lived around us. When we moved to the eighty acres on the south west corner of Mission Road and Ajo Road there were nothing but desert. I'll list the names of the families from Mission Road to Three Points. We'll start at the reservation which was four miles south of us. The Indians didn't have any automobiles just wagons and horses or mules but mostly horses and some of them were pretty scrubby. The government wouldn't give them buggies for that was a luxury. Automobiles didn't show up on the reservation until in the late thirties. They lived in mud huts made of adobe without a foundation. Some of them would smooth the floors and take out any gravel and rocks that may be in the dirt on the floor. Then they would get prickly pear cactus, put them in a vat and mash the juice out of it. The juice would then be mixed with clean dirt and spread even all over the floor. After it dried they could sweep it with a broom. Most of the Indians had their own wells. The water table was so close to the surface that you didn't have to dig very deep to reach water. I will talk about the water table later on in another story.

Opha in front of Papago adobe house, 1940

We will go north on Mission Road to a mile south of Ajo Road on the west side. That would be where the Brother's family lived they moved there in 1922 from Oklahoma. My oldest sister married one of the boys named Alton Brothers. Then on the corner of Mission and Ajo Road was the Probasco family. South side of the Ajo Road about where Kinney Road is was two families. One was the Heller family that had about five or six children and the Butts family. The Hellers had a lot of goats that ran in the hills in the area. North on Kinney Road near the museum lived the Carithers. They had two children, farther west about where Ryan Air Field is was a chicken ranch owned by the Niles family. And a little farther west was a turkey ranch. On farther west was the McBride's

Ranch. This leads us to the Three Points area where the Robles Ranch is owned by Bernabe Robles. He had a nine year old grand daughter that was kidnapped in 1934. That will be in another story later on. About twenty mile south of Three Points was a couple of ranches owned by Levi Manning. One was Pozo Nuevo and the other one was the Palo Alto. Going east of Arivaca about twenty miles was another ranch that belonged to Levi Manning and now called the Kemper Ranch. This ranch and the other two that I mentioned above were sold to Kemper Marley in 1953 for $600,000.00 there were approximately two hundred sections (128,000 acres) of leased and deeded land. Howell Manning kept the Canoa Ranch. During the World War Two the Germans cut off the rubber supply for the allies. President Wilson ordered companies to set up Guayale facilities. Guayale is a shrub that yields latex, can be made into rubber. Joseph Kennedy Sr. and two partners formed the Intercontinental Rubber Company, which established the farm community of continental in 1916. The continental school was built the following year of 1917. The continental rubber company bought the northern half of the Canoa Spanish Land Grant from Levi Manning. They planted the G uayale shrub but it never was a success, the shrubs didn't produce any latex. After Levi Manning died Howell Manning one of Levi's two sons took over the operations of his dad's estate. Howell Manning later sold the southern half of the Canoa Land Grant to some developers that started the Green Valley Homes.

There will be other stories on the Spanish Land Grant that I will get into later.

# THE TRAIL DRIVE FROM
# SELL'S RESERVATION

The only transportation the Indians has was wagons and horses some had mules and not many looked like they had been fed good. And some looked like they were well cared for. I remember one family had a pair of Spanish Mules. They were well cared for and the prettiest mules you would ever see, the Spanish Mules were small about the size of a large donkey, but so much stronger and their hide was slick and shinny. I haven't seen any of the Spanish Mules in the last sixty years. I doubt if there is any left in the United States, Spain might have some. It was quiet a sight to see four to six wagons pulling into our yard at one time with wood for us. The wood we bought came from the San Xavier Mission Reservation. We did get a few loads of wood from the Sells Reservation for they didn't have the trees there to cut.

They did have a lot of cattle where the San Xavier didn't, they had the farms.

To get their cattle to market they had to drive them to Tucson. There for the government left the land open to the Indians as a right away. It took them about a week to make the drive from Sells to Tucson. In 1938 the Indians made their last drive and it was all horses and not cattle. Howell Manning and Bud Parker went in partnership to buy all the wild horses that the Indians could round up on the reservation. Howell Manning had some holding pens near Irvington on the east side of the river. They sold what they could from the pens and the rest was shipped to Los Angeles.

My brother (Okey) and our friend Ernest Mock each bought a horse that cost them $3.00. After they broke them to ride they decided to take a little trip for about a week. They tied their pots and pans with their bed roll on the back of their saddles and left one afternoon in the rain. They got as far as about where Ryan Air Field is now. Finding a high spot of ground is where they bedded down for the night. They didn't hobble the horses just stake them out. The next morning Ernest picked up the rope that was attached to his horse. These horses now were just broke to ride and still skittish something startled him and off he took. This rope went through Ernest's hands so fast that the palms were nothing but blisters. After catching the horse they packed and headed on. They came to a ranch and got Ernest's hands doctored up and went on to the western side of the Sierrita Mountains.

A rain came up one day and my brother was down in the gulley when a wall of water came down and caught him and the horse with full force. The water was carrying both of them down toward a fence and if they got into the fence it would be bad for the both of them. The water swept them under a Mesquite Tree. That's when Okey grabbed a limb, squeezed his legs around the horse and pulled them to the bank. He jumped off and held his horse against the bank until the water went down. That was a real close call.

Before they left Ernest's mother told the both of them to take a spoon full of baking soda once a day and it would help their stomach. They had for gotten about until one morning when they were making breakfast and mixing some dough for biscuits when he was putting the baking powder in the mixture he thought of what Ernest's mother had said. Okey called to Ernest and told him that this is what your mother told us to take. So the rest of their trip they took baking powder everyday instead of baking soda.

# CHARLIE MAYSE AND THE LEGEND OF JOHN Mc PHEE

Charlie Mayse's airplane that my sister Macel went up in
with Mayse in 1928

The most famous of the early Arizona Barn Storming
Pilots was Charlie Mayse and he would perform anytime
he had a crowd of people around. Charlie's life took a
turn when he crashed landed on a rancher's field near
Safford, Arizona. The rancher's daughter was one of the
curious spectators who gathered around the plane.

During the next few days while he was working on his plane, he also has done a little courting the engaged Lola Carter. When the plane was fixed and ready to fly again, he took Lola up, up and away, landing in El Paso, Texas. With her ears still ringing from the roar of the engine, he once more proposed and this time she accepted. The two took what was perhaps the first aerial honeymoon in history.

No history is complete without telling of Mesa's famous Yuletide story, some times known as the legend of John Mc Phee, "The Man Who Killed Santa Claus". It was in 1930 during the Christmas season and times were tough with the Great Depression that just began and the business men were looking for something to get the people's mind off of the bad times and spend a little of their money.

They usually had a parade but there wasn't any luster there. The local news paper editor, John Mc Phee had an idea and he explained lets have Santa drop into town from an airplane in a parachute. After landing he could give the kids candy and things. Mc Phee became a hero to the other merchants who knew crowds stimulate business and with the children looking forward to seeing Santa Claus jumping out of the airplane and dropping to the ground, this was still the start of aviation and parachuting made it a great idea. Well there's nothing perfect even an idea that seemed to be. The stunt man that Mc Phee got to play Santa got a little Christmas cheer early. He couldn't even get off the bar stool let alone bailing out of an airplane. Well Mc Phee had to think up some other idea. He borrowed a department store dummy, dressed it like Santa and announced to his supporters that the show will go on. The pilot would push the dummy out of the plane, pull his ripcord, and Santa would float down to earth.

Mc Phee would pick up the dummy, change into the suit and arrive as real Santa. The plan was "Flawless and Fool Proof".

The people came from miles around, gathering to watch the excitement of Santa jumping out of an airplane with a parachute. Children climbed upon roof tops for a better view and some parents held their children up as the distant drone of the plane's single engine became louder, and the plane was getting in sight. Suddenly the door opened and Santa jumped out. All eyes were on Santa dressed in his red suit as he started his free fall. Down, down, down Santa fell with the unopened parachute trailing behind him, cur-pop Santa hit the ground.

The stores were empty and the streets were deserted that afternoon except for a few merchants and bawling children standing in the state of shock and disbelief.

Editor Mc Phee left town for a few days in hopes things would be forgotten when he returned. However it never was, when he died nearly forty years later the fact was mentioned in his obituary. Mc Phee will always be remembered in Mesa by the old timers as "The Man Who Killed Santa Claus".

# THE FIRST ARMY AIR FIELD IN TUCSON

The army's flying circus used this field as part of a Liberty Bond Rally in 1919 and not long afterwards Mayor Parker was advised that Tucson had been chosen as the site of one of the thirty-two official army landing fields in the United States. In July 1919 land was acquired on South Sixth Avenue and Irvington Street for the first real Tucson aviation field, the cost of the land and improvements including a well with an eight inch pipe for $5,000.00.

In the late 20's when Davis Monthan was built the army moved out there. Charles Lindergh flew in for the dedication of the new field in September 23, 1927.

Barnstormer Charley Mayse moved in the old hanger where the army moved out. Standard Airlines later American Airlines began regular scheduled flight through Tucson in 1928. Airmail service began in October 15, 1930. The first transcontinental mail plane arrived. It was exactly seventy three year from the day that the first coach of the famed Jack-Ass mail reached Tucson.

The old Army hangar that the United States Army had built in 1919. After they moved to Davis Monthan, Charlie Mayse rented it. Since the early thirties the Tucson Rodeo Committee has stored their wagons, buggies and equipment in it

There were less than 300 miles of paved roads in the whole state of Arizona in 1930.

In the turn of the Nineteenth Century all the streets in town was till dirt. It was in 1911 when they started paving Stone Avenue. It was in 1935 when South Mission Road was paved. The county doesn't have any record of the paving so they are taking my word for it since we lived on the corner of Mission and Ajo. Ajo Road from Mission to Snider Hill was paved in 1938. From Snider Hill to the reservation was paved 1947. The state highways were 16 feet side, later they added another 8 feet to make it a 3 lane road. The center lane was for passing from both directions, it was just another suicide lane, the city didn't learn from mistakes made by others that would take brain power.

The Indian school was built in 1908 at Sixteen Avenue and Indian School Road, later the Indian School Road was change to Ajo Way.

It was in early thirties when the road was built to the tope of "A' Mountain (Sentinel Peak), part of that mountain belonged to the city and some of it belong to the county.

# OLD HIGHWAY 80

In 2004 the people on the east side that are living near the Old Vail Road were having trouble getting their mail delivered. The reason was that the roads were so bad that the mailman wouldn't make any deliveries. The people called everyone they could think of for some kind of help. The county wouldn't do anything saying that it was not a designated road. Most of the old Highway 80 is still there but not marked anywhere but at South Sixth and Old Vail Highway. This road runs along side of the Arizona Feeds on the north side. It runs south east and stops at South Fourth, farther out of town the road goes by Buck Fletcher's bar and the cattle pens. On out farther it goes by a steak house at Houghton Road. Farther south east there is a "Y" one road goes south to Sonoita and the old Highway 80 goes north to the foot hills of the Rincon Mountains, this road is still in use, when the road reaches the foot hills it turns and goes east to Benson.

I decided to see what I could do because I know the road real well. I know what the county will say since all signs are gone and have been for some time. When we came to Tucson all roads out of the city was all dirt.

I called the highway department and took this issue up with them. I explained to them that the road in question was the only road going to Tucson from the east and it was maintained at that time. They told me that they didn't care if it was the only road if the county didn't accept it as a road then they doesn't have to maintain it. They never kept records back then and have no proof one way or the other. They talk with a forked tongue and when it comes to money they will not do anything to help the people. It's the people's word against them and guess who will win.

# WELLS AROUND TUCSON

There were a lot of irrigation wells on the farms that were around Tucson. These wells were less than one hundred feet deep. And they all had eight inch pumps and delivered eight hundred gallons a minute. The reason that these wells were that shallow was that the water table was pretty close to the surface of the land. I will give you an example.

Across from where we lived was a large swimming pool. It held eight hundred and fifty thousand gallons of water when I got big enough I help clean the pool twice a week. We used steel bristle push brooms. Later I was a life guard for two years. By filling this pool twice a week and pumping fifty thousand gallons of water each day from the leakage and evaporation we were pumping at least two million gallon of water in the pool each week. Now to get to the well, the well was only ten feet to water and the well was only fifty feet deep. There were a lot of people that had their own wells and they would sell water to their neighbors. My sister and her husband bought water from their neighbors back in 1937. Some of these wells were only fifteen to twenty feet deep. In the eigh-

47

Opha                     Macel    Wyvonna

Mission Swimming Pool with Probasco's children
Pictures taken about 1929

teen hundreds people would dig their own wells and some would build sides up above the ground then they would use a windless to get their water. And some would just heave their well even with the top of the ground. When it rained there was a lot of trash, etc. that would wash into their well. That was the reason there was a lot of typhoid in Tucson. Many people died from this. After Tucson established the water company and piped the water to the houses this cut down on the typhoid. As the years passed by and people moved in using more water the water table dropped. A lot of wells went dry some lowered their wells and now the water table is down around two hundred and fifty feet deep. Years ago we had the best drinking water in the world. About like Li'L Abner's water.

I'll get back to the water table later when I write about the flour mills that were built in Tucson starting in the eighteen hundreds.

# US 80 HIGHWAY INTO TUCSON FROM THE EAST

The U.S. 80 entered Tucson from the east on the Old Vail Road where it ran along side of the Arizona Feeds at South Sixth Avenue and Old Vail Road. U.S. 80 went north on 6th Avenue to Five Points went left to South Stone Avenue through town on Stone to Drachman Street. Left on Drachman to Oracle Road. Right off of Drachman onto Oracle Road to Glen Street. Left on Glen to the railroad tracks, across tracks turn right and you were on U.S. 80 going west toward Casa Grande.

# FARMING AROUND TUCSON

North of Prince and Oracle Road you were in the Flowing Wells area. From there to the Rillito River was all farm land with very few buildings. There were a few dairies scattered about. They sold their milk to a butter factory on North Third Avenue, going east from the Flowing Wells area you got into the Amphitheater District. There was a lot of farming all through the area as far east to north to Alvernon. There was no farming on the east side or the west side of Tucson. The farming on the south side started on South Mission Road south of "A" Mountain. This was where "A" Mountain Dairy was. All of the farming was done on the west side of the Santa Cruz River all the way to the Indian reservation.

On West Drexel west of the river was the Midvale Farms. They had large feed lots plus a pecan orchard. Their farm ground ran to West Valencia. This farm was owned by the John Deere family. The niece of the John Deere family said she never was going to sell her land. After she passed away her estate then was sold creating the Midvale housing.

On the north side of Ajo Way west of the Santa Cruz River was the Kennison Farm. He had a large peach orchard besides a lot of farm ground where he planted various items such as sugar cane, feed one time. He planted a lot of potatoes and I help dig the potatoes and put them in a sack. I worked all afternoon and made a quarter plus a small sack of potatoes. Depression was here so I was lucky to get the quarter. Since I was only ten years old.

# TRANSPORTATION WHEN YOUNG

When my brother (Okey) and I (Opha) twins were 10 to 13 years old and wanted to go to town (Tucson) to see the movies on Saturday we had to walk. Even a kid gets tired of walking so we tried to find some way to get to town without walking for we knew we had to walk home after the show. So some time we would look for an Indian in his wagon headed for town. When we did we would hop on the back. Some of the older men wouldn't let us ride and if we wouldn't get off he would take his whip to us. The white man put him on the reservation and he hasn't gotten over it. After getting to town one way or the other we would go to the Fox Theater to the Mickey Mouse Club. After that show we go to the Plaza Theater and saw two westerns and a weekly serial. It would be pretty late by the time we got out and a long walk home. All the walking we have done not one time did a car stopped and gave us a ride.

My sister (Wyvonna) and a neighbor Miriam Brothers would put their skates on and skate all the way to town. This was after Mission Road was paved in 1935. After

L-R, Opha and Okey during Depression days. You can tell by the dress code, with their German Sheppard dog.

getting there they would hide their skates under the Santa Cruz Bridge. When the shows were over they would skate home. I must tell you that it was five miles to town one way so it was a long walk. Since I'm talking about walking so much I want to add this. There were five of kids, only four of us went to school at this time and we were going to the Menlo Park School. Our dad would take us to school in the morning but in the evening when school let out we walked home every night. There were no buses at that time. Then after getting home two of us had to take a couple of gallon jugs and walk to Lynn's Dairy for milk. That was almost a mile from home.

Opha Probasco and his Quarter Horse, 1947

A couple of years later my brother and I got horses to ride that knocked off a lot of that old walking. We got to know a couple other guys that had horses and we done a lot of riding together.

The four of us would ride into town and right up Congress Street checking all the shows to see what was on. This would be any day except Saturday which was the day for Mickey Mouse at the Fox Theater.

There were four theaters in town and all were on Congress Street. The Plaza and Lyric were on the west end of Congress across from each other. Fox was just west of Stone and the Opera was near Scott Street, with the Rialto on the east end of Congress. After checking all the shows we'd go to Jackson and Meyer Street where there were a small stable to put our horses in. After turning our horses loose in the stalls we'd go to the front of the house and paid before going to the show. It cost us each five cents for each horse. After the show we'd get our mounts and head home.

*Opha R. Probasco*

# SANTA CRUZ RIVER CROSSING AFTER RAINS

Being the water table was next to the surface of the ground in the early days, when it would rain pretty good the river would always run. Since there was only one bridge crossing the Santa Cruz and that was on West Congress Street people had to wait till the water receded enough before they could drive across. Some people couldn't wait and started across too soon and got stuck. We would ride out to them and make a deal to pull them out. We would drop a loop over each side of the bumper and tell them to put it in gear then would take a dally on the horn with the rope then tell them lets go. After we pulled them out we would charge them fifty cents. We would do this in pairs, my brother and I would pull one car out then the next car Dean and Doug would take care of. This doesn't sound like much money but during the Depression fifty cents went a long way and a lot of people didn't have fifty cent piece in there pockets.

It was close to 1940 when a bridge was built across the Santa Cruz River on Ajo Way, around 1950 when the bridge was built across the Santa Cruz River on Silver Lake Road.

*Opha R. Probasco*

# RIDING THE RIVER

There were times when the Santa Cruz River would run bank to bank mainly if they had rain south of Tucson. Some times when this happened Bill Young, my brother and I would get out in the middle of the river and ride the river down to Silver Lake Road. We would be covered with mud and what else the river had in it. We would walk back up to Ajo Way and the river but first we'd jump in an irrigation ditch full of clear water. Some times we would go back in the river and make another trip down to Silver Lake Road. We never did ride the river any farther than to Silver Lake Road. It was fun but we couldn't wait to get all the mud off of us. We look like the Gingerbread kids.

# MOON LIGHT RIDES

Bud Mc Ghee had riding stables across the street from us and we would hang around there a lot. Luke Randolph ran the stables for Bud for he was off doing something all the time. There were a few of us that got together on moon light nights and had a steak fry. There would be about fifteen of us all together some didn't ride but did want to be involved. So while a bunch of us would take off on a moon light ride the others would go get the steaks and whatever else they wanted than meet us at a special place. After a couple of hours of riding we headed for the meeting place. They would have a big bon fire going every thing under control. We'd tie up our horses and gather around the fire to wait for the wood to run to hot coals and in the mean time we would sing some of the old cowboy songs. We taught the coyotes to howl and later they became our back us singers. We would have these moon light rides at least once a month during the summer. This was during the Depression and money was scarce but we did have a great time and a lot of fun. We made our fun in them days because we didn't have any money. Now a day's people would pay a lot of money to have the same fun. It's a funny world.

# SCHOOLING

In 1920 my oldest sister was six years old and went to a one room school a mile south east of the farm. She had to walk there and back everyday. She took her lunch in a lard pail with holes punched in the lid.

The following year the school district sent her to the New Haven School that was five miles north of the farm. A girl going to the same school horse back came by and picked her up. The following year she went to the Lone Star School and that was five miles south of the farm but this time the school district started a bus route so she and the rest of us but Bonnie rode the bus. My brother and I went to the Lone Star School the one year for we moved to Tucson in the fall of 1925.

After reaching Tucson we stayed at Verch's Tourist Court that winter and we went to the Roosevelt School. In 1926 dad bought the eighty acres on the corner of Mission and Ajo Roads and moved on it. That year we went to the Menlo School and that was five miles away. Dad would take us to school but after it was let out we had to walk home. Sometimes we would walk around "A" Mountain and at times we would go over "A" mountain. We never did get a ride. We went to Menlo Park School for two years when the school district started a bus route to our place. Jake Meyers was our bus driver and the truant officer. He became good friend to our family. He had a ranch south of us beside a home in Tucson. Checking his ranch sometime he would stop by and pick me up. We now started to the Mansfeld Elementary School. After one year my brother and I then went to the Mission View School for one year when a new school opened named Government Heights. During all this time there, there were not any cooling systems in any schools in Tucson. It was hot in the fall and spring but that went along with every thing else and we didn't complain. When the Government Heights (now Hollinger) they made the south wall to open the full length of the room. This was done on all of the rooms which did help some, but there were days when the breeze died and it got hot in all the rooms. From Government Heights' School we went to Safford Junior High through the ninth grade then to Tucson High School, the only high school in Tucson at that time. Some of the schools and the dated they opened.

| University of Arizona | 1891 |
| Plaza School | 1891 |
| Prep Scholl at Park and 10th | 1907 |
| Roskruge | 1907 |
| Safford Junior High | 1917 |
| Mansfeld Elementary | 1917 |
| Mission View | 1920 |

The Halloday, Davis and Drachman schools opened in 1903.

Safford Junior High School, built in 1917

Safford Elementary School, built in 1917 next to Safford
Junior High

Drachman School was built in 1903 with four rooms.
Four more rooms were added in 1908. Four rooms were
constructed in 1914. Two rooms were added in 1927 and
1936. In 1948 the building was 80% destroyed by fire. It

was rebuilt in 1950 with seventeen class rooms, a community room, with administration offices, and a nurse's room. Built by M.M. Sundt for $213,199.15.

Halloday School was built in 1903 with four rooms and in 1908 four more rooms was added and a single room in 1918.

This school was torn down in 1923 to make room for the Tucson High School.

Davis School was built in 1903 with five rooms. In 1908 six class rooms were added. In 1927 four more class rooms were constructed, two more class rooms were added in 1936 and in 1954 two class rooms ere converted into the cafeteria and auditorium as of this date 2005 it is still opened.

The Little Adobe School was opened as a high school in 1906 with forty five students in a two room house one large room for the class with a lean-to for laboratories, recitation rooms and halls.

The year of scandal for school district one, on March 21, 1906 this letter from Superintendent F.M. Walker reads as follows: Five teachers of the public school have been guilty of conduct unbecoming to teachers. These five teachers went to Sabino Canyon last Saturday and took with them beer, wine and cigarettes. Drank and smoked the same two of the teachers admitted it was true. F.M. Walker asked the board to deal with it for the best for the welfare of the School. The board kept it a secret while investigation was going on. But it lasted for only a short time. It came out that they were all women and no men were involved. This made it worse for those days.

Drachman and Halloday voted for dismissal of charges while Roskruge voted to sustain the charges. Roskruge didn't attend anymore meetings and resigned on March 31, 1906.

In 1901 Drachman, Halloday, and Davis were on the school board and a new school was needed. Each one of them wanted the school to be named for them, so to settle it they decided to built three schools one for each of there names.

They built the Roskruge new elementary school in 1914, alterations and additions were made in 1931.

Safford Junior High, Mansfeld, and Dunbar were all built in 1917 and completed in 1918. Safford Junior High was completely remodeled in 1953.

Dunbar School was for the black people in those days. The school name was changed to John Spring School then in 2004 it was changed back to Dunbar. Dunbar was named for Paul Lawrence Dunbar a Negro poet. He lived in the east and never saw Tucson. He died at the age of 34 years.

Dunbar School was first built with two rooms and in 1921 two more rooms were added as in 1930, 1936 and 1940. IN 1948 a junior high school was added at the cost of $375,000.00 which included twelve new rooms and remodeled the old building. The finished school had twenty three class rooms, offices and a cafeteria-auditorium combination. In 1951 segregation ended for all of Arizona schools and Dunbar was changed to John A. Spring Junior High School and in 2004 the name was changed back to Dunbar.

In 1919 the Menlo Park School and the University Heights were built. Menlo Park at 1100 West Fresno and the University Heights at 1201 South Park Avenue. Menlo Park started with two rooms and in 1921 two more rooms were added and in 1927 two more rooms as in 1930 also. The school was completely remodeled in 1949 with two more rooms, total of 14 class rooms in all.

*Opha R. Probasco*

# EARLY SCHOOLS

1860 was the first school room in Arizona territory at Sopori Ranch. There were portholes around the room where could shoot at the Indians when they came to raid the ranch.

November 18, 1867 school district number one was organized. The board named the first school community consisting of Francisco S. Leon, William Oury, and John B. Allen, (called Pie Allen because he sold pies to the army for $1.00 each).

Augustus Brichta was the first teacher the school was only open for six months because they ran out of money.

In 1870 the sisters of Saint Joseph opened the sister's convent and academy for females at the St. Agustin Church.

On March 4, 1872 the second free school opened in an old adobe building at Meyer and McCormick Street. The rent was $16.00 a month the teacher was John Spring, boy's ages were six to twenty one, bare feet and some had sandals. There were one hundred and thirty eight boys in one room. He wanted his salary raised from $125.00 to $150.00 a month so he could hire an assistant. The success of the Spring's school brought about a free public school for girls that opened February 1873 the teacher was Josephine Hughs (wife of editor of the Star Paper), L.C. Hughs. She taught for three months and had to quit due to her health.

In 1874 they started building the Congress Street School. This was built on the northwest corner of Sixth Avenue.

In 1873 the school trustees rented a building from Sam Hughs, one room for boys and one room for girls. Governor Safford hired two girls from California to teach and they were Miss Maria Wakefield and Miss Harriet Bolton. The governor said that they would stick to their job but the next spring the both of them were married. In 1874 the Congress Street School was built.

In 1886 B.C. Parker, E.B. Gifford, and W.S. Read bought forty acres and donated it for the University of Arizona. The University opened in 1891 also the Plaza school was opened the same year. The Old Congress Street School became the Indian School for a year then a store house for the military then auctioned off to L.H. Manning for $9,000.00. By 1902 the Adobe School was torn down.

In 1914 Roskruge Junior High was built.

In 1917 the Old Plaza School was torn down and Safford Junior High and Mansfeld Elementary Schools was built side by side.

In 1924 Tucson High School was built where the Holladay School was torn down.

In 1930 Mansfeld Junior High School was built on East Sixth Street and the Mansfeld Elementary name was changed to Safford Elementary.

# AMPHI SCHOOLS

In 1904 there was a one room school at Prince and Oracle.

In 1935 High School building was started with ninth grade, 1938 tenth grade, 1939 eleventh grade, 1940 tweleveth grade, and in 1941Amphitheater High School graduated their first student.

*Opha R. Probasco*

# INDIAN SCHOOLS

In 1873 the Indian School started at San Xavier Del Bac. In 1888 the Presbyterians had a contract with the government to teach each student at $31.25 for each quarter plus the expense for keep. This was at the Old Congress Street School. After nine months the school was moved closed to the University, a year later the school was moved to South Tenth Avenue and West Twenty Second Street, where it remained until 1907 then it was moved to South Sixteenth and Ajo Way. That lasted until 1960. At that time Ajo Way was called Indian School Road.

71

# PUBLIC SCHOOLS

November 18, 1867 school district number one for Tucson was organized. 1868 first public school with teacher Agustus Brichta started in an old adobe rented building, with sixty boys and girls. It only lasted 1872 a building for school was rented on the corner of Meyer and McCormick Streets for the amount of $16.00 a month. John Spring was the teacher with 138 boys of all ages in one room.

1873 public school for girls opened in the Old Pioneer Brewery building in Levin's Park. The teacher was Josephine Brawley Hughs, wife of L.C. Hughs. She taught thirty girls from three months then resigned due to illness.

1873 Governor Safford hired two girls from California to teach in place of John Spring. Safford said that they would stick to their jobs longer than a man would. At the end of 1873 and 1874 year Maria Wakefield married E.N. Fish and Harriet Bolton married John Wasson. Even if they did get married they both help raise funds for a new school building. The women sold pie, cakes, and countless other delicacies. They held dances and benefit dinners. The building was built on East Congress Street between Scott and Sixth Avenue

1886 B.C. Parker, E.B. Gifford and W.S. Read bought forty acres of ground and donated it for the University of Arizona. Which opened in 1891 and at the same time the new Plaza School opened for the kids 1 to 5 grades.

1907 Roskruge School was built and in 1917 it was remodeled. 1917 Plaza School was torn down and Mansfeld Elementary School was built and next to it Safford Junior High School was built.

1923 the Old Holladay School was torn down and a new Tucson High School was built.

1930 a new Mansfeld Junior High School was built and the name Mansfeld Elementary was change to Safford Elementary.

When the Plaza School opened the Old Congress School became the Indian School for one year, then moved close to the University for one year and from there they moved to South Tenth Avenue and West Twenty Second Street. From there the Indian School moved to Sixteenth Avenue and Indian School Road which was changed to Ajo Way.

# JOBS WE HAD WHILE GROWING UP

When we were fifteen and sixteen years old during the summer my brother and I worked as life guards at the Mission swimming pool with the owner's nephew Donald Woodman. In the winters Okey and I would work for dad in the wood business. My first job away from home was in 1937 when I went to work for Mc Bride. He had a ranch west of us in the Robles ranch area.

He had gotten a contract with the government building dirt tanks for the ranchers west of the Sierrita Mountains. This lasted two years and while I was doing that my brother, Okey, with his future father-in-law were working for Howell Manning at the Pozo Nuevo, Palo Alto and the Sopori Ranches. In 1940 my brother and I went to work for the "A" Mountain Diary. He was on a retail route delivering to houses and I had a wholesale route delivering to restaurants and grocery stores. He would go to work at two AM and I would go to work at four AM. In 1942 we went to work for the Southern Pacific Railroad. Both of us had enlisted in the See Bees. We had to get a release from the railroad before they would take us. I talked to

Okey and Opha Probasco (twins) in 1938

Mr. Bays who was the superintendent and he told me that
we weren't going no where that we were frozen to our
jobs. After World War II was over my brother went to work

for the Arizona Express Freight Company. I went to Colorado and took over the family farm and spent the summers in Colorado and the winters in Tucson. We sold the farm then I stayed in Tucson and went to work for the Arizona Express also. Later Consolidated Freight Way took over Arizona Express my brother lost the sight in one eye and had to retire.

Opha Probasco when he was driving for Consolidated Freightways

I worked until I was sixty years old then took an early retirement. After Okey retired he went to work for the Arizona Auctioneers. When I retired I also went to work for the auction company. Michael Kramer owned the auction company and Okey was in charge of the southern part of Arizona. Okey would deal with the bankruptcy lawyers and I would set up the auctions when the day came for the auction Mr. Kramer would come down from Phoenix and do the auctioneering. My brother and I have traveled all over the country setting up auctions. I was with them for over ten years, and Okey 20 years.

In 1937 I started dating Dorothy Kingla and Lee Yocum was dating Mary Jane Dorothy's sister. Lee and I with the girls double dated a lot. Lee and I began to chum around together. I would go to his house and some times spend the night. At times he would come out to my house. He wasn't a rich kid but he did have about anything he wanted. He did a lot of flying and at times he would land at a desert run way we found and pick me up and I'd fly around with Lee for awhile then he would land and drop me off. One cold day we went up and waited until we were over our landing strip before doing any stunts. We did a few wing overs and when we done a tail spin the engine died. We were up 3000 feet and to get the engine started again we dove the plane straight down to get the wind to turn the propeller. We leveled off at 2000 feet then tired it again with no luck. At 1000 feet we had to land coming in a little high Lee slipped the plane twice to lose a little altitude but it was a little too much we caught the top of a Mesquite Tree that tore a hole in the side of the fuselage about the size of your head. We landed O.K. with a dead stick. I held the brakes and Lee turned the prop we got the engine started and Lee took off for the airport. Al Hudgin the owner of the plane was sure unhappy but he never did find out Lee landed and picked me up. Lee would have lost his license if anyone found out. This flying had rubbed off on me, so I had to take it up. The cost of lessons was $6.00 an hour. We wouldn't go up for the hour only for thirty minutes at a time and sometimes just twenty minutes. I got my certificated and soled in eight hours. Money being as scarce as it was it took me one year to get in the eight hours. My solo date was October eighteen nineteen forty. After World War II was over Al Hudgin and his brothers moved their flying business to Grand Canyon. Al was trying to rescue a person in his helicopter when one of the blades hit the bank and he and the helicopter fell to the bottom of the canyon and was killed.

L-R, Buck Williams and Opha Probasco on horses in the
Mission Club Bar.
The women in the foreground are, L-R, Addie Nutt and her
two daughters Minilee Nutt and Luciele Nutt.

## MISSION CLUB BAR

A friend of mine (Buck Williams) and I had gone for a
horse back ride and after a couple of hours we decided
that a cold beer would sure go good. We decided to go to
the Mission Club since it wasn't too far. After arriving I
told Buck "Let's just ride on in on the horses". We had
someone open the door and in we went, and was served.
Some one had a camera and took pictures. After riding
out of the bar I had to do a little stable work and wouldn't
you know it the camera clicked again.

Another time I was riding near a friend's house and Elizabeth Wood was out side so I rode up to her and asked where Woody (her husband) was, she answered that he was inside. I asked her to open the kitchen door and let me ride in which she did and I told her now go and open the front door. I rode through the kitchen, dinning room and on through the living room where Woody was sitting on the couch. As I went by his mouth dropped open and his eyes opened wide he was so startled he couldn't speak. Years later he still talked about it, same way with Elizabeth.

Opha Probasco riding in the Rodeo Parade. L-R, Sally Fletcher, Opha, Wayne, Buck Williams and Bill Williams

We road in the Rodeo Parade about every year during the late forties and after the parade we would ride down to the Ozark Bar and Café. We would eat a bite then ride on down to the rodeo ground, watered our horses then sat in the bleachers to watch the action.

One year Hank Conley who had a riding stable asked me if I would ride with his group in the parade, and I told him I would and later on he gave me a number to pin on my arm for him advertising his stables. While we were riding during the parade a fellow was riding a burro next to me and I was cutting up with him unbeknown we were gong pass the judges. Next day Hank told me that I had won a prize to go down to the Chamber of Commerce and get it. After I got there I was asked how long had I been in Tucson. I told them that I had come in 1925. They told me that they couldn't give it to me. It should have gone to a new comer. The prize was for "The Most Typical Dude" and the prize was anew Stetson hat. I told them either give me the prize or pay me later. I got the hat.

I was in on a rodeo committee meeting a few year ago and Cele Peterson and I both mentioned that the parade route should go back through town like it always had before. They came back with a lot of excuses that didn't make sense but the big reason the parade route had changed to where it is today is if the truth was known that it is a lot easier to clean the streets and very few streets that has to be blocked off besides it is a lot cheaper. The city really doesn't give a damn about the parade or the people. All they think about is what it is going to cost them.

I have a friend in Germany that is a freelance writer for a hundred newspapers and magazines. I gave him copies of the pictures and the story of riding into the bar on horse back. He sold the story to a monthly magazine and sent it to me. I had the story translated into English.

# TUCSON, ARIZONA
## Historical Population Growth

| | Tucson [1] | Arizona [2] | Pima County [4] |
|---|---|---|---|
| 1821 | 395 | | |
| 1831 | 465 | | |
| 1860 | 929 | 6,482 [3] | |
| 1864 | 1,568 | 4,573 | 2,517 [5] |
| 1870 | 3,224 | 9,658 | 5,716 |
| 1880 | 7,007 | 40,440 | 17,006 |
| 1890 | 5,150 | 88,243 | 12,673 |
| 1900 | 7,531 | 122,931 | 14,689 |
| 1910 | 13,193 | 204,354 | 22,818 |
| 1920 | 20,292 | 334,162 | 34,680 |
| 1925 | 25,000 | The Probasco family arrived in Tucson, Arizona | |
| 1930 | 32,506 | 435,573 | 55,676 |
| 1940 | 36,818 | 499,261 | 72,838 |
| 1950 | 45,454 | 749,587 | 141,216 |
| 1960 | 212,892 | 1,302,161 | 265,660 |
| 1970 | 262,933 | 1,770,900 | 351,667 |
| 1975 | 331,000 | 2,245,100 | 452,000 |
| 1980 | 360,537 | 2,700,000 | 531,443 |
| 1990 | 402,506 | 3,665,228 | |

(1) Tucson was first incorporated in 1871. Population figures after 1870 are for incorporated (city) area only.

(2) Arizona became a separate territory in 1863. (3) The population figure shown for 1860 is for Arizona County of New Mexico Territory.

(4) Pima County was organized in 1864.

(5) Population figure shown for 1864 was the result of a census of Judicial District 1 which was a predecessor of Pima County.

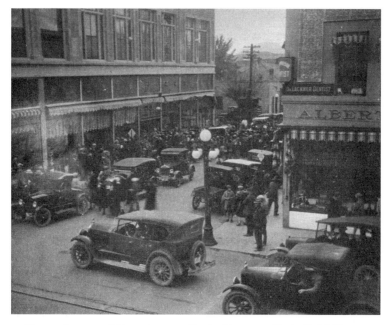

Stone Ave. and Pennington St. in Tucson. Steinfield Dept. Store on the SW corner, Steinfield Grocery Store on the NW corner and north of the grocery store was the lumber yard.

When we arrived in Tucson, the population was 25,000, there weren't any signal lights anywhere in town. It took years before it became a city. The first signal lights were put up at the intersection of Stone Avenue and Congress Street. The second signal went in at the intersection of Sixth Avenue and Congress Street.

There was only one fire station and it was located on South Sixth Avenue between Broadway and 12 Street on the west side.

There was only one under pass and that was on 4th Avenue built in 1916.

Sixth Avenue under pass opened up in 1929. In the same year a bond was sold for $400,000.00 and construction was started on the Broadway underpass.

Stone Avenue was opened up to the public in 1934, just one half blocks north on the east side was the street car barn. Tucson was incorporated in 1877, in 1883 Tucson became a charter city.

St. Mary's Hospital was built in 1880. Southern Pacific Railroad went to Bishop Salpointe and asked him if he would build a hospital for they knew there was going to be some injuries with there men and they would need medical attention. So in 1880 a hospital was built on 60 acres of ground on west side of the Santa Cruz River. The two story hospital was the first non-military hospital in Arizona. It had eleven beds with three of the seven nurses that came from Missouri. They left the mother house Carondelet on April 20, 1870 arriving in Tucson on May 26, 1870.

In 1880 Southern Pacific Railroad reached Tucson, 1881 was the first telephone exchange. The first water went through the mains and the first gas lights were turned on in 1882 in Tucson.

Tucson had their first fire department in 1883, 1895 the first electric was organized.

When Tucson constructed the Sixth Avenue under pass they put in a speed bump to slow the cars going into the under pass. This bump isn't like the ones they use now a days with a short hump. The ones that they put in had a long hump. Leave it to a teenager, we wouldn't slow down, we would speed up when we went over those speed bumps all wheels would leave the ground. The city found out what we were doing it didn't take then long in removing the hump. Some times when the traffic wasn't heavy, there were a couple of guys that were heading into the under pass they would switch and go through the wrong side. They were lucky they never had a mishap. This is something I never done. So you see the teenager weren't much different then they are today only thing the automobiles didn't run as fast as they do today.

We never did get into any bad trouble we were only mischief like at the Mission Pool one day during the Prohibition Days when my brother and I was in the dressing room of the men's when one of them ask us if we knew where they could get some whiskey. I told them sure but it would cost them a dollar a pint. They said O.K. we'll be back in a little while. We were about eleven or twelve years old. Any way we found a pint bottle, that was easy for dad was in the moon shine business. My brother and I peed in the bottle and put the cork in and headed back. We walked up to the guys and gave them the bottle and they gave us the dollar. We got out of there and ran around the building and peaked through a knot hole just as one of them took a mouth full. The words he started using my brother and I headed for home.

Tucson and its saloons, gambling and tough characters Tucson was as Will Barns said, "A Sorry Looking Mexican Town with Narrow and Crooked Streets". The houses were of adobe with dirt floor s and roofs. There were two classes of business, gambling and prostitution. Some of the saloons had women faro dealers, not only were they pretty, they were a tough bunch along with it. Being Mexicans they took a fancy to the American men. A Mexican didn't have a chance. The women were good and faithful nurse to their lovers. The older women wore a Rebozo to cover their heads while the young ones covered their faces with flour paste to protect their skin from the sun. Even in those days the people knew that the sun was hard on their skin. They play faro and not poker in those days, they were illiterate.

There were a café in Tucson that was owned by a woman, which is very rare, all business was owned by men. This cafe was named Shoo-Fly with dirt floors and a mud roof. On the inside there was a muslin ceiling, the muslin was used to catch any dirt that may drop down from the roof. There were pine table and chairs that was held together with raw-hide. The diners enjoyed their meals by ignoring the dust and flies. There were a couple of young boys with white jackets on that had fly swatters to keep the flies at bay. The café got its name Shoo-Fly because the flies there wouldn't shoo.

The menu was jerked beef, which went into a stew and has, chicken, bacon and ham served with red chili. As for fresh vegetables they had tomatoes, lettuce, oranges, lemon, limes and apricots that came by burro train from Mexico.

The town of Tucson in the 1860's was filthy, garbage thrown out into the streets laid there forever. If some one would ask where the governor house was, the answer would be, just keep going down there to the manure pile on your right, then keep take left past the post-office and you will see a dead burro in the middle of the road and a mesquite tree on your left near a Mexican store. Just beyond that is the governor's house.

The saloons and gambling rooms stayed open twenty four hours a day. There were ten years between 1860 to 1870 where Tucson didn't have any army troops or any kind of law, men would walk up and down the street with shot guns just looking for some one to kill. During that ten years period there were forty seven graves of white men and out of the forty seven only two died a natural cause. The rest were murdered in fights and bar room brawls.

Mark Aldrich was a successful businessman in Illinois but the gold fever got him and he headed west. He was the first American to have a permanent mercantile in Tucson and he also was the first post master. He was also the first American arcade replacing Juan Elisa. There wasn't a jail in Tucson so he rigged up a whipping post in the plaza. For the wrong doers he would order so many lashes for punishment. This was done by a strong arm city Marshall. The practice was to give the culprit half of the lashes and tell him to come back the next day for the rest. Before sunset he was out of town. It was one way to get rid of people that wasn't wanted. An unarmed man was murdered in front of several witnesses but no one would come forward to testify so Mark resigned stating that they had no use for a judge or court. Aldrich never did go back to his wife and children. He lived with Trefoil Leon until he died in 1873. In the 1870's things got better but the gambling and prostitution stayed around.

Mark Aldrich's whipping post was found in the basement of the old court house in 1928 when it was torn down to make room for the present one that is on the corner on Alameda and North Church Street.

# SAN AGUSTIN CHURCH

Father Solano Leon arrived in Tucson, Arizona in 1862. A year after he arrived the cement foundation was poured for the new church, and it was time to build the walls. The church as being built on the corner of Church Street and Broadway Avenue, facing west. The adobes was being made on the property of Solano Leon, later on Levi Manning would acquire the same property. Every morning after the congregation was over they started making adobes for the walls. Each one carried one adobe to the foundation and the walls started up. Before the walls were up, father Solano Leon left for New Mexico, and in 1864 he was killed by the Apaches on the road between El Paso and Chihuahua.

In 1866 the archbishop sent John Baptist Salpointe to Tucson to take charge, he had a letter of introduction and upon his arrival he gave the letter to William Oury and Juan Elias.

The church was just like it was when Solano Leon left. Salpointe didn't waste any time in getting started on the job of finishing the church. In 1868 the roof was installed, and the school building was built next door. The construction of Agustin continue through the years. The tower was installed in 1881, and the windows of rosette design were installed in 1883.

Bourgade succeeded Salpointe as bishop. In 1895 the foundation for the new church was formed on South Stone Avenue to take the place of the old San Agustin Church. In 1896 the Saint Augustine Cathedral was almost finished when Salpointe died in St. Mary's hospital, July 15, 1898. He was buried beneath the altar of the new church. Years later his remains were dug up and reburied at the Evergreen Cemetery.

The year after Salpoint's death, bishop Bourgade and Pope Leo XII sold the old Agustin Church to Dick Brady. It was soon turned into a hotel. Dick Brady leased the building to Col. W.S. Low. He and his enterprise brought about change, providing Tucson with the first place of entertainment. Low had many diner parties and dances.

It was also a musical center with concerts. A lot of bachelors lived there.

In 1901 Levi Manning and Col. Epes Randolph with a group of other business men made plans for the Santa Rita Hotel. It was under construction for a year and opened in 1904, it was the finest hotel in the west. The building was six stories high with the roof garden on top where the dancing took place with two orchestras, the partying lasted all night.

After the Santa Rita opened the old San Agustin Church, converted to a hotel with night time dining and entertainment started to decline rapidly. The Brady family retained ownership but there were a lot of lessees. The rooms were used by the lower and lower income levels.

One pioneer said it was for tin-horn sports and whores. The patio was covered with a roof and seats were installed for a prize fight ring. It was the first sports center in Tucson, called "Cabinet Pool Hall" located at the plaza park with Church Avenue on the east and Meyer Avenue on the west. Congress Street was on the north and Broadway (use to be Camp Street) on the south. I remember there was root beer stand on the north east corner just north of the church. They drew the root beer from kegs at that time.

The had was turned into a garage which had a taxi stand and a service station in front of the church with a sign "In God we trust, all others pay cash".

The paint peeled, roof leaked, only the façade stood defiant. The city condemned the place for the lack of sanitary facilities.

In 1938 the end came to San Agustin Church, it was demolished. The cross in the tower is in the Arizona Historical Society front room as you walk in.

A couple of years before the church was torn down my brother and I was going to the sports center and doing a little boxing. Our dad and a good friend got their heads together and decided that my brother and I should take up boxing since my dad's friend was a trainer. There was only one purpose for this and that was to teach us how to protect ourselves in everyday life. They didn't want us to be prize fighters. We worked out and boxed for three years. While we were training the church was torn down and the sports center was moved to the labor temple on South Stone Avenue. While we were training at the labor temple a group of us went to Sasabe, Mexico to put on an exhibition. There weren't any electric lights any where in town just candles and lamps so the boxing exhibition was held in the afternoon. Earlier in the day the people had a picnic for us with ice cream for desert, there weren't any cows there only a lot of burros and the ice cream was made out of burro milk, it was real sweet. It wasn't too much longer when we both quit the boxing and training at the labor temple. They held boxing and wrestling at the temple it wasn't but a couple of years after we quit that the sports center was built off of west Congress Street, west of the Santa Cruz River on the south side. There wasn't any boxing, just wrestling matches. My dad loved the wrestling, he didn't miss a match.

# THE WOMEN SUFFRAGE AND PROHIBITION

A state hood bill passed the house in 1910 six months later President Taft signed an Enabling Act. Governor Richard Sloan called a special election to choose delegates to a constitutional convention. The convention assembled in Phoenix. And they worked diligently to finish December 9, 1910. The Democratic Liberals and labor representatives dominated the session, and produced a constitution featuring many provisions the people could pass laws independently of the legislature, could reject measures passed by the legislature, and could turn public officials out of office by popular vote. President was opposed to these provisions and vetoed the state hood bill. Arizona circumvented him by voting on December 12, 1911 to leave out the offensive propositions. Taft signed on February 12, 1912, and nine months later the voters restored them.

Tucson sent five of its citizens as delegates to the convention all republicans. The liberal democrats led by George W.P. Hunt dominated the convention and when the documents were completed the republicans wouldn't sign it. Two measures that were dear to the women were omitted from the constitution which was women suffrage and prohibition.

The saloons use to have private rooms where families could get together and enjoy an afternoon. That was done away with along with not allowing women in the saloons. The women suffrage begins to grow.

L.H. Manning was elected mayor and he had been known to gamble a little and said if he was elected mayor he would close the gambling down. He did change the hours from running twenty fours hours a day to 10:00 Am to 6:00 PM with permit limited to thirty days. This was too much for the gamblers and they left town.

The women suffrage was given to the voters in 1912 election. The people voted in favor of the women and they were permitted to vote in the next election.

In 1914 election they voted Arizona dry. On December 31, 1914 was the last day the saloons was open. January 1, 1915 was the first day of prohibition.

Five years alter in 1920 all of the states went dry. This created another problem for Tucson. There were at least 250 moon shiners (Whiskey) and a lot of bootlegger, rum runners and mescal moon shiners. The whiskey moon shinning was pretty good business, I think that was the reason dad got into it for money was scarce and with a family to feed a person had to do something.

A campaign was mounting against bootleggers and prostitutes, the first of many. Three squads of officers led by the mayor and the Sheriff arrested thirty two suspects.

The activity was at the San Agustin Hotel, once a church and convent of the sisters of Saint Joseph, later a boxing ring, where my brother and I use to box. Along with this it had a garage and service station. In 1938 it was torn down. The new Saint Agustin Church was built on South Stone Avenue where it is today. Twenty men and women faced the judge on April 9, 1917, they were fined and turned loose. On June 12, 1917 the law arrested a big fish, a mister, Jeff Cole, who owned Cole's Auto Service. He was known as the king of the bootleggers. The title seems to fit for they picked up forty cases of whiskey at the business and 1080 pints at his home. Also arrested was a woman bootlegger named Cruz Carrillo.

Business got so good they had gotten careless. Ingacio De La Vega was arrested when he tried to make a customer out of a deputy sheriff Sid Simpson. They passed a law to confiscation of a smuggler's car if he was arrested, this proved fruitless.

There was so much smuggling going on that they tired to slow it down by putting out 3% alcohol beer, known as near beer so the nation's supply of bonded whiskey would last longer and slow the bootlegging down. Many of the people living at that time claimed the near beer was the horrors of war.

Prostitution was also running out of control without a solution. Tucson administration admitted July 1917 that they didn't have laws to deal with Sabino Alley (Gay Alley). The girls were picked up fined like they did in the eighties but couldn't run them out of town.

The army was planning on coming to Tucson and putting in an air field and they were concerned about their soldiers. It took them six months to come up with some thing else to fight gay alley (Sabino Alley). The town passed an ordinance forbidding loitering. Which means women as well as gamblers living in Tucson had to have the means of support, like a job or a bank account, if they didn't have they could be ordered out of town. In February 1918 they started enforcing the new law. The (Law) went house to house telling the gamblers and prostitutes they had to get out of town. Before long they were back in Sabino Alley.

The citizens were meeting at the Y.M.C.A. to listen to Popenoe's report on the prostitution. He said that there were two hundred prostitutes in Tucson and 90% were infected and needed a clean up.

When we came here in 1925 it was just as bad. You could drive down Ochoa Street and Sabino Alley and the prostitutes would be sitting on the front step. They would hold up two fingers showing you what it would cost to play house. It was in the late thirties when the houses of prostitution begin to end. The last place to go was Mary's Place which was located at 398 West Alameda Street. She had nine to ten girls working for her and they all were great lookers. Mary had a black lady that done the cooking for all of them. This place was a two story house and it had a lot of rooms, the girls operated on the second floor. The police knew all about Mary and her girls but never did bother them. There could be a reason for that this, I don't know.

I was going with a girl that was in high school and I had just gotten out. We went together for a couple of years and during that time I got to know all the family. The oldest sibling was a girl, they came here from Texas being money was short and no job, so she went to work being a prostitute. She went to San Francisco and worked in a hotel.

She put her brothers and sister through school and kept food on the table at all times. She was a big hearted person, she bought her family a brand new car one time. She would come here three or four times a year and stayed a couple of week on each trip. She told me her and the family's history. Even if it was the wrong profession to be in I still admired her for taking care of her family. She also knew Mary real well for she had worked for her. I went with her to visit Mary one time and got to see all the girls and met Mary, being a young kid I was nervous and felt out of place being there. I was glad when we left. All I thought about while I was there was, what if the cops would raid this place while I was there and my name would come out in the paper. That's when I learned the cops would never raid her place. She had the connections and that is what it takes just like being a moonshinner. You were better off being in the country than in the city.

The gambling was wide open just like the prostitution and it lasted longer. One reason was that most of the gambling was done in private clubs such as the Elks, there were some saloons that had back room gambling. Red Chitwood had a large place on the Old Nogales Highway he ran during the forties and the law caught up with him in 1059 and forced him to close down. He had the gambling up stairs and there was a hole that went through the floor to the basement where a person could pick it up and go through the tunnel to the reservation where the law couldn't touch him.

The Chinese had a lottery with numbers that cost a dime each, I use to play it every week with no luck. There was always some kind of gambling going on around town at all times.

There's a large open field across from the Catalina Park on the west side of the highway going up Oracle Road. Back in there every Sunday was a week end jack pot roping and rodeo. After the activity was all over you would go and have dinner then head for Oracle Junction.

I made a lot of trips up there but I never got into the gambling part. I went there for the dances. There was always a good crowd for the dance. You could always bet there was going to be a fight and maybe a couple. Some time with the same two and other times not. The dance was held in the main building in front where there was a bar and a small store. The gambling took place in the back where some cabins were. It was in the fifties before the gambling stopped around Tucson. I think every town in Arizona had some gambling going on if you knew where to go. A lot of gambling was going on in Globe, Arizona. I never did know where but a few of the gamblers that I knew told me about them.

Moon Shinning during the twenties along with the gambling and prostitution. I told you about the prostitution and the gambling now I will tell you about the bootleggers, moon shiners and mescal makers.

# MESCAL

The moonshinners making mescal would search for the Agave (Century Plant) when they found an Agave with the stalk starting to grow out of the plant they would cut the stalk off and look for another one, when they find all they were going to use and have all the stalks cut off they would cut all the leaves off except one, they would leave it on to use as a handle when loading and unloading the Agave. They would use burros or mules to transport these where the pit is. You had to use canvas or blankets on the backs of the animals to keep the Agave juice off for it was very toxic and would make sores on the back of the animals.

The moonshinners would dig a pit (also called Malla) about three foot wide and three foot long and approximately six foot deep. You would fill the pit about half full of wood, the other half you filled with big rocks up to the top of the pit. The moonshinners would wait till dark before setting the wood on fire, the reason for that is they can't see the smoke after dark.

The Agave heads are unloaded off of the mules or burros what ever was used. After the wood had burned down and rocks are on the hot coals the leaf that was left on for a handle is cut off that was used for a handle and laid in the pit on top of each other bringing the heads up to the level of the ground. They are then covered with a tarp of some kind then dirt put over the tarp to keep the pit air tight. After three or four days the pit was uncovered. It released an appetizing smell. The finished product was called (Biguata) it was sweet and good tasting. Next the moonshinners would place the baked heads in a wooden trough (carved out by the old timers) and mashed with wooden mallets. The pulp and juice from the heads was put into forty gallon wooden kegs with water added they waited for fermentation to start. The length of fermentation depended on the weather, if it was hot it wouldn't take it as long as it would if it was cloudy and cool. When the bubbling stop and the pulp moved away from the sided of the keg it was time for distilling.

The fermented Biguata was transferred to a copper still. Eventually the steam would liquefy and drip through the copper coil into a bottle. The last quart was weak so it was saved and poured into the next batch. Mescal came out about 80 proof, if they wanted it stronger proof, sugar or honey was added into the fermentation. For taste, acorns and spices were added after it was bottled. Some of the one that made Mescal were Matt Culley, Morales, Robles and Miguel, Mendez who made whiskey also three of them had their still in the canyon. Mendez had his still at the foot of Tom Boy. There were others that were making Mescal, only one was ever caught in the ten years of operation. His name was Morales. The revenue confiscated his still. Other wise he got off scott free because he was a widower with four small children. The agents asked him where did he get the still? He told them that he had found it. The agent told him if he ever found another one just run, toward it he asked.

Doctor Latta in Sterling, Colorado which was my father's doctor told him before he went to bed to take and once of whiskey, that it would help him. Being that the states were dry my father had to go to a doctor and get a prescription for the whiskey, and it was expensive. It was either Doctor Smelker or another doctor told him that he would come by and pick him up and take him to Nogales for he made a trip there every month. My dad went with him and the both of them brought back a gallon. For years everyone was allowed to bring back a gallon of anything they wanted, years later this was changed to just a quart.

A friend of ours was staying in our court and he was a bootlegger. He would take three suit cases catch a train to El Paso, fill them with assorted brands of whiskey, catch the train and go to Phoenix. After getting rid of his merchandise back to Tucson he would come, his name was Joe Banks. He and my father went in together and started moonshining. They made good whiskey by distilling it twice. They were getting two dollars or more a gallon than the going price. The Sheriff Department enjoyed it. They would come out and nip all day, take a quart with then when they would leave. The still was pretty close to the neighbors and there was one that would call the Sheriff office and report the odor of a still. They would send a deputy out and the first place he would go to was to dad's place. He would nip awhile and report back that he couldn't find anything. Some times the complaints got so bad that the Sheriff had to make the trip out and you guessed it, he headed for dad's place. He would do like the deputy did, nip awhile, then take a bottle with him.

The complaints got so bad that Joe and dad decided to move the still to the east side of the Santa Rita Mountains to his son-in-laws brother's place in Fish Canyon. With a spring there made it a perfect spot. That was forty miles away and it was inconvenient. When we would go there to pickup a load of whiskey we'd take a truck and trailer, loaded the wood around the kegs. Since we were in the wood business it worked out fine. Dad had customers that bought wood and whiskey so he would hide the bottles in with the wood.

Dad would use to make home brew for his own personal use. One time when it was ready to be bottled dad ask my brother (Okey) to do the bottling. That made my brother mad for he didn't want to do it. Dad told him to put one teaspoon of sugar in each bottle when he filled it. Being angry Okey put two and sometimes three teaspoons in each bottle. Boy about midnight or there after those bottle begin to explode. What a mess that was. He never asked Okey to do any bottling again.

My dad's moonshining partner had a keg of whiskey on the back seat of his car and while going around a corner a cop standing there said hey Joe what do you have in that keg? Whiskey what do you think it is? The cop thought he was kidding but he wasn't, if he had said nothing he would have been checked out and caught. He did finally get caught. He spent a year on the Catalina Highway building the road to Mount Lemon.

# JOKES ABOUT MOONSHINNING

There was a fellow that made very bad liquor and he gave his friend a bottle of it. Meeting him later he asked Rufus how did he like the liquor? Rufus answered "Fine" it was just right, had it been any better you wouldn't have given it to me, and if it was any worse it would have killed me.

On another occasion the moonshinner told Rufus "Here take a drink" when he refused the moonshinner took out his pistol and demanded Rufus to take a drink, he took a drink, then the moonshinner took the bottle back and gave Rufus the pistol, now he insisted make me take a drink.

After the Agave plant blooms it dies, so when the plant started to put out the shoot for the bloom the moonshinners would cut off the small stalk this process was called "Caper". Even after prohibition some die hard moonshinners still went around capering the Maguey, also called "Agave Plant or Century Plant".

*Opha R. Probasco*

# GORDON SAWYER'S KIDNAPPING

There has been a lot of things happen in Tucson and a couple of kidnappings to go along with every thing else. I happened to be around when both them took place. The first took place February 4, 1932.

Gordon Sawyer came to Tucson in 1909 and had been a cashier and Vice President of the Southern Arizona Bank and Trust Company since 1912. A thin-haired, middle age, mild-looking man with a cheerful countenance and a ready smile which showed a battery of gold teeth, he looked inoffensive but was in reality, a hard nosed, to-bacco-chewing executive. His inner toughness, however, did not prepare him for what happened on the night of February 4, 1932. He had been to a meeting of the Masons, returning home just after 11:00 p.m. He gave three gentle toots on the horn to let his wife know that he was home. When he got out to open the garage doors two men stuck guns in his ear and ordered him back into his car. They put him in the back seat on the floor with a man sitting on top of him. He didn't come in the house. His wife checked on him and he was gone. She got worried and called the police. The big man covered Gordon's eyes with a large rag. Gordon Sawyer didn't know where they were taking him. He told them if they are going to kill him don't drive this car too far for it is about out of gas. They told him to shut up and pushed his head down on the floor. It was then that they began to threaten him. He was told if he made a false move they'd put a bullet in each ear.

The third party met them and Gordon Sawyer was transferred into another car, a green Ford Roadster. They left his car, Packard Sedan, in the brush. The three men took Sawyer to an old farm house. Threw him on the floor and told him to go to sleep. A little hope came to him toward morning when the big guard said "I'll try to save you Mr. Sawyer, but they will probably kill you". Mr. Sawyer was let to an old well a ways form the house and was told to descent to the bottom. He told them if they are doing this for money they had better take good care of him for it was cold down there. They told him if he didn't sign the ransom note he'd be a lot colder.

This is what the note read. This is to warn you that we want $60,000.00 Saturday night or Gordon Sawyer will be killed. We have killed and robbed other people, and another killing is nothing to us. Early the next morning the letter was delivered to Fred J. Steward, President of the bank.

In the mean time the Tucson police went into action.

Charlie Mayse, an aviator, had a flying school at south Sixth and Irvington. It was in the same metal building where the U.S. Army Air Force was located before moving out to Davis Monthan. And now it houses the rodeo equipment. The next morning about day break Charlie Mayse took off and in no time he had located Sawyer's Packard car. Officers Al Franco and Jesus Camacho were sent to the site of Sawyer's car, to find out what they could. The tire marks on the old dirt road way were easy to follow. This was on West Grant, but at that time the road was named De Mos Petrie. On one side of the road the Demo Family lived and on the other side the Petrie Family lived and to this day my sister still keeps in touch with one of the Petrie girls.

A mile or two down the road they came upon two men sweeping out the tire marks with brooms. One of them took cover behind an old Chevy car and opened fire with a rifle. A lively interchange of gun fire followed. But the two policemen had only pistols and were over matched, and had to retreat. They came back with more men. They followed the road to an old house and inside showed signs of leaving in haste. The coffee on the table was still warm. Sawyer was still in the well and afraid to come out until he heard the voice of Dallas Douglas Ford a detective and a friend of our family. In a few minutes he was back in his house but still shaken, but unharmed.

They found a packet of letters addressed to Billie Atkins by a Tucson boy. Through him they found her and she was jailed. She wouldn't give out any information except she was living there with her dad and brother, it had to be Colonel Cole Atkins and his son Clifford whom both had record having served time in California, for bootlegging. The colonel, originally a Kentucky barber, was an experience sinner and his twenty nine year old son Clifford had just taken his first steps.

The third person was never positively identified. The next day after the abduction there were a lot of men 1500 searching the hills for them. The Colonel got completely away and it took nine days to find Clifford who was hiding in a friend's house name Joe Baker near the old Yuma mine in the Tucson Mountains, west of Tucson. Joe became bored with his company and told Clarence Houston the County Attorney about his predicament. Don't breathe a word or I will get killed but I want that S.O.B. out of there. The officers flushed him out with out any trouble.

Clifford's trail was held in May. Harry Juliani was in charge of the defense. The jury could not agree on the validity of the defendants alibi but he was tired again in June, convicted and sent to Florence with a life sentence. He was a model prisoner and was granted an out of state parole on December 1941. An account of his further adventures would be interesting, but he left no forwarding address.

# JUNE ROBLES KIDNAPPING

This is the second kidnapping for ransom that Tucson had and they both happened with in two years. The Robles family lived on West Franklin Street between church and court. June Robles (six years old) was going to Roskruge School on East Sixth Street.

The Kenglas Family lived on North Second Avenue and Barney Kengla six June's cousin also was going to the Roskruge School. Both of them were in the first grade. They left school together at 3:00 O'clock in the afternoon. June would go to the Kengla's house and her mother Mrs. Robles would pick her up there and go to their home. Barney was in a hurry so he had gotten ahead of June. When he passed this one car a man got out and tried to get Barney to get in the car. He had a ball game that evening so didn't pay to much attention to them and kept on going. When June got to the car a man got out and told her that they were told to pick her up and take her home, so she got in the car with them, Barney looked back and saw her get in the car, and they drove off.

Her father Fernando Robles received a note at this business Robles Electric Company. A small boy who delivered the note was to wait for an answer. It said that June was safe and would be released for $15,000.00. When the boy took the reply back he was gone. The next day the second note was received by Bernabe Robles, June's grandfather instructions were included and the ransom was reduced to $10,000.00. For several days no one knew what was happening. Rumors were that Bernabe Robles had gone to Mexico following some lead. This was never verified. Public interest remained high and large crowds gathered at the Robles's residence on Franklin Street. The parents were trying to establish some communication with the kidnappers to determine if June was alive and could be ransomed. They asked the citizen paper to print some questions that only June could answer. Like "What do you do with your bunnies in the morning?" The right answer came back.

The ordeal ended after nineteen days of abduction. A letter came from Chicago to Governor B.B. Moeur giving direction where to find June. On May 14th County Attorney C.E. Houston and June's uncle Carlos Robles began searching an area in the desert east of Wilmot Road that was miles form town in those days. They looked for a long time and started to go home when they stumbled upon a sheet-iron box six feet long and four feet high buried in the desert and covered with dirt. She was inside chained to a stake and the key was on top of the box. She was alive and well, and soon at home with her mother. There was a large crowd gathered in front of the home offering congratulations. The whole country was interests, newsmen and photographers were there.

Two Hollywood visitors wanted to take June on a tour for public appearance. It took the family very little time to decide that wouldn't be the best interest for the child.

There were never any indictments returned by the grand jury. The curtain was quickly dropped on one of the west most puzzling dramas. The record remained permanently close. The rumor was that it was an inside job by a distant relative from Mexico who was trying to get even with the grandfather from some past incident.

I met Dorothy in 1937 and dated her for a couple of years. Her family and the Robles were close nit and proud of their heritage.

The media or anyone else has never interviewed either one of the families. Bernade Robles made the statement "No one is going to use his name to kick around". The only new the public read is what the paper printed.

After World War Two was over I only saw Dorothy a couple of times and that was in the sixties.

In the summer of 2004 I called Barney for one thing or another, and in the process I asked him how Dorothy was and he gave me her phone number and I guess we talked for a two hours. When she got back in Tucson she gave me a call we went out to dinner and had a few lunches together. She's a great person to pass the time of day with.

June is still living and staying in Tucson, and a couple of months ago Dorothy gave June a picture of the two men that had kidnapped her. Dorothy told me that she should have it for she was the victim.

There have been a lot of people that have tried to interview June and or any one of the family with no success. They are still very private people and I respect them for it.

The siblings were born in the U.S.A. but before they started school Mr. Kengla took a job with the Southern Pacific Railroad in Mexico as a bookkeeper. They traveled all over Mexico living in the rear car of the train. Down in Mexico Dorothy started school and after the semester her mother told her husband to go back to the states for she wasn't going to put her kids through school in Mexico. He quit and the family moved to Tucson on North Second Avenue and Mr. Kengla took a job with the Steinfeld Department Store as a credit manager.

# RAILROADING

My brother (Okey) and I went to work for the Southern Pacific Railroad in 1942 we had to put in thirty day student trips, that's thirty days without any kind of pay or subsistence. This was for any one that wanted to hire out as switchman, brakeman or a fireman. After you made your thirty day trips you then had to write the book of rules. This took all day the brakemen and firemen not only had to write the book of rules but also book on steam engines and the book on diesel engines and that took a day for each book after you wrote the book of books you were allowed to put your name on the board to be called out. It was strictly seniority. That started the day you are called for work. My brother and I decided to be a switchman so we would be in town all the time. But if they ran short of brakemen then they would call a switchman to make a run which I did a couple of times. You could either bid on a regular job or you could bid on the extra board. I did both. On the extra board they worked us sixteen hours on duty we would have to take ten hours off but if you wanted to come back to work in eight hours you had the foreman to mark you off at fifteen hours and fifty nine minutes. A lot of them did that only to make extra money. I always ran a job and was home after my eight hours.

My brother-in-law Joe De Vos hired out as a fireman he had to spend thirty days the same as a switchman, but he had to go to El Paso and spend two weeks on a coal burner engine, the engines in Tucson was oil burners. After the thirty days where the switchmen had to write the book of rules, they had to write the of rules, book of steam engines, and the book of diesel which took him three days a day for each book. After the books are written then you can tell the dispatcher to mark you up, you go home and wait for a call.

The conductor picked up his paper work at the yard office and the train orders from the train dispatcher. Whether you are going to Lordsburg, New Mexico or Yuma, Arizona you will pick up orders along the way. About every fifteen miles there will be a telegraph shack that used the Morris-code. If the telegrapher had an order for the train he would raise an arm on a high pole next to the shack. If there weren't any orders the telegrapher would leave the arm down and the train would continue on. But if he had a message he would raise the arm on the pole which the engineer could see from a long distance he would slow the train down either the head brakeman or the fireman would reach out with his arm and run it through a bamboo loop with a long handle attached to it, at the base of the loop would be a clamp that held the message. He would drop the bamboo loop off at the next station as they go by.

When the railroads were lying the steel ribbons across the country there were a lot of accidents and people got killed. One thing that was bad was the head on collisions, caused by bad signals. Also they had a lot of boilers that blew, bad water gauges and water stations too far apart. In forty to fifty years it has to get better when we went to work for the Southern Pacific. Even after we went to work for the Southern Pacific had an engine to blow up. This was in November, 1946. This happened out of Gila Bend going to Tucson. The Steam Road Engine picks up a helper engine (this one happen to be a diesel) to help them over the mountain east of Gila Bend. Just outside of Gila Bend they passed a train in a siding waiting for them to go by and they all waved and it wasn't but a short distant when the steamer blew. Harry Hall was the engineer on the steam engine recollect who the firemen or the head brakeman was, on the diesel the engineer was John Roads (his brother Frank Roads use to own the Saddle Sirloin Steak House on Benson Highway) and it is still there) the fireman was Frank Bogulas, the engine number was 5037. All were killed except the head brakeman. Every one thinks that both gauges were defective, the fireman's and the engineer's.

Cab from Engine Number 5037 after it blew up just east of
Gila Bend when the boiler ran out of water

Another photo of Engine Number 5037 after it blew up

When Southern Pacific Railroad reached Tucson in 1880 the companies officials went to Bishop Salpointe and asked him if he and the sisters could build a hospital for some of his employees are going to get hurt and would need medical attention. That's when Saint Mary's Hospital was built. They started with eleven beds with three nuns and the first doctor was Doctor Handy.

The railroad had an engine shop, back shops that they could make anything you needed if it was made of metal. One of my brother-in-laws was a pipe fitter, another engineer, another switchman along with my brother and me. I had a sister and two cousins that worked in the yard office.

After the World War Two was over they moved the shops in Tucson to the El Paso Division, closed down the switching yard, they still have a couple of crews to spot some cars and do a little switching but not like it was when my brother and I was working there.

The Southern Pacific did a lot of changes. Like when we were switching we use to get on top of the cars to ride them from one yard to another. There was a cat walk they called it that ran from one end of the car to the other end. Many times when we would have five, ten, or fifteen cars I'd run the length of those cars going twenty to twenty five miles an hour. When you get up to that speed the cars really rock back and forth.

During World War Two out in the east yards a friend of mine was standing on top of a cut of cars waiting to shoved into the yard tracks when he looked up as a plane was coming in for a landing, he lost his balance and fell off of the top of the car he was standing on. He wasn't hurt bad a little bruised and shook up.

Another time a plane (bomber) coming in for a landing at Davis Monthan and it under shot the field and crash landed, all of us ran over to the plane and about that time it caught on fire the men in the back couldn't get out and started to yell we were going to knock a hole in the side with an axe but the captain was out and kept us away from the plane. When he found out that the men couldn't get out the captain started yelling for some one to do something. It was too late we couldn't get close due to the heat, the poor men burned up.

Tucson was a training center for the bombers and fighter planes. I saw a lot of crashed and the men burned up. When one of those bombers crashed it meant twenty lost. I noticed the paper in the past and mentioned about some of the crashes and I would call them and asked why they didn't write about all of them like when there were two bombers hit each other and both went down on the north side of the Catalina's. Some of these fighters would come in and land at Consolidated this was before the International Airport took over. Two of them in a row over shot the air strip and crashed into the brush.

Arizona had sixteen different railroads in the state. Three of the main ones were interstate, and the rest (13) were intra-state and were owned by the mining companies.

Listed below are the railroads with the first three being interstate:

Southern Pacific R.R.
Union Pacific R.R.
Santa Fe R.R.
El Paso and Southwestern R.R.
Santa Fe, Prescott, and Phoenix R.R.
Arizona Central R.R.
Arizona and New Mexico R.R.
Apache R.R
Arizona Eastern R.R.
Atlantic and Pacific R.R.
Mineral Belt R.R.
Clifton and Northern R.R.
Peavine R.R.
Maricopa and Phoenix R.R.
Salt River Valley R.R.

Southern Pacific bought up all the railroads in the southern part of Arizona and the last being El Paso and Southwestern in 1924 and the other twelve railroads the government gave Southern Pacific permission to pull up all the railroad tracks in 1930.

Sunset Limited Train. Sister to the one that was involved with Crescent City Express in a headon collision (called cornfield) meet by the railroaders

# THE TRAGIC TRAIN WRECK OF 1903

George McGrath didn't have a worry on his mind in January of 1903 for on Sunday February first, he was going to marry his true love. He was twenty seven years old with good looks and great character with a secured job as a fireman with the Southern Pacific Railroad's Sunset Limited passenger train. But the night before he was to make his run, he had a bad dream, he dreamed that the engineer Jack Bruce and he were going to have a head on collision, "Cornfield" in a railroader's slang was called. His fiancé begged him to lay-off but George refused, he told her if he ever came in on a stretcher it would be due to a careless dispatcher.

In 1901 alone, more than 50,000 people had been injured and 8,000 killed in railroad accidents.

With the increase of passengers and freight business starting in 1898 put a strain on their resources to keep cars moving, adding cars to the trains and adding trains to the same identification numbers. It was confusing to all who was involved, this clogged the rails putting strain on every one involved in the running of the trains, especially when there isn't any signal lights to control the movement of the trains.

When a telegraph operator received orders he completes a form in duplicate and the southern pacific rules are called for him to hand the forms directly to the conductor, who singed the orders and read them aloud while the operator verified them against the duplicate. If everything is correct then the operator issued a clearance order allowing the train to proceed. John "Jack" Bruce sat in the hog head's (engineers) seat on the southern Pacific's sunset limited headed into Tucson from the east January 28,1903 running twelve hours behind schedule. By the way John Bruce was the engineer on engine number 31 when the first train entered Tucson in 1880. After picking up his orders in Vail to pass an east bound freight at Wilmot, the Sunset Limited sped downhill, entering the sharp curve just west of Esmond siding, fourteen miles form Tucson, at forty five mile per hour and at the same time, unbeknownst to Bruce the east bound number 8 Crest City Express was chugging it's way up hill at twenty five miles per hour. As the rain rounded the curve, engineer Eugene R. "Bob" Wilkey spotted the head lamp of the on coming Sunset Limited. He pulled hard on the long emergency brake lever big holing the whole train and yelled to his fireman to jump and save your life, I will hold the throttle.

It was just an instant when the two locomotives slammed together fireman Gilbert leaped from the cab and tumbled into the darkness. He had a bad cut, broken shoulder and leg. He was unable to speak for several days. He survived and related his story of his heroic engineer. Wilkey a big man had applied the emergency brake will seated and was found in the wreckage trapped in his chair behind the brake handle.

Conductor O.H. Scriven had not quite finished collecting all the ticket in the day coach on number 8, when the blow came. Just as he reached for the cord to signal passing the flyer at the Esmond siding. The coach began to come in from the car behind climbing over its back. Scriven manage to keep his balance and jump to the ground with his passenger's right behind him.

The Sunset Limited conductor G.W. Parker was staggered by the crash but quickly recovered and leaping to the ground he dashed forward to crumpled mass of steel that had been the engines of both trains. He located engineer Bruce's burning body, minus an arm and a leg, beneath the oil tank. Next to Bruce lay fireman George McGrath, his skull mutilated and his right arm extended toward his trusted companion.

Realizing there wasn't anything he could do for the men, Parker raced ahead to the first two cars of the Crescent City, both engulfed in flames. After ordering the passengers off the train and away from the blaze, he began working to free the injured.

Parker retuned repeatedly to the burning cars until he finally collapse, bleeding and exhausted to the ground. The fire raged with fuel oil quickly saturated most of the wreckage, flowing in streams down each side of the tracks and torching the cars as it flowed by on both trains. Flames could be seen for miles and the smoke visible from Tucson.

Just before the collision Southern Pacific fireman and news butcher Tim Donahue had been enjoying a smoke in the Crescent City's smoker car and chatting with O.M. Stewart a Phoenician going to Bisbee.

At impact the smoker car rolled on its side and was drenched in burning oil. Donahue fighting to free himself from the fiery tomb remembered the door at the top of the car. He quickly flung it open and got out. The stricken news butcher was gasping for breath when he felt Steward's hands grab at his feet. Donahue with his cloths afire fought desperately to save the terrified passenger, but to no avail. It wasn't long before the coach was devoured by flames, he kicked himself free and dropped to the ground W.B. Keely, editor of the Bisbee Review threw his coat over Donahue and smothered the flames. But it was too late he died later in St. Mary's Hospital in Tucson.

Around 4:00 A.M. a relief train carrying physicians H.W. Fenner, W.P. Purcell, and W.V. Whitmore along with Southern Pacific division superintendent C.C. Sroufe in his private car, arrived at the scene and began loading the injured to bring back to Tucson. Chaos and panic ruled as day light broke over the Rincon Mountains. The screams of the dying and injured mingled with the smell of burning flesh. A brakeman from the rear of the Crescent City ran on foot to Vail, where he notified head quarters in Tucson on the wreck.

*Opha R. Probasco*

According to the Arizona Daily Star paper, twenty one year old night telegraph operator E. Frank Clough greeted the brakeman with the "Is anyone killed" Clough added I don't care much about the cars being destroyed, but I'm sorry I killed anyone.

Back at the wreck there was a pullman car still upright, but hitched to a flaming car. The passengers banded together to unhook the pullman from the flaming car. They soon lost control and Pullman headed down hill toward Tucson. There was a Negro porter inside and he tried to apply the hand brake but that was useless. He knew in a short time that there was going to be a H— of a wreck. He started thinking quickly, he piled up the sleepers mattresses to form a breastwork, to a padded wall. Then he wrapped himself in blankets, held on tight and waited for the conclusion.

At the Southern Pacific yard in Tucson the runaway Pullman car slammed into the locomotive of a wrecking train that had just entered the main line on its way to the Cornfield "Head on Collision". Sixteen year old fireman Maynard Flood recalled being thrown from the cab back onto the tender as the car hit and began to climb on top of the locomotive. The petrified porter ashen face but unhurt emerged from the mangled sleeper to tell of the awful accident up the line.

At the scene of the tragedy Tucson Daily Citizen reporter was spotted among the mangled wreckage, several spots of pure white ashes and in numerable small bones that were thought to be human remains.

Coffins lined the track as investigator battled the odds to make positive identification. Locating engineer Wilkey's body was heart wrenching. As Wilkey's ten year old son wandered among the ruins. Investigators gathered what they thought were his father's remains into two separate piles. One small pile, minus the head and some limbs, was found beneath the Crescent City's engine, while the other pile contained body parts.

Some of the survivors had consumptive and were traveling west to regain their health. They had gathered along a fence coughing uncontrollably in the cold morning air. Capitalist J.M. Hilton had been conversing with a Mr. Glidden of Cambridge, Massachusetts, when suddenly hurled through the window of a smoker and slammed to the ground. Hilton regained his composure and hurried to help the man, only to find him pinned beneath a flaming mass of metal. He watched helpless as Glidden burned to death. Jack Dwyer a tramp from Benson, described how he and three pards had hitched a ride on the Crescent City's engine tender. The collision threw Dwyer to the ground and had crushed his less fortunate friends.

By early afternoon workers had erected a Shoo-Fly. It's a temporary track that diverts the rail traffic around the heap of wreckage.

News of the wreckage reached Bruce's family late in the morning. Thirteen year old son George recalled that Judge William Angus came to the door saying "There's been trouble down the line". George never went to the wreckage site, but it seemed like every horse and buggy did.

The sequence of events leading to the head on collision quickly unfolded. Tucson dispatcher Charles Gray had sent two orders to the Vail station in the early morning hours of January 28th. The first instructed the west bound Sunset Limited to wait at Wilmot for an east bound freight to pass. The second order, issued ten minutes later and twenty one minutes before the train reached Vail, directed the Sunset Limited to pull out on the Esmond siding and let the east bound Crescent City Express go by. Operator Clough acknowledged receipt of both telegrams, to which he had signed conductor Parker's name.

At 2:50 A.M. Clough telegraphed Tucson saying he was unsure whether conductor Parker on the Sunset Limited had picked up both orders. About five minutes later, he notified head quarter that a large sheet of flame had flashed on the track west of Vail. He believed there was a wreck.

Clough had only gone to work as a telegrapher a week prior to the accident. Still he wasn't new with the telegraph his pass record of four years were good with other lines. He worked until noon answering almost sixty telegrams and maintained his innocence. He boarded the train to Tucson.

When questioned about the event of January 28th, Clough claimed that when the Sunset Limited "tied up" or stopped at the Vail station. He had placed the orders on the counter and hurried outside to load mail and express on board, returning to his office, he discovered the conductor Parker had taken only the top order, "Parker you have left one of your orders on the counter", Clough had yelled out. Parker did not respond instead the conductor boarded the train and signaled the engineer to proceed. According to Clough, Parker had violated company rules. The conductor had not read the orders aloud for verification. Clough appeared calm and sincere. While judging him a truthful and conscientious young man, the unknown rail predicted you will not see Clough in this part for a long time, there is no use of the coroners waiting for him to come and testify for he will not show up.

Clough however did report to the Southern Pacific superiors that day. The Tucson Citizen reported on January 30th, that Clough arrived on Wednesday afternoon and went directly to Mr. H.G. Bonorden, the chief dispatcher in Tucson, asking for his vouchers so he could get his pay and leave. That afternoon superintendent Sroufe called a conference of all surviving employees involved in the head on collision. Clough came into the meeting with some display of bravado then broke down and admitted his responsibility. He was ordered to appear before an inquest the following day. He was never seen in Tucson again. Rumors were that a friend of his had slopped Clough a roll of bills and he headed for Mexico. The Tucson Citizen accused the Southern Pacific Railroad of aiding and abetting in the escape. Clough's deliberate absence is accepted as a guilty plea, the police of the company are plainly obscurantism. Clough should have been taken into custody at once. With a sly wink of his employers he simply took a train to the International Line and disappeared.

There was confusion in how many casualties there were as people poured into Tucson looking for their dearest. Bruce,Wilkey, and Mc Garth's remains went to Parker's funeral home, while the corpses of eleven passengers were sent to the Reilly's Mortuary. Some of the people that were listed as dead turned up on other locations. A sterling silver pocket knife with the inscription "Eugene P. Willard" was found under a hand of a man who had been burned beyond recognition. Investigators assumed the young San Francisco cigar maker and his wife, close friends of the Sam Drachman and his family had perished in the conflagration. Fortunately, the couple soon turned up in Jerome. A citizen reporter asked for a passenger list but was told by the Southern Pacific officials that people traveling west had turned in their tickets at El Paso and no record had been kept of the east bound passengers, an exact count will never be known.

Vail station agent H.A. Mann received a telegram from Ethlyn P. Clough, intended for her son Frank it read "It is horrible be brave for my sake everything will come out alright".

The train wreck caused a battle royal between the Tucson Daily News Papers. The citizen charged the Southern Pacific with murder claiming that company had crammed as many as five bodies in each coffin to hide actual number of passengers killed in the collision. "The railroad company will attempt to cover up the facts", the paper predicted, but this is natural. It's not the fault of the tired and over worked employee. It's the fault of the improperly managed system.

The star jumped to the company's defense. It seems they want the responsible head of the Southern Pacific executed, quartered, and cremated as a partial atonement for the terrible disaster. The star lectured, this is nothing to be gained by exciting acrimonious feelings on such occasions simply to gratify an abnormal appetite which fattens on the abuse of corporations.

Ceremonies honoring the dead diverted Tucsonans attention for the next few days. Jack Bruce the Sunset Limited engineer and former Territorial Legislator, left a wife and five children. Bob Wilkey of the Crescent City Express, a member of the local Masonic Lodge was eulogized as a good citizen and a reliable railroad employee who was trusted by every one who knew him. A procession of Masons and at least thirty members of the local brotherhood locomotive firemen escorted George McGrath remains to the depot for shipment to his Connecticut home. On February1st passenger John E. Cassidy was buried in Tucson. His brother explained that it was useless to take his remains home as he could not be recognized.

In the mist of the funerals, a fight broke out over jurisdiction in assessing responsibility for the tragedy. A squabble in which is instilled no little bitterness, has risen between the justice of peace culver and O.T. Richey as to which has the power to act as coroner in this case, the citizen explained. Culver prevailed and jury soon announced its findings. It identified only three corpses, engineers Bruce and Wilkey, along with fireman McGrath, the remaining victims were listed as eleven unknown supposed male bodies. The jurors placed the blame for the collision squarely on the shoulders of telegraph operator Frank Clough.

On February 9th Judge Richey's jury rendered its own wordy decision. It concluded that fourteen bodies were recovered, that there were other killed but the number is not ascertained. They also found Clough at fault in the disaster, but went onto chastise the railroad officials for not placing guards at the wreckage. The flood of visitors at the scene made off with all sorts of matter and articles of value. Conductor parker admitted under oath, to the Culver jury that he had broken the rules by not repeating back to Clough the order to pull out on the Esmond siding.

Although the Southern Pacific concedes that Parker's violation had been of purely technical nature they none the less fired the well liked conductor. In a semi-official statement to the Arizona Daily Star the company explained that the action was necessary in order to maintain the rigid discipline in the army of employees. Parker quickly found work with El Paso Southwestern Railroad.

On February 10th the Star published a long letter from Mrs. Clough defending her son's departure from Tucson. In her opinion, conductor Parker was as much or more to blame than Frank. He is an older man and had been with the company for a long time. He knew the rules better than Frank, Mrs. Clough wrote again the following month claiming she had indisputable proof of her son's innocence but wouldn't tell of his where a bouts.

The wreck had generated at least one legal skirmish and it was a corker. Twenty eight year old Hugh MacKenzie, a wealthy and finely educated young Australian mining engineer, was reportedly on board.

The Crescent City Express on his way east from Los Angeles to claim his inheritance of an immense estate in Aberdeen, Scotland when he failed to arrive, MacKenzie's wealthy parents spared no expense looking for their son. After ten full months of futile searching the MacKenzies reached an obvious conclusion young capitalist had surely been incinerated in the Esmond rail disaster.

After one year after the Esmond wreck Thomas Wilson special administrator of Hugh MacKenzie's Estate, filed a $5,000.00 law suit against the Southern Pacific Railroad. The out come of the suit remains a mystery, and does not ultimate fate of Hugh MacKenzie.

The Cornfield disaster poignantly emphasized an improvement on traffic control on the rails. The most horrific of four serious wrecks across the nation with in a twenty four hour period, it sparked heated discussions of railroad safety on editorial pages from coast to coast. As the southern pacific hustled to put the finishing touches on a new edition of its "Book of Rules" (the company bible). Tucson division Superintendent Sroufe responded to the tragedy by calling together his assistants to discuss ideas for preventing such wrecks. He personally carried their views to a meeting with company officials in San Francisco. Suggestions included no longer requiring conductors to sign orders that had been dead for hours and demanding that dispatchers regularly remove train orders from their often cluttered desk. The Southern Pacific reacted promptly and decisively to the Esmond tragedy. In April the railroad issued a new schedule that called for passenger trains to proceed at a slower pace. It hoped the slower speed would allow the engineers to adhere more closely to the printed time table. The following month the company took another significant step towards improving safety on the road by placing train agents on all passenger trains. Drawn from the baggage and brakemen corps, the assistants to the assistants to the conductor were assigned to collect tickets and fares. Railroad executives hoped the move would reduce the duties of the conductors, allowing them to put their full attention toward managing the train.

Captain James H. Tevis of Bowie Station have for years studying the safety problems. After the Esmond wreck he submitted his proposal to several railroad men. Tevis suggested installing electric wire along the tracks in Tucson division, powered by a dynamo at every pumping station. The electricity conveyed along wire would illumi-

nate bulbs suspended form every second or third telegraph pole. An agent who detected an error in handling
orders could press a button that would signal every train
affected by the mistake to stop and proceed slowly until
the trouble is cleared. Tevis had already applied for patent
protection for his idea, though there's no record that indicates a patent had ever been granted. Although a block
system such as Tevis proposed had finally been installed
and greatly improved the safety on the Tucson division.

The Star paper predicted that the wreck of Esmond
will never be forgotten. On the tablets of memory, anguish,
suffering and death has been written ineffaceably the horrors of the worst railroad disaster that ever occurred in
the territory of Arizona. But memories are fleeting, and
today the story of the desert train wreck is buried in local
archives. The site of southern Arizona's worst train disaster is all but forgotten in the back yard of the Rita Ranch
subdivision west of Houghton Road and north of Rita
Road. A century ago, the Esmond collision helps change
the face of railroading in Arizona.

# SOUTHERN PACIFIC RAILROAD
# ROBBERIES

Wilcox lies in the heart of the Sulphur Springs Valley. The valley is about fifteen miles wide and about a hundred miles long, stretching from Douglas on the south to Fort Grant on the north. When the cattlemen first arrived in the area in the 1870's the native grasses were stirrup high, and the Riches Valley in the west. At one time there were 40,000 cattle grazing in the valley. It was so over grazed that the valley never did return to normal. All the valleys in Southern Arizona were a cattlemen's dream with so much native grasses, and every one was over grazed. A couple years of drought and it looked like all the grasses in the valleys just disappeared, never to return. At one time only Tucson shipped out more cattle than Wilcox.

One of the west's most humorous train robberies took place just five miles west of Wilcox on January 30, 1895. Cowboys Grant Wheeler and Joe George decided to raise their station in life by holding up the Southern Pacific Railroad they purchased a large box of dynamite in

Wilcox, to be used in prospecting and went out to meet the Southern Pacific train. They stopped the train, uncoupled the two head cars mail and baggage and ordered the engineer to take them several miles down the track. They broke open the express car but found the Wells Fargo messenger had gone out the opposite side of the car and escaped. The robbers placed some sticks of dynamite around the two safes. The first blast demolished the small safe but the big sturdy Wells Fargo safe remained intact, so they tried again without success. Finally the frustrated punchers packed the rest of the dynamite around the large safe and piled eight sacks, each containing $1,000 in Mexican silver pesos, on top to act as ballast. The blast that followed shook the mountains near by. The safe was blown apart but so was the express car. The air was filled with shrapnel as $8,000 adobe dollars were hurled in all directions. Impregnating everything they hit including nearby telegraph poles. It was said that for the next thirty years folks were still picking up silver pesos in the surrounding desert. The damage created far exceeded the loot, which was estimated at between $200 and $1500.

Although the heist left a lot to be desired, wheeler and George were happy with their handy work and decided to try it again.

On the evening of February 26th they stopped another Southern Pacific train at Stein's pass near the New Mexico line. The two cowpunchers just grinned. Following their last plan, wheeler and George uncoupled the cars fro the train and ordered the engineer to head down the tracks to where the horses were staked. In their haste the two robbers unhitched the wrong car. After getting the horses and dynamite they realized the car with the money in it was still hooked to the train. With frustration they ordered the engineer to reverse his engine and rejoin the train. They then lit the fuse to the dynamite and rode off in disgust.

Another train robbery took place a few miles for Wilcox on the evening of September 11, 1899. The heist was planned by none other than the good humored Wilcox town Marshall, Burt Alvord a bald headed man was good ole boy if there ever was one. He had a big grin, and a sense of humor, along with that of a prankster. He made friends easily from judges, merchants, and even cattle rustlers, but wasn't blessed with any intelligence. What he did have was from hanging around the pool halls in Tombstone, where he was raised. Burt Alvord was good with a gun and wasn't feared of anything or anybody John Slaughter the sheriff of Cochise country from 1886 to 1892 deputized him for his prowess in chasing outlaws.

Alvord had befriended an ornery bunch of coharts that included the deputy constable at Pearce, Billy Stiles along with Bill Downing, Matt Burts, three finger Jack Dunlap, and Bravo Juan Yoas. Collectively their I.Q.'s wouldn't add up to a hundred, but they were as mean and nasty as any bunch that every rode the Arizona country.

At about 11:30 P.M. on September 11, 1899 Billy Stiles and Matt Burts climbed aboard the west bound Southern Pacific train just as it was pulling into Cochise Station, ten miles west of Wilcox. While one of the gunmen covered the engineer and fireman the other uncoupled the engine and express car from the rest of the train. The Wells Fargo messenger was ordered to open the door and vacate the premises. Next they ordered the engineer to take the express car and engine down the tracks a few miles at the prearranged point, the outlaws jumped off and picked up a box of dynamite. Then they climbed into the express care piled explosives around the safe, lit the short fuse and headed for cover. The stillness of the night was shattered by a resounding blast as the interior of the express car was blown to splinters. The blast blew open the Wells Fargo safe, and the outlaws quickly emptied the contents.

Burt Alvord took the gold and buried it, in a secret hiding place. He was feeling pretty good about the perfect robbery and his alibi he had established. However, he didn't count on the persistence of Wells Fargo detectives and a lawman name Bert Grover. Bert Grover suspected Alvord early on probably because he was acting a little too innocent. Grover questioned the porter at the saloon and he had made a confession in his role as establishing Alvord alibi but before he could bring charges his star witness got cold feet and left the territory.

Burt and the boys felt so good about their train robbery that they decided to try another Estimate of the loot was range from $3,000 to $300,000 in gold. An educated guess would be $30,000. They loaded the gold on the horses and headed for Wilcox.

Mean while the engineer rejoined his train and backed all the way into Wilcox to give the alarm. The town Marshall was sitting innocently in the back room of Schwerner's Saloon playing poker with his pals

He deputized Bill Downing, and rode out to Cochise, cut the trail of robbers and followed it back to the out skirts of Wilcox, where the tracks were lost in a herd of horses. Feigning great frustration the two returned to their poker game.

Obviously, the card game had been a clever ruse to establish an alibi. During the evening Alvord and friends exited through the window and headed to the out skirts of town, where Downing had left some horses. Burt and Stiles then rode to a spot two miles west of Cochise where a Cache of dynamite was waiting. They then hobbled the horses and jumped on the train as it slowed down going up a long hill grade of the station.

The porter at Schwerner's had been bribed to take drinks to the back room every few minutes and return with empty glasses creating a illusion that the long running poker game was still in progress. By the time the train had returned to Wilcox, Alvord and friends had returned through the back window and resumed their poker game. Just to make sure the boys didn't squander their new wealth around town and arouse suspicion; Bone, this time they let Bravo Juan, Three Finger Jack, Bob Brown, and the Owens brothers do the dirty work, but the robbery at Fairbanks didn't go as planned. They didn't figure on the gun fighter Jeff Milton on being in the express car.

Milton opened fired on the gang from the inside of the express car, mortally wounding Three Finger Jack and sending the rest away empty handed. The outlaws left Jack on the trail to die and when the lawmen found him, he bitterly gave all the details of both robberies.

Burt and his pals claimed their innocent claiming Dunlap had tried to frame them. So many people like Burt Alvord that they thought he wasn't smart enough to pull off a robbery of that kind.

Burt Alvord was the only one who knew where the gold was hidden. So afraid they wouldn't get their fair share they stuck with Alvord. But Billy Stiles broke under pressure for exchange for his freedom.

With Billy stiles confession the gang was locked up in Tombstone. Since the gold had not been found the charges against them was tampering with the U.S. mail only.

On the morning of April 8, 1900 for reasons known only to him Billy Stiles walked into the jail, shot the jailer in the leg, opened the cell door for Alvord and Bravo Juan, not surprisingly he left the troubled Bill Downing sitting in his cell, cursing as they ran out to their horses.

Burt Alvord and Billy Stiles hid out in Mexico for a couple of years until ranger Burt Mossman, working under cover, enlisted their help in capturing the notorious bandit Augustine Chacon. In return they were to surrender to authorities and be given light sentences. Despite the short jail term Alvord and Stiles broke out of jail again this time digging their way out. Alvord was captured but Stiles was never caught. He moved to Nevada and took the name of Larkin, got into a gun fight and was killed.

Matt Burts served his time then went back to cowboying at his brother's ranch near Wilcox. Burt Alvord did his time, returned to Wilcox for a few days, said howdy to his old cronies, than left town for good. Old timers said that he had dug up his gold and moved to Honduras, where he married and settle down.

Downing had married a pretty young lady from a good family in Texas. While he was in prison, she'd been forced to sell their ranch and move to Tucson, where she worked as a domestic. Before his ten year term (three years off for good behavior) was up, she died. The coroners report said that it was heart failure but perhaps it was a broken heart.

Bill Downing came out of prison in 1907 as despicable and mean as ever. He returned to Wilcox and became a proprietor of the Free and Easy Saloon. It became a place for prostitutes, brawlers, tin horn gamblers, and the general riff raff. Customers complained about having their wallets picked by the ladies, but nobody in town was brave enough to press charges. Downing boasted he'd kill anyone who got in his way and that lawmen would never take him alive. Finally the Arizona rangers were called in, Captain Harry Wheeler dispatched ranger Billy Speed to Wilcox to keep an eye on the Free and Easy Saloon.

In 1907 the territory legislature had passed a law against allowing women in a saloon. Downing was charged with violation of this law, and fined $50.00; he went home and beat up his live in girlfriend to vent his anger. She went to the Wilcox constable Bud Snow and give evidence about the customers being robbed at the Free and Easy Saloon. Snow asked ranger Speed to help arrest Downing. At 8:00 A.M. On the morning of August 5, 1908 Ranger Billy Speed armed with a 30-40 Winchester stood in front of the Free and Easy Saloon and ordered Downing to step outside with his hands up. Downing had been drinking a lot and feeling mean, ignored the ranger, when Speed called the second time, Downing headed for the back door, as he moved past some early morning drinkers, one reached over and snatched the revolver out of Downing's holster. The outlaw went out the door, around the corner only to meet the ranger coming the other way.

*Opha R. Probasco*

"Throw up your hands" the ranger yelled, Downing a left hander, reached for his pistol but came up with nothing but an empty holster, at the same time Speed fired, putting a bullet into Downing's chest. The outlaw fell to the ground mortally wounded. Nobody in Wilcox was remorseful over the demise of Bill Downing.

# TUCSON GOES TO WAR

War was in the air and war fever was rising. The university offered early graduation to seniors who wish to volunteer to join the National Guard. Everyone in Tucson almost showed up to march at the armory. The civil war veterans were there dressed in their old uniforms of what was left of them. Everyone had a flag including the boy scouts and the Red Cross girls.

Governor Campbell ordered every male between the ages of 18 to 45 to report at the court house to register for possible enrollment in the state militia. The next morning there were 100 patriots there and more showing up. There were some conscientious objectors as always when it came to war. Not all the soldiers were too eager to fight the Germans. Nogales became a concentration point for the slackers since there was an avenue of escape to Mexico. There were attempts to bring them back and make them enlist or go to jail. Some of the people recommended they be shot. There were other attempts launched in the sacred name of liberty to defend them of their rights as conscientious objectors. Pancho Villa and his troops had raided

Columbus, New Mexico on March 9, 1916. Fear of invasion was uncomfortable real so deeply ingrained that after1916 the boarder was guarded and patrolled.

It was peaceful and quite and boring that the men of Company M marched up and down the Naco streets shouting they want to go home. Six months later the unit lost ninety nine men through desertion.

It was believed that the Germans had infiltrated and were planning to attack the border communities and these fears were not with out foundation. In 1917 the Zimmerman telegraph revealed that Germany was prepared to return to border states to Mexico in exchange for military alliance. The people of Tucson were afraid that there were German spies and saboteurs that were going to interfere with communications and supply lines. This alarmed the Major and the City

Council, and they reacted to do something about it.

The Star paper carried this head line "Auto Shot Gun Squad to Guard City".

Mayor O.C. Parker was a muscular, tough, aggressive fellow that would take actions instead of pointing a committee. He assembled a posse of volunteers in twenty four automobiles prepared to repel all invaders. Ninety fighting men in twenty four autos with a driver and four armed men with sawed off shot guns in each car, they will patrol all roads leading into the city. A big supply of buck shot was purchased by the safety committee for the arming of the shot gun brigade. The Red Cross, all ambulances, motor cycles, and wagons have all been put into commission for an emergency notice. The mayor went to Monte Mansfield and told him that he wanted an automobile with just the chassis for he wanted to mount tow machine guns on the front.

O.C. Parker the mayor and the council did get the shot gun shells but not the guns, and we still don't know what happened to the shells.

The same, new faces, same old ideas. If this mayor and council were in on this shotgun brigade they would have shot themselves in their foot.

Look how they tore down our history, they bull dozed it all down because it was an eye sore. I remember the old convento that stood along side of the Old Simpson Road that crossed the river from South Main over to South Mission Road. A couple of years ago they were searching for the spot where that old convento stood. The state capital was here on Ocha Street in two buildings, you would think they would save the capital buildings for history, they just had to have the space for the community center, which they could have put it out side of the city. They moved Mission Road farther south and extended El Grande south of Congress. They are always wanting to change things, if they would just sit in their chairs and do nothing they city would be a lot better off.

They moved the parade out of the down town area to South Park. Cele Peterson and I both with everyone else think the rodeo parade should go back in town where it originated. You ask the city why they moved it and they will give you a big lie of everything but the truth. The real reason they moved it was it saved them a lot of money in blocking the streets and cleaning up after the horses. It's the people's money and we should have some say in how it is spent. But they want to spend it on some Pork

Barrel Project. If they did move it back down town there isn't a person on the city's pay roll that could handle it. They have to have something simple.

After we came here in 1925 the army was stopping all cars into Tucson, on West Ajo Road where Kinney Road turns off of Ajo was a tent with a lantern hanging out side on a pole. Stopping the cars going into town, also on Nogales Highway the soldiers were doing the same thing. This lasted to 1930.

# THE ARRIVAL OF THE FIRST AIRPLANE

During the early part of aviation the planes were called aero planes. It was February 17, 1910 when Charles Hamilton loaded his air plane on a rail car and shipped it to Tucson from Phoenix, Arizona. Along with Hamilton was Glen Curtiss who was the mechanic, the engine was an eight cylinder Curtiss with a pusher blade.

It was on the ball park in Elysian grove that Hamilton made his flight on Saturday and Sunday, he was guaranteed $1500.00. Saturday he had made a good flight, then on Sunday he came in a little too fast or a little too high for he over shot the field and couldn't stop before he hit a post. He damaged the front of the plane but had fixed it up and went on to Douglas and from there to El Paso, Texas, where he was killed.

Due to fear of the Germans invading us through Mexico the army planes patrolled the border from California to Texas. Always eager to do their part the members of the Tucson Chamber of Commerce leased and graded an air strip between Oracle and Stone Avenue, where Amphitheater High School was later built. The Chamber of Commerce saw to it that they had gas and lodging.

# FLOUR MILLS IN TUCSON

The Rowlett Brothers came to Tucson in 1857. There wasn't a flour mill in Tucson at that time so they decided to build one. This all took place where the river runs through Silver Lake Road. There were some low lands in that area. The Rowlett brothers built a big dam on the back side enclosing a large area of ground. Then they build a dam that ran out into the river to divert some of the water coming down the river. With the dam on the back side they got the flour mill built and running and later sold it to William Grant for $5500.00 Grant then enlarged the mill and built another one next to it.

In 1861 the Civil War broke out and the union army gave William Grant thirty minutes to gather his personal papers and leave. The union army then set fire to both flour mills, supplies, and equipment. William Grant and the Rowlett brothers disappeared from Tucson never to be heard from again.

Charles Hayden came to Tucson on the first Butterfield Stage Coach in 1858. He took over the abandoned flour mills and fixed one up that wasn't damaged too badly from the fire. Later he sold both mills in 1864 to James Lee and W.F. Scott. They ran the one mille and in 1870 they built another mill on the corner of Broadway (use to be called Camp Street) and Main. It was the tallest building ever erected in Tucson, called the Eagle Steam Flour Mill. Later Scott sold out to Lee then Lee sold the mills to E.N. Fish, who was married to Maria Wakefield. In 1898 E.N. Fish sold the mill Leo Goldschmidt a few years later Goldschmidt build another steam mill on Tool Avenue above Sixth Avenue, under pass. In 1940 he quit making flour and made just feeds. In 1963 the Eagle Mill was torn down and a new one was build at Jaynes Station and was called Arizona Milling Company. Sometime later that name was changed to Arizona feeds as it stands today.

# SOLOMON WARNER

Solomon Warner was born in Warnersville, New York in 1811. He drifted to the Mississippi River, worked on boats, then went to California during the gold rush. From there he sailed to Panama and stayed there in Nicaraque for two years. Then he went to San Francisco in 1853 then moved to Yuma, Arizona and built the fort there.

After hearing about Tucson, Arizona he decided to open a store there. He took merchandise from Hooper and Hinton who had a store in Yuma, on consignment. He hired Sonora Trader Joquin Queroga with his fourteen mules to haul his goods to Tucson. The price was 300 miles at $30.00 a cargo. One cargo equals 300 pounds.

Solomon Warner opened his store in 1856 and made trips back to Yuma for more merchandise and he also made trips to Mexico. The Apaches seems to be always waiting for him. The trips coming back from Yuma was the worse. Besides getting injured the Apaches destroy every thing including the merchandise. In 1861 Civil War broke out and the Union Army destroyed both flour mills and anything else that would help the confederacy. In 1862 Captain Hunter captured Tucson and ordered Solomon Warner to get a rifle and join his troops or get out. He took off for Mexico and the army destroyed his store.

Solomon went to Santa Cruz, Sonora, Mexico. He soon had a farm and many head of cattle. He started a freight business running from Guaymas to Hermosillo. He also started a flour mill and married a Sonora widow with a beautiful daughter named Eulalia. They had many servants with all the comforts of life. He bathed in love of his wife and step daughter and was admired by the Mexico business men. His home was filled with guest on all holidays. One of the guests was John Spring an Untied States army officer in 1866. He was on leave from Camp Wallen in Arizona. He was 22 years old and fell madly in love with Eulalia, but she was already engaged to a young Mexican youth.

John Spring and Solomon Warner remained close friends through out their lives. They went to Tucson together and John was the second teacher the public school had in Tucson.

Augusta Brichta was the first teacher in 1868 and the school only opened for six months and closed for the lack of funds.

Solomon Warner saw a lot of Mexican freighters heading for Tucson with as many as forty burros loaded with merchandise. This brought back memories and Solomon's love for Tucson was the reason he left his wife and step daughter, and the good life he had. He opened his old store and got it well stocked with European goods and merchandise from Mexico and San Francisco. The prices were high but he gave a discount to the ones that paid him in gold. All the money he had was "Dobe" dollar or Mexican silver.

In 1874 and 1875 Solomon built a flour mill at the base of "A" Mountain he had built a dam out into the river as the Rowlett brothers had done which he created a dam with control canals and ran water to his mill. He also built his home just north of the mill. When the farmers below him ran short of water and it was during a thunder storm they would blast a hole in his dam to get some water people would just think it was thunder. This was probably the reason Solomon decided to change over his paddle wheel to a steam power mill. This was in 1878. This did not solve his growing problems. He had been in competition with Lee and Scott and their steam mill, plus his old wounds were giving him trouble that he had to sell his mill.

In 1891 a big flood had come and wiped out all of the dams that were never rebuilt. Solomon died in 1899 his good friend John Spring was the only one at his side when he died. The Arizona Pioneer's Historical Society was in respect. He had the largest funeral than anyone in those days.

The foundation of the mill is still there and his home is now owned by Diana Hadley who is living there now and a good friend of mine.

There is no record of his wife, step daughter, or her husband. Solomon Warner died in poverty at the age of 88.

# WHITE HOUSE CANYON

Harry E. Heighton was born in Marshalltown, Iowa on October 7, 1867. He was sixteen years old when Harry left Marshalltown and went to Santa Ana, California to be with his mother. He worked as a clerk but the economy wasn't good so he left and went to Phoenix, Arizona in 1893. He worked as a cashier and bookkeeper for the Henry Kemp Company. The following year he married twenty five year old Frances Lynn Clardy.

The slump of the 1890's forced his employer into bankruptcy. In 1899 he had the job of liquidating the business then he moved to Tucson, Arizona. He opened an office for the New York Insurance Company. He did very well and in 1904 Harry bought a full partnership in a real estate and insurance company of Franklin and Heighton. Previously it was the under wood and Franklin real estate and insurance company. The following year he bought the Citizen's building and loan association, and became the sole owner of the company in 1925.

In 1921 he was president of the Chamber of Commerce, a member of the Sunshine Climate Club, served on the county and city planning and zoning commission. Following the life time service to Tucson, Harry E. Heighton passed away on August 23, 1948 at the age of eighty.

He recorded this story of the trip to the Santa Rita Mountains. In October 1910 Harry Heighton and Dave Cochran, left Tucson in a light spring board wagon with a good team of horses. They went through Greaterville ( a mining camp) on the Box Canyon Road up to Fish Canyon through Snider's Mine to Gardner Canyon. They left the wagon there and packed their supplies on the horses and hiked up to Anderson's cabin. This was to be a two week trip. They had gotten plenty of deer meat and decided to climb to the top of Mount Wrightson Peak (Old Baldy or Mount Baldy named after Captain Richard Ewell commandant of the Buchanan Fort by his troops for his receding hair line and their respect for him). After Heighton and Cochran got to the top and looked down, there was a ridge that ran around the peak with four canyons running down and coverging into the White House Canyon. The canyon names from west to east are Johns, Little Shots, Madera, and Big Springs.

After returning to Tucson Harry Heighton reported to some of his friends of what he had seen from the top of the Wrightson Peak. They were so interested that Harry and two of his friends took a trip to the White House Canyon to inspect the ground. There were plenty of water and shade. They selected a site then got a permit from the forestry for five acres.

In June 1911 after school was out all the families amounting to six adults and fourteen children got the supplies and everything they needed to last for three months stay. They built six cabins and for the next five or six years the summers were spent at the White House Canyon. During that time the roads got better and automobiles came into use and more people were building cabins.

How the canyon came to be known as White House Canyon. About 1880 a Sheepman named Walden was living there behind some large boulders with his sheep. He finally build a house and lived there for two years and left in 1882 never to be heard from since. Theodore Welisch who owned the White House Mercantile in Tucson saw the cabin had been abandoned so he decided to take it over for himself. He painted it white, then used it for his summer home with his family. Since then it was known as White House Canyon. It was still called that after we came here in 1925. In 1922 Corydon Dunsenberry built a store in the canyon and just opened it during the summer. A few years later he decided to stay open the year around and established a post office. White House Canyon was to long so he changed it to Madera Canyon. He was a deputy earning $12 a month, he kept horse to rent and sold fire wood. Dunsenberry sold his business in 1935, the post office closed in 1942, and in 1983 the store burned down. The old timers still called it White House Canyon even after the name changed.

During the 1980's the forestry cancelled all the cabin permits and gave the people ten years to Tear the cabins down.

1985 twenty nine cabins were torn down. 1991 twenty three remaining cabins were torn down.

The remaining cabins are:

Three people own their cabins on the Susie Load Mining Claim. American Smelting Mining Company has three cabins on their lots. Four people own their cabins on the Iron Cap Claim in which includes the Big Rock the lodge with several cabins to rent is owned by the forestry.

# SANTA RITA MOUNTAINS

In the middle of the 1850's the Untied States – Mexico boundary commission change the name of Sierra De LA Madera to Santa Rita Mountains. The reason for the change from Sierra De LA Madera (mountain range of the lumber) to Santa Rita Mountains was that it was too long of a name.

The Big Shear Cliff is named Elephant Butte which the top side runs up to Mount Wrightson. The country around it was known as Tom Boy Range. Mount Wrightson is also known as Mount Baldy for Captain Richard Ewell who was in charge of the Fort Buchanan. He was bald on top with a heavy beard. His troops respected him so much that they gave him the honor. After the Civil Was broke out he defected from the Union Army to the Confederate Army and they made him one of their top generals.

In 1857 a Captain Tarbox from Maine established the first lumber mill in Arizona. The lumber was whipped sawed and this was done by digging a ditch approximately four feet wide, seven feet long, and six feet deep, with a man in the hole and a man on the top side using a long two man saw. After the lumber was whipsawed it was transported to the Canoa Crossing. He had build a house and a corral there and sold the lumber for $150.00 per thousand feet. Captian Tarbox used oxens to pull the timber down off the mountain to the whipsaw mill.

The Presidio had one black smith shop and needed an anvil. They used a meteorite from the Valle De Hierro (valley of iron) this was the only meteorite that was known to have a hole through it. It weighed 1400 pounds and they transported it on a stone sled which was two long poles with a cross plank pulled by a mule or an oxen. In 1849 Gold Rush Ramon Pacheco decided another black smith was needed so he went to the Valle De Hierro (valley of iron) and got another meteorite for another anvil but this one was a lot smaller than the other one was, it just weighed 633 pounds. The Valle was known to all of the settler. In 1850 J.F. Velasco wrote that there was several pieces of iron meteorites in the Valle De Hierro. There was very little interest shown. Later the Smithonian Institute in Washington D.C. received both fragments. In 1976 the Smithonian Institute returned the big meteorite briefly to Tucson, Arizona. The visit started an interest in the meteorites and the rock hounds started their search for any of it they could find. None was ever recovered and it is a mystery to this day to what could have happened to any or all of it.

# CABIN ON TOP OF WRIGHTSON

In 1914 assistant forest ranger Olof (Olie) Olson build a cabin on top of Mount Baldy a short distant form the summit of Mount Wrightson. Carl Scholefield was the look out guard. He would sleep in the cabin then in the morning he would go to the summit to the look out post and check for fires. When the fire season was over the hunters would take over the cabin. By 1948 the look out post wasn't needed so the cabin was pushed over the ridge. The cabin was still popular as a shelter for hikers and back packers. The cabin was in despair until 1962 when Southern Arizona Hicking Club supplied the labor and the forest service hauled up the supplies to fix the cabin up. In 1973 the cabin burned down.

# A FEW MORE SANTA RITA MOUNTAIN STORIES

Everyone talks about the Catalina Mountains, more so than they do about the Santa Rita Mountains, I guess it's because there is a ski slope up there, and the paved road up to the top. I remember going up to Mount Lemon from the back side in a model T Ford, This was before the road was built on the front side. There's more history that came out of the Santa Rite Mountains than came out of the Santa Catalina's. The forest service had a look out post on top of Mount Baldy, named for Captain Ewell with his bald head. The correct name is Wrightson Peak. The White House canyon now it's Madera Canyon changed by the Post Master Corydon Dusenberry, to make it a shorter name.

The first Cavalry's Company K moved form Fort Mason, near Calabasas to west of the White House and established Camp Cameron on the Canoe Road in 1866. In 1877 some of the soldiers left for Fort Lowell in Tucson and by March the rest of them left and that put the end to Camp Cameron.

# RANCH OPERATION

Operating a ranch has changed from what it was eighty years ago, right along with everything else. There was a lot of riding to do, not only during the roundup but every day or so when nothing is important to do around the home place. There is the fence line to check to see if any part of it has been knocked down from some cause or other. Water tanks to check and some times you have to climb a windmill to oil and check.

Mister Davidson and his wife owned a Doctor Pepper franchise in Trinidad, Colorado which they sold and bought a ranch west of Three Points on Ajo Road. They had about two hundred head of mother cows, steers and calfs. Three of us–Buck Williams, Frank Clark and I– worked all the cattle which included branding, dehorning, cutting the bull calfs, checking for screw worms, plus getting a count of all the stock. This was done back in the days when it was done the hard way.

A very dear friend of mine, Virgil Mercer and his wife own the Camp Stool Ranch across the river from Mammoth. He's the third generation living at this ranch. He used to do a lot of riding doing everything that I mentioned above plus getting ready for a roundup when that time rolls around. That is getting thirty, thirty-five head of horses shod, fed to get along with some grain, corrals to repair if needed.

My brother had the franchise for the Japanese Hodaka and the Montessa that the Spanish made. Virgil changed from riding horseback to riding dirt bikes in checking the fences and the water. Virgil was a pilot during the World War Two and he took up flying the ultralight airplanes. Then he changed from dirt bikes to the ultralights. Also his son Gary flies a helicopter and instead of rounding up the cattle on horses and dirt bikes the two of them do a pretty darn good job with the helicopter and the ultralight. His sons finally took over the ranch but Virgil still flies the ultralight checking the water and fences.

Gary Mercer in his helicopter rounding up cattle at the Camp
Stool Ranch on January 18, 1990. Courtesy of Gary Gaynor,
Tucson Citizen

Virgil Mercer in his ultralight plane rounding up cattle at his ranch "The Camp Stool". Courtesy of Gary Gaynor, Tucson Citizen

In the early days when there weren't any fencing to keep the cattle from straying, the old time cowboys led a different kind of life. His work was harder and the hours long, with chuck wagon eats, thirty dollars a month was considered good pay. Cattle belonging to different ranches roamed together and during branding time the cowboys separated the cattle by their brands. Each ranch had their own cowboys that took care of their cattle, branding and cutting the calves, plus dehorning the ones that needed it.

After all the branding and etc.. had been done the mother cows with calves were turned back and the yearlings with older cows that they wanted to get rid of were driven to the market. They usually have a round up twice a year mainly to get a count on what they have and brand the new born calves. When a calf get six months old he's been on grass and not following their momma anyone could put their brand on him.

During the round up the work was dangerous, especially during the long drives to the market, the cattle are tired and restless and about anything could cause a stampede like thunder, gun shots and any unusual noise. The cowboys would talk and sing to the cattle try to keep them calm. On a dark humid night when the cattle horns rub together it causes static electricity. The balls of light, called St. Elmo's Fire, produced and eerie and spectacular show. It follows the horns and jump across the spurs and bridle bits. Even the sparks would fly when the cowboy would pop his quirt.

A cowboy may ride for a few days before going home. The food they carried usually was jerky, bread, or tortillas along with some salt. Their bed roll was always tied behind the cantle of the saddle. Of course they always had coffee which was called George Washington, it was a syrupy concentrate. You could use sugar if you want and all you had to do was to add water.

After the soldiers left Camp Cameron the cowboys took advantage of the shelter they had. On one occasion the Apaches surrounded the camp. The cowboys decided to fool them by pretending they escaped from one side of the camp. They tied a young boy Manuel Sanchez to a fast mare and sent them to the opposite direction toward the Canoa Crossing. Realizing help would soon arrive they departed.

The cowboys also built a one room cabin a mile northeast of the White House, between two peaks of the mountain. There were a lot of wild mavericks around there. Most of the cowboys had two horses, one to scout on and one to rope from. After they roped a maverick they would bore a hole through the horns by using a hot iron, then put pegs on the holes after they ran a rope through to keep the rope from slipping when they tied two animals together so they wouldn't run away.

# CHARLES PROCTOR

Charles Proctor bought a ranch at the Sopori also La Testota Ranch near Sahuarito where he had a stage coach stop. My nieces Janet Probasco Mathews and Judy Probasco both went to the La Testota two-room school house in their third grade. They had grades one through eight. In 1885 he became a foreman for Maish and Driscoll. He held this job for about ten years and became well acquainted with the valley. Living at the White House (this would be where you entered Madera Canyon) now and then were Atondo, then Rufina Paz. Later Proctor met a fellow named Smith, who had to flee because he got caught butchering a beef belonging to Maish and Driscoll. During his days, Proctor came across all sorts of characters and this includes Billie Stiles who was a good cow puncher. In time he became a deputy sheriff and a train robber. He also met Manuel Sanchez of Camp Cameron Fame who was then a young man and a good cowboy. Proctor greatly admired him.

When he was running the Box Canyon Ranch, Proctor baled grama grass at the "Y" where the Box Canyon forks off. He used the grass to fatten the beef when he had a contract with Helvetia Mine.

One day he came home late after delivering beef, no one locked their house in those days so he wasn't surprised to find two fellows in their bed rolls on the floor asleep. He went on to bed without saying anything and the next morning he saw who his visitors were. His fellow cowboy, now an outlaw, Billie Stiles, and a Mexican friend. This was the second night they stayed there. A neighbor stopped by after breakfast and Proctor asked his quest "How shall I introduce you" Stiles answered "My name is Stiles, and introduce me as such". Proctor did and soon the neighbor left. That evening the Sheriff arrived but Stiles was long gone.

# TREASURE HUNTERS

Over a period of years there have been a few treasure hunters through out the valley. Shrubs and trees have covered their holes but some dowser rods of various types have been found at some of the sites.

One out standing story tells of a Spanish treasure. Around the turn of the century a cowboy named Joe Garcia stumbled upon gold bars in a caved in tunnel. He would bring his wife (Lupe) with him to remove some of the gold then cover up the opening. Jose would melt the gold and pour it through a screen into a bucket of water to make it appear as nuggets.

Later he brought his good friend Atenojenes to the tunnel. When Jose made a trip to Spain a fellow named Miller followed Atenojenes. When he went to get some gold they got into a fight. Miller killed Atenojenes and at the same time the slain man's son arrived. He killed Miller and left both bodies there.

When Jose returned from Spain Atenojene's son told him what had happened. Jose tried to poison him but instead of dying he lost his mind. Jose removed a lot of the gold and he and his wife moved to Mexico where Jose died.

Lupe who was eighteen at the time of the discovery returned in 1924 when she was forty eight. She had two partners Parks and Howell from Nogales and they went looking for the tunnel. They rented three horses for one day thinking they could go right to the tunnel. Not finding anything they rented the horses for the second day. Still not finding anything again they rented the horses for a week only failing again to find the tunnel. To keep from paying anymore on the horses they took the owner of the horses in as a partner. After three more weeks they gave up and left.

A fellow by the name of Cluff learned of Jose Garcia's treasure from Parks. For about five years in the 30's Cluff and his son camped, at the foot of Tom Boy. Their search proved unsuccessful.

# CONFUSING NAMES

I think every state has some confusion about their cities, counties, and state. Arizona has them as well like the town of Pima is not located in Pima County, but Graham County. The town of Navajo is in Apache County, while Fort Apache is located in Navajo County. Arizona had even lost a county, to go with numerous "Lost" mines. The county named Pah-ute isn't really lost rather taken away from the new territory in 1866 by congress and given to Nevada.

The wind seldom blows in Winslow. Copperopolis was a metropolis that didn't metrop. Snowflake was not named after the weather, it was named after Eratus Snow and an early pioneer William Flake, whom the both founded the community in 1878.

Oraibi a Hopi Village in Navajo County is considered to be the oldest continuously inhabited community in the United States.

Bush Valley in the White Mountains rests on an elevation of 8000 feet and said to be the highest spot in the United States where farming is successful.

Mount Lemon near Tucson boasts its skiing area is the southern most in North America.

Bisbee is a mining community and most of the homes are built on the sides of the mountains. You can jump from your yard to your neighbor's roof below. According to Ripley Bisbee High School is the only school in America that stands four stories high and has a ground floor entrance to each level.

# CATTLE RUSTLING

Butchering a neighbor's cow was done about every-day some where. A neighbor might ash when was the last time you had some of your own beef? The answer would be "Not since I was at your place and ate". This rancher was out riding one day and came upon some fresh dirt and cart tracks leading to and from the spot. So he decided to a little digging and he came up with a cow hide with his brand on it. He rolled up the hide and tied it behind the saddle and started following the cart tracks and it led him to the White House (that would be the entrance to the Madera Canyon) Morales was staying there at the time and he told Morales Chato, you have butchered one of my cows. Morales said yes, Chalito, and I will pay you for it and how much do you want? Thirty dollars was the reply and Morales since I paid you for the cow I would like to have the hide. He dropped the hide and rode away.

He probably made rawhide gelatin, the recipe is simple. First you singe and scorch the hair then scrape and rinse the hide real good. Boil the hide in water for one hour then throw the water away and rinse again. Add more water and boil it until it jells.

Cattle rustling was common in those days. This rancher I'm not going to mention lived pretty close to Byrd Yoas his brand was /P\ and after Byrd Yoas moved in he registered his brand as /B\ When this rancher started losing cattle he changed his brand making it more difficult to alter the brand. Some years later this rancher found some fresh tracks where there were four cows and a horse behind. He tracked them across the mountains to the east side of the Santa Rita Mountains to the Santa Rita Ranch that was owned by Keith Brown and confronted him about it. Keith Brown's cowboy had started his ranch in the Sonoita area. The following day Keith Brown went to see the rancher and told him he could be sued for accusing him of steeling his cows.

The rancher told him that he wasn't accusing him of stealing the cows he was accusing his cowpuncher and if I thought it was you I would have kept quiet and start taking your cow's one at a time and you would never finish paying me off. You had better check his place, which he did just that. Two weeks later Keith Brown showed up at the rancher's place with his four cows and a gift of a young registered bull with his apologies.

I knew Byrd Yoas real well and had been to his place many times. He had two brothers, one Dick Yoas had a ranch west of the Santa Cruz River and what is now Green Valley. The other brother was Juan Yoas and Dick and Byrd didn't have too much to do with him. He was getting into trouble all the time. He got to running with a gang in Wilcox which high jacked a Southern Pacific train and robbed it. You will read that story in the book later.

My brother, sister and I would go with Bud McGhee to the Kinsley dance and on our way we would stop by Dick Yoas and take him along.

Otho Kinsley had a small ranch where the Cow Palace is now. Some of the bathroom fixtures are still in use that were there in the forties. Otho had a large building where the dances were held which had a great hard wood flooring to dance on and with his bar there was a restaurant. The place was packed every weekend. There were a lot of pictures that were taken there and were displayed in the Ozark Bar on South Sixth Avenue in South Tucson. Attaberry owned the place and later sold out and the building torn down. The Mountain Oyster Club has a lot of those pictures. A jack pot rodeo was held on the weekends and Byrd Yoas one of the officials and he took care of the starting gate for the ropers and doggers. And for sure he was always there when the band started. The first lady he would head for was Beth Aycock, he would get an arm hold around her neck and about choke her and with his false teeth being so loose and a mouth full of tobacco juice while jumping up and down talking she would go back to her seat polka-dotted with tobacco juice. When she did see him coming her way she would head for the ladies room. Once in awhile she would lose track of him and that's when he'd grab her for a dance. They were very good friends but she sure hated to dance with him.

One time she was at his ranch with a few of the cowboys and it was about lunch time for all of them and decided to make some coffee. She found the coffee pot and it was a mess he boiled his coffee and never washed it just rinsed it out. There were stains, coffee oil, and grease all over the coffee pot. It took her a long time to get it cleaned up enough to make some coffee. The next day when Byrd was going to make himself some coffee and found his coffee pot had been scrubbed clean the roof of the ranch almost flew off of the house, he wanted to know who ruined his coffee pot. That almost ruined their friendship but as time passed on it was something they laughed about.

Byrd had the biggest fig tree I have ever seen. A lot of people would gather figs when they ripened up. There were plenty to go around.

# GREATERVILLE MINE

Placer gold was discovered in 1874 and the town of Greaterville sprung up at the site. Population reached 500, mostly Mexicans. Miners were making around ten dollars a day. There were several dance halls, saloons, and mercantile stores. The jail was a deep hole in the ground, and they used a rope to let them down.

The cowboys working at the Empire Ranch went to the dances to court the pretty senoritas. One night the miners decided not to share the ladies and locked the door. One cowboy not to be denied climbed upon the roof and dropped a hand full of cartridges down the chimney. A few seconds later all hell broke loose. The doors broke open and the miners ran for cover. The cowboys moved in quickly and took over the dance hall. One jealous miner followed his girlfriend with his knife as she was swept around the dance hall by the cowboy. Following the miner was another cowboy with a cocked pistol. It was a stand off no body was hurt.

When the dance was over the cowboys invited the miners and their wives and girlfriends to the Empire Ranch for a big barbeque and dance.

Water was scarce and had to be hauled in goat skin bags on a burro from Gardner Canyon. Greater was located on a road known as Renegade Route. Men fleeing the law camped in the area on their way to and from the Mexican border. The post office closed in 1946, school started in 1882, teacher was Patrick Coyne, only two other schools in Pima County.

*Opha R. Probasco*

# THE MORMON BATTALION'S MARCH ACROSS ARIZONA TO CALIFORNIA

General Stephen W. Kearny with Captain Philip St. George Cooke (later Lieutenant Colonel) recruited the Mormon Battalion mainly in Iowa. The Mormons wanted both to demonstrate their patriotism and secure free passage to California. This battalion under General Kearny was to make a wagon trail along the 32$^{nd}$ parallel line in Southern Arizona from New Mexico to Colorado River.

It was a rag tail outfit numbering nearly 500 men, 25 women and some children. They left Council Bluffs in July 1846 and reached Santa Fe, New Mexico on October 13$^{th}$ and proceeded to trim roster by excluding 86 men, all the children, and all of the women except the wives of two Mormon captains and three sergeants. This excluded group of about 150 in all was sent north to Pueblo, Colorado on the Arkansas River and the next year became part of the newly founded Mormon Colony at Salt Lake City, Utah.

General Stephen Kearny and Captain George Cooke split up and General Kearny went direct to the Gila River and followed it to the Colorado River.

On October 19th Captain George Cooke with the remaining men and five women started from Santa Fe, New Mexico to blaze a wagon road to California. After leaving the Rio Grande River the battalion was guided southwest across the present international boundary by Pualine Weaver and Antoine Lerour. Turning northwest the Mormons passed through the old abandoned ranch of San Bernardino and a week later reached the San Pedro River. The valley was full of wild bulls. For two weeks the battalion lived off of bull meat. The battalion had engaged in its first and only battle. Not with the Mexicans or the Indians but with wild bulls. The bulls attacked the wagons, gorged some of the mules, and injured some of the men. The battle lasted several hours.

The wild bulls came from the San Bernardino Land Grant where the Apaches killed most of the men and the rest of the family left the ranch in the 1830's. In 1884 John Slaughter bought the Spanish Land Grant that was on the United States side. In 1917 Mexico passed a law that no foreigner will own land with in 62 mile of the border.

They marched on toward Tucson and before getting too close they prepared for a battle that never happened.

Captain Cooke sent word to the Comandante Antonio Comaduran of the Mexican troops in Tucson, Arizona, that the Americans came as friends and only wished to purchase flour and other provisions. The Mexicans refused to surrender but evacuated his army from the town to San Xavier Mission. On December 17, 1846 the Mormon Battalion entered Tucson without firing a shot. They raised the stars and strips for the first time in Arizona. They were kindly treated by the people of Tucson. After restocking their supplies they left the next day October 18th. After a three days march they reached the Gila River. Following the Gila River to the Colorado River and after crossing it they continued through the California desert and arrived in San Diego, California on January 29, 1847. Captain Cooke, now Brigadier General was in the union army, but his son and son-in-law were loyal to the south.

The department of war assigned Lieutenant John Parke to learn more about the 32$^{nd}$ parallel route. In 1854 and 1855 he surveyed alternative route between El Paso and Thepima Village. Instead of following Captain Cooke's wagon road south into Mexico, Parke's crew located short cuts through passes in southeastern Arizona. Lieutenant Parkes said that the 32$^{nd}$ parallel route had a level terrain but shortage of water and timber.

Andrew Belcher Gray worked for the Texas Western Railroad Company to survey a route across the Southern Arizona. Gray had 19 men in his crew and most of them were Texas Rangers. Gray recommended that the Texas Western Company build a railroad from El Paso through Apache pass to Tucson, Pima Village, Fort Yuma, and on to Los Angeles, no rails were laid.

It was a California company, Southern Pacific that built the railroad through Southern Arizona between 1877 and 1881.

Leach's wagon road was the first wagon road across Southern Arizona in 1858. The road ran from El Paso to Fort Yuma, missing the settlements of Tucson and Tubac. Leach followed Parke's railroad survey route down the San Pedro Valley. The road turned westward and followed the Gila River through Maricopa Wells to Yuma. Part of the Leach's wagon road was used by the stage lines.

The first mail and passenger stage line through Arizona started in July 1857, it ran from San Antonio, Texas to San Diego, California. It was called "The Jack-Ass Mail" for the reason when you get to Yuma, Arizona you had to ride a mule through the sand dunes and when you get to the mountains it was the same thing.

The larges stage station besides Tucson was the Maricopa Wells most other stations were merely a camping place. They had mud huts with brush corrals. The San Antonio and San Diego mail made forty trips across Arizona the year they were in operation. No one was really pleased with them, but they did open a trail for the Butterfield Stage Line. They started in 1858 on September 16th. Their route was from a railroad terminal near St. Louis, Missouri to San Francisco, California. They had a twice weekly service on a twenty five day schedule. There were 26 stations from the New Mexico line to the California line. John Butterfield's instructions to his drivers were "Nothing on God's earth can stop the U.S. mail". During the Butterfield Stage existence the mail was late only three times.

A total of 168 people met violent deaths as a result of Indians attacks and other causes. The Butterfield Stage arrived in Tucson on October 2, 1858 and on board was a New York Herald reporter named Waterman L. Ormsby. During his short visit he noticed that Tucson had a few adobes houses, most of the people were Mexicans, a hand full of Americans that ran some stores and were elected to the town offices. William Buckley was in charge of the Tucson operations. In March 1861 a month before the Civil War started, the Butterfield Stage Line was shifted north through Utah.

Congress had commissioned the Texas and Pacific Railroad to build a railroad line from Marshall, Texas to San Diego, California along the 32$^{nd}$ parallel. By 1873 they got as far as Fort Worth, Texas. They had financial problems and couldn't go any farther west.

Southern Pacific had build a line as far as Yuma, Arizona on the Colorado River, and waiting to get into Arizona and build a line across Arizona and pick up some grants and loans the congress offered the railroad. The government awarded twenty sections of land for every mile of track they laid, free right of way, free use of timber and mineral to build the line, and a loan of $16,000.00 if the track was laid on flat land, $32,000.00 if laid across foothills, and $48,000.00 if they laid the track in the mountains. Southern Pacific had secured a right away to El Paso from the Arizona New Mexico legislature. Southern Pacific had reached the Colorado River in 1877 ad spent the summer constructing a bridge to the other side with the permission of the federal government. When the bridge was completed the railroad was refused permission by the secretary of was to cross over a federal stream or cross the military reservation on the other side. There were two versions to what had happened next.

One story has it that the Southern Pacific engineers drove an engine quietly across the bridge in the night when the fort was fast asleep, and soon as they were on the other side the engineers tied down the whistle valve and used all the steam he had to celebrate the advent of the Iron Horse into a new territory.

Another version was that the entire military force at Yuma was fine people. Major Tomas Dunn, the Commanding Officer Leonard Loring the assistant surgeon, a sergeant, an enlisted man and a prisoner.

To avoid any trouble with the military, the company decided to lay the tracks to the bridge at night. Major Dunn was suspicious so he placed a guard at the end of the tracks until 11:00 o'clock each night. The railroader waited until the sentry went off duty, and then went to laying track toward the bridge. Every thing went fine until someone dropped a rail on the bridge. That woke the Garrison up and all four of them rushed to the scene of the crime, to prevent anymore construction. The soldiers standing with fixed bayonets were no match for what happened next. Some one started a rail car full of material down the tracks toward the startled troopers.

Major Dunn realizing he had done the best he could to carry out his orders and was defeated, they retreated back to the fort. By morning the work was completed and the engine rolled on into Yuma.

The Franchises were granted and the railroad started laying its steel ribbons across the Arizona desert, creating boom towns along the way such as Maricopa, 35 miles south of Phoenix and about 8 miles south of Maricopa Wells, a stage coach station.

On March 20, 1880 the Southern Pacific Railroad reached Tucson and there was a big celebration. Richard Gird of Tombstone presented the City of Tucson a silver spike form the tough nut mine in Tombstone, for the occasion. There were a lot of drinking going on and someone decided to send a telegram to the Pope, a lot of telegrams were sent all over the United States they wrote this message and signed it Major of Tucson. The telegram reads

Pope Leo XIII at the Vatican "To his holiness the Pope of Rome, Italy" the mayor of Tucson begs the honor of reminding your holiness that this ancient and honorable Pueblo was founded by the Spaniards under the sanction of the Church more than three centuries ago and to inform your holiness that the railroad from San Francisco, California now connects us with the entire Christian world signed R.N. Leatherwood.

Before the telegrapher could send the announcement some of the locals advised him to reconsider and slipped him a couple of bucks to "Can" the telegram and forget the whole thing.

The telegrapher was feeling guilty about not sending the telegram sincere there was such a gala celebration, he decided to give the city fathers a reply even if it wasn't genuine, after all that's how legends are born and he didn't want to cast a sour note on the celebration, so he penned a reply suitable for the occasion. He carried the message over to the group and handed it to Mayor Leatherwood. Not reading it first, he read aloud to the people. His holiness the Pope acknowledges with appreciation receipt of your telegram informing him that the ancient City of Tucson at last has been connected by rail with the outside world and send his benediction, but for his own satisfaction would ask, "Where the Hell is Tucson?" "Antonelli"

The people in Phoenix had to take the stage coach to the new Maricopa town. This lasted seven years till 1887 before Phoenix got a steam locomotive engine and that was by the Santa Fe Railroad. They ran a line from Phoenix to Maricopa Station and called it Maricopa Phoenix and Salt River Valley Railroad, it was in 1926 before Phoenix got a through railroad by Southern Pacific. The railroad line ran from Yuma to Phoenix then to Tucson and on to Lordsburg, New Mexico. When the railroad reached Tucson it put most of the merchants out of business, Zenkendorf went bankrupt, Solomon Warner closed his store, while Tulley and Ochoa went out of business.

Vail, Arizona was named for Walter Vail, he and his two partners H.R. Hislop and John Harvey owned the Empire Ranch. During the 1890's drought and hard times hit the ranges, and to make things worse the Southern Pacific Railroad raised the freight rates. Walter Vail and his brother, Edward, refused to be pushed around by the Southern Pacific Railroad.

So, Walter, Edward, eight cowboys, and a Chinese cook drove their herd of cattle to California. That was the last of the great trail drives. When the rest of the ranches begin to follow suit the railroad dropped their freight rates.

Later on the Southern Pacific raised their rates to the mines. Doctor James Douglas who was the president of the Phelps Dodge Corporation which also is the Copper Queen consolidated decided to build his own railroad. He built a spur off of the Santa Fe Lines at Deming, New Mexico. He ran the line to Douglas, Bisbee, and down to Benson, Arizona. He also ran a short line from Benson to Tombstone, Arizona.

From Benson he was going to by-pass Tucson and follow the Gila River to Yuma and on to California. The big shots of Tucson put the pressure on Douglas to come through Tucson, he finally changed his mind to their way of thinking, Doctor Douglas Railroad was called "El Paso and South Western". E.P. & S.W. he had the line built to Tucson in 1912 and by 1913 he built the depot Rail linkage with Mexico was in need of up grading. It was possible only by using the Santa Fe Line from Benson to Guaymas. This was done in 1882. Jacob Isaacson a traveling salesman arrived and saw the opportunities for a store next to the railroad station. The community consisted of a few tents, mud huts, and a box car railroad station. He built his store on the international boundary line.

On May 31, 1882, a post office opened in the store and the place became known as Isaacson.

Jacob Isaacson on stayed for three years and in that length of time he became a respected community leader, entrepreneur, linguist, and a musician. In September 1882, he was given the honor of driving the last ceremonial railroad spike. This spike was made of silver from tough nut mine in Tombstone.

After a year the people decided that they wanted to change the name of the town. There were a lot of suggestions and they decided to name it Nogales. The Nogales name had been around a long time. In 1850 Major William Emory of the army corps of engineers camped on the site while surveying the land acquired through the Gadsden Purchase. Two big walnut trees were straddling the border. Nogales is walnut in Spanish. This provided the inspiration for the name change.

In 1887 the Maricopa, Phoenix, and Salt River Railroads were built from Phoenix to Maricopa where it joined the Southern Pacific. In 1926 the line was moved Maricopa going just south of Tempe and then to Picacho, and on to Tucson, and that is the route of the Southern Pacific today.

On January 22, 1892 work started on a line from Ash Fork to Phoenix, called the Peavine, it reached Prescott in 1893 and Phoenix in 1895.

The Santa Fe Railroad that ran through the northern part of Arizona didn't have regular stops for dinning. The people would eat at hash houses whenever the train would stop. The food was terrible and the service was worse.

It took a gentleman from England named Fred Harvey to bring the real cuisine to the southwest. After checking out the conditions along the rail lines, Harvey went to the Santa Fe Railroad in the 1870's with an idea to provide the passengers with good food and service. The railroad accepted his proposals and agreed to supply the building along with the transporting of food, furnishing the personnel free of charge and Harvey would receive all profits.

The first Harvey House opened for business at Topeka, Kansas in 1876 ad was immediately a success. French chefs were hired away from some good restaurants in the east and paid good salaries, more than the managers of a local bank. They bought the food from the local farmers.

During the next twenty years, Harvey opened his Spanish-style restaurants at a hundred mile intervals through out the southwest.

Arizona had five Harvey Houses on the main line in the early days. They were located at Winslow, Williams, Ash Fork, Seligman, and Kingman. The Harvey House in Winslow has been remodeled as a motel and restaurant. If you go through there it's a must to stop and check it out. It is beautiful there are a lot of them that are being redone across the country.

In the southwest where the women were scarce Harvey would bring in young women from the east furnish them with room, meals, and a salary. He wouldn't bring in the prettiest women only the more common looking ones for he knew the prettiest wouldn't be there long before she would be married, even the common looking ones wasn't there long before they got married.

Like Will Rogers said one time "Fred Harvey kept the west in food and wives". The girls were required to live in dormitories like the universities had. They had to be in by 10:30 P.M. on week nights and 11:30 P.M. on Saturday nights.

The girls were called biscuit shooter by the locals. Before reaching the station the brakeman would take orders then wire ahead the information. When the train was a mile away it would blow its whistle. When the uniformed employee heard the whistle he would ring a gong and it would signal the waitress to set up the first course. By the time train arrived the meals were ready to serve. The waitresses were not allowed to serve men without a coat on in the dinning room. If a man didn't have a coat he was loaned one. The waitresses couldn't talk to each other while the train was at the station. However, they learned how to communicate through the use of signals and codes. They learned to talk out of the sides of their mouth to escape detection from the company's inspectors who were passing through. Sometimes Fred Harvey would pass through and he had been known to fire the manager on the spot if all wasn't up to his standards.

*Opha R. Probasco*

# THE CIVIL WAR AND ARIZONA GOVERNORS

The territorial capital buildings on Ochoa Street when the capital was in Tucson for ten years

Arizona and New Mexico were very important to the confederate. The people of New Mexico were pro southern while the people in Arizona were sympathetic to the south, especially Sylvester Mowry. Many of the north's officers defected to the south and became southern generals.

Major Henry Sibley organized three regiments of the Texas volunteer cavalry and made preparations for the New Mexico campaign. The invasion had already started. On July 1st Lt. Colonel John Baylor reached and occupied Fort Bliss (near El Paso). These men were recruited to hunt buffalo and furnish their own horses, saddles, guns and ammunition.

July 25th the Texans took possession of Mesilla.

Major Isac Lynde advance with his troops toward the town from near by Fort Fillmore. July 27th the panicky Lynde abandoned Fort Fillmore and headed toward Fort Stanton. The soldiers didn't have adequate water supply and by the time Lt. Colonel Baylor caught up with him and the thirty stragglers, they were quiet willing to surrender in exchange for a drink. It has been told when Major Lynde left Fort Fillmore on their way to Fort Stanton they captured a saloon and liberated their supply. The confederates cut the main body off at San Augustine pass in the Organ Mountains and that's were Major Lynde cowardly disgracefully surrendered his entire command with out firing a shot. The south won its first territory.

Lt. Colonel John Baylor proclaimed the territory of Arizona with the capital at Mesilla and himself as military governor. Everything south of the 34th parallel, the east and west line passes through Socorro, New Mexico and Wickenburg, Arizona.

When the union troops left Fort Breckenridge they destroyed the forts and left the people to their mercy of the Apache Indians. The people wanted protection from any government. The union troops headed for Fort

Fillmore, but were warned to stay away from there and go to Fort Craig located on the Rio Grande.

Several months later a major conflict, the first of the civil war at Valverde a few mile up from Fort Craig.

When General Sibley was preparing to march up stream, he detached Captain Hunter with a company of mounted rifles to take over Tucson. In 1862 Captain Hunter raised the confederate flag over Tucson and gave everyone their choice either swear allegiance to the confederacy or leave town. Solomon Warner left for Sonora. Hughes left for California.

Hunter confiscated everything. We went to the Indian Villages on the Gila River and arrested Ammi White A. Miller and a federal agent who had been buying grain and supplies for the union troops. He confiscated 1500 sacks of wheat and gave that to the Indians.

Captain Hunter learned that every old Butterfield Station was provided with hay and supplies for use by the union army on their march east from California. They burned six stations, and Captain Carleton in Yuma had been informed of Captain Hunter's activities and dispatched Captain William McCleave with a squad of cavalry to learn the strength and disposition of the confederate forces. Colonel Carleton orders were for him to go to Pima Villages and construct a building to store wheat and flour in from the Ammi White's mill, also to take the town by surprise and arrest Captain Hunter. McCleave and his men were sighted by the confederate scouts in time to lay a trap. Unaware of Mr. White had been arrested. McCleave knocked on the door and was greeted by Captain Hunter posing as the Miller. In the mean time the confederates surrounded the Yankees and easily made them prisoners. McCleave and Ammi White were escorted to the Rio Grande by Lt. Jack Swilling, a man that will reappear often during Arizona history.

When the news of McCleave's capture reached Fort Yuma, the officers and men were eager to find out what was going on in Arizona. Captain Galloway was dispatched with 272 men, established a base at the Pima Village then made a dash to Tucson before McCleave was taken Mesilla. Near Stanwix Station Captain Calloway's men encountered some Texan trips destroying stored hay. Shots were fired and exchanged, but not much of a battle. The Texans took off and were caught up with at Picacho Peak. The Yankees were ordered to charge by Lt. James Barrett. There was some fierce fighting for a few minutes. Lt. James Barrett was shot in the neck and died instantly. Two Union privates were also killed and three others wounded. All the confederates escaped except two that were wounded and three were taken prisoners. That was known as the "Battle of Picacho Peak". That was also known as the western most action in the Civil War, though we have seen a conflict nearly a hundred miles west of there.

Colonel Carleton reached Tucson June 7, 1862 and on June 8, 1862 he declared Arizona a territory of the United States of America and designated himself as the military governor. All citizens of legal age were compelled to take an oath of allegiance to the U.S.A.

Colonel Carleton let his axe fall on the confederate sympathizers. The most notable man arrested was Sylvester Mowery. In 1860 Mowery purchased a mine in Patagonia, Arizona Mountains seven miles form the Mexican border. The mine was supporting a camp of 400 people by 1862.

Colonel Carleton confiscated Mowery's silver mine and place Mowery under arrest and brought him to Tucson. Colonel Carleton confined him to the Yuma prison where he remained until November 4, 1862. His case was investigated by General Wright, commander of the department of Pacific. Mowery was acquitted and given his unconditional release. Carleton went beyond Mowery's arrest and sold his property at a public auction for a mere $2,000.00.

Mowery wrote letters to influential people, published newspaper article, and south vindication through legal channels. In 1862 Mowery filed for more than a million dollars against Colonel Carleton and others. In 1868 he received $40,000.00 from the federal government.

Mowery went to London to raise money for refinancing his properties. While there he became ill and died in October 1871.

A detachment of 126 men under the command of Captain Thomas Roberts left town July 10th and about July 15th the advanced troops were ambushed near Apache Pass by Indians led by the tow most feared of all Apaches, Mangas Colorado and Cochise. The battle of Apache Pass that followed was one of the largest engagements ever fought between federal troops and Apache Indians in Arizona history. Casualties of Captain Robert's troops were two killed and three wounded. The Indian losses were estimated from ten to sixty eight.

This battle got the attention of Colonel Carlenton in controlling the pass. On July 27, 1862 he gave orders for the establishment of a military camp there. It was named Fort Bowie, in honor of General George W. Bowie of the fifth California cavalry.

Colonel Carlenton stayed in Tucson for a couple of months then left for Santa Fe, New Mexico.

President Abraham Lincoln appointed John A. Gurley as first territory governor of Arizona. He died in his home before he could take office. President Lincoln then appointed ex-congressman John N. Goodwin form Chief Justice of the Arizona Supreme Court to governor of Arizona territory. Richard McCormick was appointed secretary. Goodwin's party traveled over the Santa Fe Trail to Santa Fe, New Mexico. Their destination in Arizona was unknown, General Carlenton suggested near the Walker's gold diggings. He also advised against Tucson because the people were sympathetic to the south. Mentioning of gold excited the group so much that is where they headed for. They arrived at Fort Whipple January 22, 1864. Governor Goodwin picked a lace that was a mile high on Granite Creek for the capital and named it Prescott for Mexico Historian, William H. Prescott. The capital was moved from Prescott to Tucson in 1867 where it stayed for ten years. The capital was moved back to Prescott in 1877 where it stayed for twelve more years. In 1889 the capital on wheels moved to Phoenix for good. Out of the sixteen governors there were three democrats and thirteen republicans. The first Arizona state governor was George W.P. Hunt a democrat and his first term was for five years. He spent four different terms as governor and the last was in 1933.

# TERRITORY GOVERNORS

|  | Dates Governing | Governing Party |
|---|---|---|
| John N. Goodwin | 1862 – 1866 | Republican |
| Richard C. McCormick | 1866 – 1869 | Republican |
| A.P.K. Safford | 1869 - 1877 | Republican |
| John P. Hoyt | 1877 – 1878 | Republican |
| John C. Fremont | 1878 -1882 | Republican |
| Federick A. Trittle | 1882 – 1885 | Republican |
| Conrad Meyer Zulick | 1885 – 1889 | Democrat |
| Lewis Wolfley | 1889 – 1890 | Republican |
| John N. Irwin | 1890 – 1892 | Republican |
| Nathan O. Murphy | 1892 - 1893 | Republican |
| Lewis C. Hughes | 1893 - 1896 | Democrat |
| Benjamin Franklin | 1896 – 1897 | Democrat |
| Myron H. Cord | 1897 – 1898 | Republican |
| Nathan O. Murphy | 1898 – 1902 | Republican |
| Alexander O. Brodie | 1902 – 1905 | Republican |
| Joseph H. Kibbey | 1905 – 1909 | Republican |
| Richard E. Sloan | 1909 – 1912 | Republican |

Nathan O. Murphy served two terms as territory governor.

First term was 1892 - 1893
Second term was 1898 – 1902

# LIEUTENANT NED BEALE

Lieutenant Navy Officer Edward Ned Beale was with General Stephen Watts Kearny at the siege on San Pasqual. During the siege, he, Kit Carson and a Delaware Indian sneaked through the Mexican lines reaching San Diego in tie to bring back a rescue party.

When gold was discovered in California Beale was chosen to carry the news to President Millard Fillmore. Beale dressed up in miner's clothes and a large Mexican sombrero and a poke sac of gold nuggets, he started across the continent. He took a shop to San Blas, on the west coast of Mexico then over land to the Atlantic coast. There were several attempts of robbery, but he out rode the pursuers including riding down a steep mountain side where the bandits wouldn't follow.

After reaching the capital he dumped the gold on the president's desk with the story of gold discovery in California.

The next major survey of the 35th parallel was the Beale camel experiment in 1857. Jefferson Davis was secretary of war from 1853 to 1857 and was responsible for the camel project. IN 1855 congress appropriated $30,000.00 for the purchase of camels to be used for military purpose. Jefferson Davis place Major Henry Wayne and Navy Officer David Porter in charge.

Porter and Wayne traveled through the Middle East selecting their camels. On the first ship's load several of the beasts died on the rough ocean trip. They did realize the mule skinners and camels were going to clash so they hired several Arabs, Greeks, and Turks to care for the camels. The first ship load of thirty four arrived on the Texas coast in Mary 1856 and the second load about year later increased the herd to over seventy.

The camels passed all tests including a race with horse-drawn wagons. They carried a heavier load and still finished first. When it rained and the slick gumbo got so bad that the mules couldn't go, the camels had no problems. This whole experiment fell on Beale's shoulders

He was dressed like a circus rider and riding on a bright red wagon when a New Mexican asked "dis show wagon, no?" Beale answered "yes" "Ah Ha! Be dee show means, no?" Beale answered "yes, sir" "What you gotee more on camelos? Gotee any dogs?" Beale answered "yes, monkeys too, and more". "Whatee more?" Beale "Horse more" "Whatee can do horse?" Beale stand on his head, and drink a glass of wine". Valgarne dios! What a people these are to have a horse stand on his head, and drink a glass of wine".

Lieutenant Edward Fitzgerald Beale became interested in the possibilities of using camels in western United States after reading Abbe Hue's "Travel in China and Tactary".

Beale went to the secretary of war Jefferson Davis with his enthusiasm to use camels to transport supplies to army post in the southwest. The present secretary of war John Floyd chose Lieutenant Beale to chart a route on the 35$^{th}$ parallel for a wagon road and conduct the experiment with camels.

The camels were shipped to Indianola, Texas. Lieutenant Beale took one of the Turks Hadju Ali , but he was known as Hi Jolly and he wasn't a Turk, he was a Syrian and twenty four of the camels to make up his crew of 8 mule drawn covered wagons, 56 men, and 350 sheep. The caravan left San Antonio, Texas, June 25, 1857 two months later they arrived in Zuni, ready to start charting the 35$^{th}$ parallel, but first they had to start from Fort Defiance to make it official. Lieutenant Beale took 20 men and rode into Fort Defiance through Navajo country and returned to Zuni. The legal requirement having been met the party moved along the 35$^{th}$ parallel. The route was close to the Little Colorado River and turned west near the northern out let of Devil's Canyon. The trail was marked by the wagon wheels and distances were recorded with an odometer. The route westward lay north of the present towns of Flagstaff and Williams. The Colorado River was reached north of the site of Needles, California.

Lieutenant Edward Beale couldn't have been more pleased with his camels. While he was camped at the foot of the San Francisco Peaks he made a note of them.

The camels are so quiet and give so little trouble you'd almost forget they were with us. There wasn't anything as patient and enduring and so little troublesome. They pack twice as much as the mules and accept any food offered to them and always up with the wagons. Perfect docile and quiet. During the stretch of thirty six hours without water the horses and mules suffered, but the camels took all the hardships stoically. With all the work the camels were content to eat anything from the driest greasewood bush to a thorny prickly pear and get fat on it.

After crossing the river Lieutenant Beale moved in camels to his ranch ninety miles north of Los Angeles to Fort Tejon. This was to test their ability to thrive in several feet of snow. The camels did fine, so much better than the mules in everyday. The bad thing was the rocky shale that cut the camels pads. The Wagon Road was a great success and not only the Wagon Road, but the railroad also was built along side of the Wagon Road.

Lieutenant Beale's experiment with the camels showed they could go along distant without water and arrived in good condition. However, there were factors that prevented further experimentation by the government.

For one thing the men, horses, and mules did not like the strange odor. Pack trains and wagon trains often panicked with the approach of the camels. Most of the camels that Beale had taken to his ranch were later transferred to the quarter-master at Los Angeles and sold at public auction. Some were bought for parks and circuses and by ranchers who hooked them to buck boards. Many of the camels were abandoned to live in a wild state.

All sorts of tales were told about these roaming camels and their descendants which were encountered in Arizona. One of the stories was reported to be captured near Phoenix in 1905 and sold to a saloon keeper. One day the camel escaped from the corral he was in and trotted through the saloon out into the street. All hell broke loose, the horses bolted and scattered wagon loads of farm produce over half the town. Many more yarns were told and undoubtedly true. Another story is told about Hi Jolly's name was left off of an invitation list for picnic sponsored by the German Colony in Los Angeles. Knowing the reaction of horses to camels Hi Jolly harnessed two huge beasts to a cart and drove into the midst of the picnic area. When it was all over with the disturbance, the results were broken halters, disable buggies, and the country side was strewn with Wienerwurst and etc.

Hi Jolly was married and living with his wife in Los Angeles. He wasn't used to be cooped up and left his wife for the Arizona desert. He settled around Quartzsite and done some prospecting. While he was out in the country from town he ran into his pet camel he named Topsy he took care of Topsy up to the time of his death then Topsy was sent to the Los Angeles zoo. Hi Jolly was cremated and Hi ashes was put on a monument at the side of the highway in Quartzsite. Topsy died in 1934 at the zoo, they cremated Topsy also and his ashes were placed in the same pyramid monument above Hi Jollies ashes. There is now a copper camel image on the top of the monument.

Opha R. Probasco

# TUMACACORI–CALABASAS–GUEVAVI

Tumacacori goes back to the Jesuits, but it was 1784 when it became a head mission. Guevavi and Calabasas were visitas, but they were abandoned near the end of the eighteenth century. Tumacacori continued to prosper as herds of horses and cattle increased. The lands originally bought from the natives became insufficient. The title papers to these lands had been lost before 1806. Juan Ligarra, governor of the Pueblo of Tumacacori, petitioned the intendente of the province Hon Garciaconde for an adjudication and survey of the land for farming and grazing to replace the old title. Conde complied with the request and issued a royal patent to the Indians of the Pueblo of Tumacacori and giving them land that amounted to about 26,000 acres. After the surveying the actual amount was less than one fourth of a square league, about 5,000 acres. In the new title it was stipulated that if the land was abandoned for three years then any one cold claim it unless the Apaches ran them off. During the 1830's and 1840's all missions declined. In 1842 the Mexican government began selling abandoned church lands valued at $500.00 or less. Tumacacori was sold in 1844 along with

199

the stock farm of Calabasas and adjacent lands to Francisco Aguilar for $500.00 at a public auction. All land was sold at a public auction even the land grants.

Aguilar was a brother-in-law to Manual Maria Gandara who was governor of Sonora off and on for twenty years, who later transferred the title into his name.

The Civil War in Mexico during 1840's until 1846 was started between a Tucson born military hero of the Texas was, Jose Cosme Urrea federalism against Manuel Gandara a centralism government.

Through out the conflict the Apaches stepped up their depredations, with the Apaches in control of the Sonoran frontier. It was 1853 before Gandara could capitalize on the lands.

On December 9, 1852 he entered partnership with a German named Federico Hulseman and three others to develop a hacienda with live stock which he supplied.

The live stock included 5,000 sheep, 1,000 goats, 100 cows with calf's, 100 brood mares, 10 yokes of oxen's, 6 pack mules, and 10 horses for use. This recorded in the old records of Pima County, Arizona.

The old Calabasas church was converted into a ranch house. Soon there was Mexican herdsman watching over the large herd.

A large band of Apaches struck the ranch one morning, but an Apache woman warned the Mexican commander at Tucson what day the attack would be. On the day of the attack Gilanin Garcia the Tucson commander was waiting for them with sixty Mexicans dragoons and forty friendly Apache Mansos from Tucson. When the Indians begin their attack, the Mexican cavalry charge taking them by surprise, there were very few shots fired. The Apaches were all killed mostly by lances and knives. The wounded ones were finished off by the Apache Mansos. Peter Brady and Andrew Gray were camped near by and told of the slaughter. Don Federico invited them over and showed them some more evidence. A guy had what looked like a string of dried apples two and a half to three feet long, on close inspection they were the ears of their dead foes.

Eventually the Apaches were successful in forcing Gandara to abandon all operations of his ranch. This was months before the Americans troops arrived after the Gadsden treaty. The Americans rushed in to the newly acquired land to seek their fortunes. Sylvester Mowery wrote in 1859 that the rich land around Tumacacori was being cultivated by squatters.

After the Civil War there was again an influx of American people into the region. In 1869 Agular formally sold the Tumacacori and Calabasas Grants to Gandara for $499.00.

# CHARLES P. SYKES

In 1878 Charles P. Sykes of San Francisco, California paid $12,500.00 in gold coins for the Tumacacori and Calabasas land. The same year Charles Sykes sold a 3/16TH interest to John Currey an ex-judge of the California Supreme Court for $9,000.00. In 1879 Charles Sykes and John Currey transferred their interest to some Boston men for $75,000.00. The new owners organized the Calabasas land and mining company, later the Santa Rita Land and Cattle Company. Charles remained as director of the company. Charles Sykes tried to attract capital to Calabasas with exaggerated advertisements and illustration including one picture of a line of steam ships coming down the dry Santa Cruz River. Charles Sykes built a two story brick hotel called the Santa Rita and supplied it with walnut furniture and Brussels carpet through out. Excellent cuisine was served to gala parties form Tucson who came by railroad by the way of Benson. Some of the distinguished visitors were from far away England. The hotel was a beehive of activity until 1893 when business slackened and the name "Pumpkinville" was given by the Tombstone epitaph. The Sykes' heirs lived at Calabasas until 1915 then moved to Nogales. The hotel later was used by ranchers for storing hay until it burned down in 1927. This land was a part of the Boca float number three and the courts denied a title for the land.

# SALERO MINE

Mexicans first worked the Salero Mine in the early 18th Century. The priest at Tumacacori expecting a visit from the bishop of Sonora planned a great feast in his honor. The bishop appeared delighted with the chicken, fruit and wine. But one luxury was missing, a saltcellar. The padre in charge deeply mortified at his over sight dispatched a few men to the Santa Rita Mountains with orders to mine some native silver and fashion a saltcellar. The saltcellar was made and the mine which supplied the silver received its name (Salero).

In 1857 the property passed to the ownership of John A. Wrightson of The Cincinnati Inquirer, and his brother William, and in 1858 these men formed the Salero Mining Company, comprised of John Wrightson, manager, H.C. Grosvenor, engineer, Raphael Pumpelly, geologist, and Gilbert W. Hopkins mineralogist, of these four men all but Pumpelly were slain by the Apaches.

During the mines period of activity under the American ownership, the old Hacienda De Santa Rita (abandoned, June 15, 1861 following a fierce Apache battle) again became the center of a small community.

Salero contains many interesting ruins and tourist not allowed without permission, reports Mrs. Wirt D. Parker of Patagonia, Arizona, owner.

# LOUIS ZECKENDORF

Louis Zeckendorf came to the U.S.A. in 1854 at the age of sixteen. He joined up with his brother Aaron who had a small general store in Santa Fe, New Mexico. Another brother named William who also joined up with his brother Aaron. The three of them formed a partnership under the name of A. and L. Zeckendorf and moved to Albuquerque, New Mexico.

Sometime later Louis loaded twelve (12) wagons of merchandise from their store in Albuquerque, New Mexico and hauled it to Tucson, Arizona and sold it all to Charles Hayden. The next spring he loaded twelve more wagons and hauled it to Tucson, Arizona. He couldn't sell any of the merchandise so he opened a store on the corner of Pennington and Main Street.

Aaron Zeckendorf died in 1872 and the remaining brothers hired Albert Steinfeld their nephew who lived in Denver, Colorado. He accepted his uncle's offer and traveled to Tucson, Arizona by the way of San Francisco by train, a boat to San Diego, and a stage to Tucson. He looked at Tucson and just knew he was in no man's land, he was just seventeen years old and didn't quiet know how to handle it. He decided to do the best he could.

After working for his uncle for six years they made him a partner and also the manager of their business.

The Zeckendorf brothers and Albert Steinfeld invested into some mining operations even though it was risky there was a chance to make some big money. About the same time William's wife Julia Zeckendorf became the owner of the Old Boot Mine (no one knew how). Julia Zickendorf made Albert Steinfeld the trustee of the Old Boot Mine and in turn leased the mine out to Carl Nielson and let him charge supplies that he used for the mine. After the bill had reached $16,000.00 Albert Steinfeld decided to incorporate before the bill got out of hand. So in 1899 Albert incorporated the Old Boot Mine and called it he Nielson Mining and Smelt Corporation. He appointed James Curtis as mining superintendent with other directors being Carl Nielson and Ralph Shelton. Albert Steinfeld and the directors bought the Silver Bell Mine for $5,000.00.

Louis Zeckendorf told Albert Steinfeld that he wanted to withdraw from the corporation. In 1903 the Silver Bell and the Old Boot Mine was sold to the Imperial Copper Company. They were paid $115,000.00 cash and a note for the amount of $400,000.00 that would be paid in twelve months. Papers were drawn up which showed Albert was paid $18,117.00 for the purchase of the Silver Bell Mine plus expenses from the Englishmen. The board of directors mailed a copy of the contract to Louis Zeckendorf after Louis read the contract he got upset at Albert for charging labor. This couldn't be settled, so Louis took

Albert to court and this wasn't resolved until 1912. This was the first case the state Supreme Court had since Arizona became a state. The Supreme Court ruled in favor of Louis Zeckendorf.

On March 14, 1906 Louis Zeckendorf closed the doors on his store at Main and Pennington Street forever. The very day March 15, 1906 Albert Steinfeld opened the doors on his brand new store located at Pennington and Stone Avenue.

In 1876 Louis Zeckendorf wanted to build a powder magazine. The board of trade wouldn't allow it in town it had to be a safe distant out of town. A few years later the powder magazine blew up, and everyone just knew that the world was coming to an end. The San Agustin Church filled with hysterical weeping people, admitting their sins and you could hear the sounds of prayer.

Louis went back to New York to live out his life. He died in 1937 at the age of 99. Albert died in 1935 at the age of 81.

After Albert's death his son Harold took over the operations of the business. The Steinfeld department store continued business on Stone Avenue and Pennington until 1970 when Harold sold the property and moved the business to the El Con Shopping Center. Also in 1970 the Pioneer Hotel caught on fire and Harold and his wife died in their room where they were living.

Harold's two nephews took over the business and operated it for another 15 years, then closed the doors on a 135 year old company for good. Arizona auctioneers disposed of the fixtures I was working for them at the time.

# SASCO

In 1901 Frank Murphy organized the D.C.A. Development Company of America, Murphy's partners were Elipthlet B.Gage, Henry Mauris Robinson and William Fields Staunton. Under Robinson direction the D.C.A. purchased the major holdings of the Tombstone Mines. IN 1901 the mines were organized as the Tombstone Consolidated Mines Company, with E.B. Gage as president. Later they bought the Poland and Lookout Mines in the Bradshaw Mountains. IN 1903 D.C.A. purchased the Union and Mammoth Mines in the Silver Bell Mountains and formed the Imperial Copper Company with E.B. Gage as president and W.F. Staunton as general manager. One of the biggest problems with the Silver Bell Mine was the transporting the ore to a processing plant where it was refined into pure metal. Originally the ore was transported by mules and wagons. The ore wagons were tall with every large and high wheels. Twenty mules were used to pull those wagons, it depended on how steep the grade was to how many wagons were hooked together. They would haul the ore to Red Rock and load it on S.P. rail cards and ship it to El Paso to the smelter. In 1904 the D.C.A. built the Arizona Southern Railroad to haul the ore to Red Rock. In 1905 the D.C.A. decided to build their own smelter plant. In 1906 with Gage as president and Staunton as vice president and general manager, Murphy and Robinson wee the heads of the board of directors. Mead Goodloe was made superintendent.

In 1907 the smelter was built and a small town was formed. They came up with the name of Southern Arizona Smelting Company. S.A.S.C.O. was born for the town and post office. Wages ranged from $4.00 to $5.00 a day for foreman and engineers, $1.75 a day for labors work-

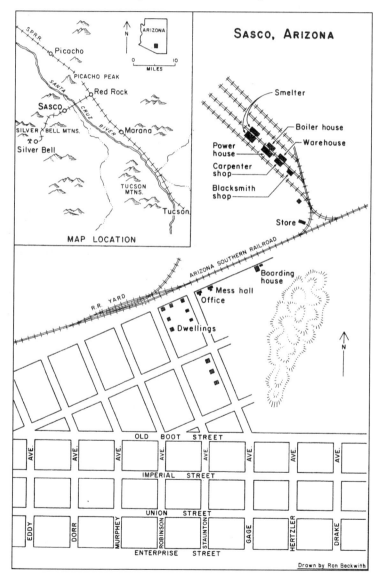

Drawn by Ron Beckwith

ing 10 to 12 hours a day. The company built homes at $700.00 each and rented them for $10.00 a month.

The stage coach that ran from Tucson to Sasco and to Silver Bell Mine, the stage station was located where the Li'l Abners Steak House is now. They are still using the same well that was there at the turn of the century. If you will check the Pima County map dated 1893 at the Arizona Historical Society Library you will find on the map (water tank) this is where Li'l Abners is now and where the stage station was.

Back in the 40's they use to hold weekend rodeos. I participated in some of the events they had.

Dean and Ardith Armstrong played at Li'l Abners for 44 straight years.

Dean Armstrong came to Tucson in the mid forties and around 1960 he started playing at Li'l Abners. He had played there ever since. Making it the longest stint that anyone has ever done. He still has the oldest active band in the country baring no one. His band is called the Arizona Dance Hands.

Arizona Dance Hands–L-R, Toni Clack, Dean Armstrong,
Don Johnson and Earl Mock

Waitresses at Li'l Abner's Steak House helping Opha
Probasco celebrate his 86th birthday

The Li'l Abners is owned the by the Hoffman's Family and managed by Connie Gilbert and Shawn Bell with the prettiest waitresses in town to attend your needs.

Getting back to Sasco and the Silver Bell Mine, we'll start with the Tombstone Mines first, the Tombstone Mines were flooded and the expense of pumping out the water was so great that the Sasco Company had to file bankruptcy one by on the company properties were sold off including the smelter it was the end of D.C.A. Company but not the end of Sasco.

In 1915 American Smelting and Refining Company (ASARCO) opened the Silver Bell Mine also briefly the smelter. In 1918 and 1919 the world wide flu epidemic hit the Sasco town filling the cemetery with rows of concrete crosses. The post office closed in 1919 the price of copper in 1921 forced the mine to shut down. The train tracks were torn up and the smelter demolished in the middle of the 1930's.

## BUTTERFIELD OVERLAND STAGE STATIONS
## (26 STATIONS IN ALL)
From New Mexico across Arizona to California

San Simon
Apache Pass
Ewell's Station
Dragoon Springs
San Pedro
Cienaca
Tucson
Point of the Mountain
Picacho
Blue Water
Oneido
Sacaton
Casa Blanco
Maricopa Wells
Desert Station

Gila Ranch
Murderer's Grove (later Kenyon)
Oatman Flat
Burkes
Stanwix (also Flat Creek Station)
Henry Grennell's Station
Peterman's Station (later Mohawk)
Anelope Peak & Anelope Hill
Filabuster Camp
Mission Camp
Snively Station

Opha R. Probasco

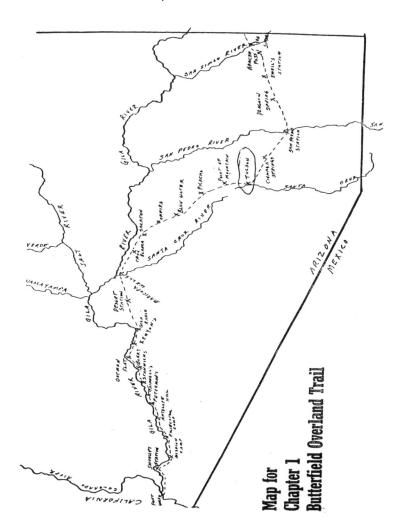

Butterfield Overland Stage Stations (26 in all) from New
Mexico, across Arizona, to California
See list previous page

215

# AGUIRRES FAMILIES

Don Pedro Aguirre was a freighter and a rancher in Chihuahua until 1852. The United States troops crossed the border and stayed over night at his ranch. Don Pedro was a good host and didn't see anything wrong since the soldiers were chasing the Apaches. A Mexican officer in the area had a different perception and accused him of being a traitor. Don Pedro was given a choice of being shot or moving to the United States and he chose the latter.

He settled in Mesilla, New Mexico and went into the mercantile business with Estevan Ochoa that ended in 1860. He then went into the freighting business on the Santa Fe Trail.

Later he moved to Tucson, Arizona and established the Buenos Aires Ranch, one of the famous early ranches. Gill owned the ranch after that and I was working for McBride, he had a contract building dirt tanks for the ranchers in that area and we build a large one for Mr. Gill. The forest service later bought the ranch and they control it as of today.

During the 1880's one of Don Pedro's sons, Don Yjino Aguirre started in the freight business around Wilcox, Arizona. In 1892 he moved his freight business and cattle operation to Red Rock, Arizona and established the El Rancho De San Francisco. All over the Avra Valley the grass was up to the horses belly which was watered by the over flow of the Santa Cruz River.

During the good days of the Aguirre Cattle Company, Don Yjnio and his son Higinio ran thousands of head of cattle in Southern Arizona. During the same time Aguirre's freight wagons was hauling ore from the Silver Bell Mine to the Red Rock spur of Southern Pacific Railroad.

Yjnio build a beautiful Spanish style adobe house eight miles north of the San Francisco Ranch.

The Aguirres and other Spanish families such as Elias, Robles, Pachecos, Redonods, Otes, Amados, and Samaniagos socialized, intermarried, ran their cattle and build a life style that's only a memory of the good old days.

Today,Yjinio and Enrique, grandsons of Don Yjinio Aguirre are retired, but these younger generations of the Aguirres still carry on the family traditions.

# WISHING SHRINE IN THE BARRIO LIBRE

The wishing shrine on south Main Street

This shrine was dedicated not to a saint but to a sinner who died violently and dishonorably.

This is a story told by Mrs. C.B. Perkins, daughter of a pioneering father, doctor F.H. Goodwin (not the first governor of Arizona territory).

Doctor Goodwin had a sheep ranch near the town of Tucson in 1875 in his employment were a young herder named Jaun Oliveras and the herder's father-in-law. Juan, his wife, and father-in-law all lived at the ranch, but the mother-in-law lived in Tucson. Juan was infatuated with his mother-in-law and often visited her. One day the father-in-law followed Juan into Tucson and surprised his wife with her lover. The men fought and Juan was thrown out of the house. The father-in-law followed and picked up an axe from the wood pile and killed Juan. The husband fled to Mexico and Juan was buried in a shallow grave where he had fallen. The mound was marked by desert mesquite, creosote bushes, and cat claw, soon by tin cans stoves and glass jars.

The spot where this took place is not the present site of the wishing shrine, which is 300 block of South Main Street, but was at the southwestern corner of South Meyer and West Simpson Street.

It was believed for years by the Mexicans that their wishes would come true when they burned candles over and around a grave. Some say the custom started when members of Juan's family began burning candles at his grave for the expiration of his soul. Probably some coincidence of a wish coming true after the burning of a candle at the grave, was recounted and others would slip through the shrubs at night to light candles. The superstition spread through out the village, more and more people went to the site and cheating a little, put scraps of iron and tin up to protect the candle flames from the wind. It must burn all night and into the day, if a long one, to make the wish materialize.

Another story of many was that some said "The spot marked the grave of a loyal son of a woman who had been murdered in Mexico". The son followed his step-father to

Tucson and stabbed him fourteen times once for each year the son had searched for the murder of his mother.

There are a few more stories, but the one that the city of Tucson always tells id the one about Juan the ship herder.

Mayor C.M. Straus ordered Simpson Street to be cut through Main Street and down to Santa Cruz River so there would be a better drainage on the muddy streets. That's when the grave of Juan's and the shrine were moved to the 300 block of South Main. The Tucson land marks an association in 1927 succeeded in obtaining a deed from Teofilo Otero for the lot on South Main Street so the shrine might be improved. The Tucsonans talked about beautifying the rubbish heap that was the shrine, and in 1940 The National Youth Administration accomplished that goal. The lot was cleared of rubbish and a wall built to out line three sides of it.

It was ugly by day light, but a touching beauty at night when kneeling figures wrapped in black rebozos were silhouetted dimly by the many flickering candles.

No community seems to have developed without a slum district, and Tucsonans called it Le Barrio Libre. This was at the southern end of town, particularly at the terminal of Main and Meyer Streets. The entire business district concentrated in a few blocks between Broadway and Alemeda, Main and Church Street. The residential areas circling that region and to the north were the Chinese Shanties and to the south El Barrio Libre.

On South Main Street, south of Congress were the homes of Governor McCormick, Pete Kitchen, The

Drachmans, Oteros, and other fine families. Just on the west side of the wishing shrine was the little eye springs, (Ojito Springs) watering place for the travelers. After the water table fell it shut off the water supply to the springs.

El Barrio Libre, explained the Tucson City directory for 1881, was not for the cultivated Mexicans of the city, but only for the lower classes. Then it gives this description, "Here the Mescalian could imbibe his fill and either male or female could, in peaceful intoxication, and sleep on the side walk or in the middle of the street, with all their ancient rights respected. Fandangoes, Monte, chicken fights, broils, and all the amusements of the lower class of Mexicans were, in this quarter, indulged in without restraint, and to this day much of the old-time prevails, although the encroachments of the American element indicate the ultimate doom of the customs of the Barrio Libre".

Also in this region were shacks occupied by Indian wood cutters who came from San Xavier Del Bac and villages west, on what is now the Papago Indian Reservation. They bought their loads of wood to town, usually arriving in the evening and staying over night in the shacks, and the next day drive their wagons through the streets, every once in awhile you'd see a dog walking under the wagon to get out of the sun and into the shade, selling their wood. A lot of the Anglo Americans joined the Spanish American in poverty and sin. Some lived off the earnings of a common law-wives and some lost their jobs and respect of not only the community, but of themselves, drinking themselves into early graves. One pioneer claimed Tucson served the worse coffin varnish that could be found in America.

# PHOENIX

The Hohokam culture reached its peak about 12:00 A.D. The Hohokam people began to leave the Salt River Valley around 1250 A.D., and by 1400 A.D., they were gone completely. There were a lot of reasons that were discussed about their leaving, but some thought they didn't leave that their descendants are the Pima and the Papago Indians of today.

Salt River Valley lay unclaimed for nearly 500 years. At the close of the Civil War in 1865, Fort Mcowell was established near where Sycamore Creek joins the Verde River. Lieutenant John Y.T. Smith mustered out of the army about that time and decided to stay as a hay contractor and post sutler. He'd seen the fields of wild hay growing on the flood plains of the Salt River, eighteen miles to the south and decided to set up a hay camp. The place became known as Smith Station and was located on the road he built to Fort McDowell. Today in Phoenix it would be at 4oth and Washington Street.

John Smith was just a common John Smith and meeting so many with the same name and getting into politics in 1874 and he ran for Congress a newspaper commented unfavorably for a man with a name John Smith. He went to the legislature and added Y.T. "Yours Truly".

September 1867 thirty seven year old Jack Swilling visited the Smith Station. He was an Indian fighter, adventurer, hellion, confederate officer, and recently a member of the famed walker party that discovered gold in the Bradshaw Mountains. He saw the opportunities for irrigation the rich soil by cleaning out the old Hohokam Canals and ditched.

Jack Swilling went to Wickenburg fifty miles northwest and organized a company called it the Swilling Irrigation Canal Company.

He also raised $400.00 to fund the project and recruited a party of sixteen strong back workers and headed for Smith Station.

Swilling and his companions arrived in December 1867 they began to dig in the north bank across from Tempe, but caliche and rock moved them down the river to 40th Street and the river bed near them Smith Station.

By March 1868 the wheat and barley crops were in and the population reached fifty. The watering system was called Swilling ditch that ran for one and a half miles then curved back toward the river. Later on it was called Town ditch. It was used to bath in, drink, irrigate, and do laundry, it turned out to be one of the riches agricultural regions in the world.

The first from was Frenchy Sawyer. There is a small plaque on the southeast corner of Washington and 24th Streets.

Population in 1870 was 61 women and 164 men ages ran from 21 to 30. There were ninety six that listed themselves as farmers, and there wasn't a single doctor, lawyer, banker, or a teacher among them.

October 20th 1870 a committee of citizens gathered to select a town site. Among the members of the section committee was Bryan Philip, Darrell Duppa, better known as "Lord". Duppa reported to be a British Lord who'd been something of an embarrassment to his family and been exiled to the colonies. He received financial support on regular basis as long as he remains out of England. Lord Duppa was also a well traveled, educated man who spoke five languages fluently. His friends complained, however, that he was hard to comprehend, because he remained in a drunken state most of the time and spoke all five languages at once. Sometime between 1868 and 1872 "Lord" Duppa built a two room adobe house at 116 West Sherman, three blocks south of today's Central Avenue under pass. Today this house still stands and it is the oldest house in the capital city.

The spot that was selected was Seventh Street and Seventh Avenue parcel. The town sites that were voted on were Sixteenth and Van Buren, Thirty Second and Van Buren, and Thirty Second and Van Buren and 7th. It was the down towner's that won out. A task for the settlers was to choose a name for the town site. Several were proposed including Stone Wall, Salinas, Punkinville, and Milleville. "Lord" Duppa is credit by some historians with providing the inspiration, but credited for naming the city after the mythical Phoenix Bird that rose from its own ashes to Jack Swilling. He found the description in his Webster's dictionary and thought the name suited the place. Ashes of the Great Hohokam were reborn.

1871 Maricopa County was organized and Phoenix became the county seat. The first election for Sheriff of Maricopa County set an early political fire works. Three candidates tossed their hats into the ring. Jim Barnum sat back and let the other two "Whispering Jim" the favorite and J.M. Chenowth fight it out. Each claimed the other was immoral, and hated kids, and was rude to the ladies. So much attention was given to these two that Jim Barnum was almost forgotten and seemed like he didn't have a chance.

Day before election, Whispering Jim and Chenowth grew tired of arguing politics and went for their six shooters. When the smoke was cleared Whispering Jim laid dead and the city fathers suggested Chenowth leave town, Jim Barnum was elected by a land slide.

Bill Kickland moved to Phoenix from Tucson in 1871. He was the first Anglo American to bring cattle to Arizona. He first brought 200 head from Sonora to the Canoa Ranch 1857. The Apaches had stolen them by 1860. He and his family wife and two kids moved into a small adobe house on Washington Street. August 15, 1871 his wife gave birth to a baby girl. The first Anglo American child born at the Phoenix town site.

In 1872 Phoenix opened its first school, adobe building with a mud roof and the first wooden floor in town. The first teacher was Ellen Shaver. She didn't last long, the first year she married John yours truly Smith.

By 1877 they had funds to build roads to link them to the outside world. There were nothing but cattle trails to Globe, Prescott, Yuma and Wickenburg. By 1879 they had a road across the Salt and Gila Rivers to Maricopa, link-ing Phoenix by stage coach to the new Southern Railroad. It was a sixteen hour ride from Maricopa to Phoenix. By 1880 Phoenix population was 1708. In 1885 William Murphy came in and built a thirty five mile long Arizona canal, to water the thirsty desert north of the Grand Canal. There were four canals north of the Salt River. They now challenge Prescott and Tucson for the capital, two years later Phoenix got the capital 1889.

Phoenix still faced serious water problems. Floods in 1890 and 1891 nearly wiped out the town, followed by long droughts in the 1890's, either too much or too little water, people leaving the valley and moving out.

The Theodore Roosevelt Dam was completed in 1911 and the future of Phoenix was secured. The dam was paid in full in 1955.

Phoenix didn't have a through railroad. They had the Santa Fe Prescott, the Phoenix
and the Maricopa Phoenix Railroad. Finally in 1926 a Southern Pacific line ran from Maricopa to Phoenix ten back to the Southern Pacific line to Tucson.

Jack Swilling a generous and big hearted man was the product of the violent frontier. Originally from South Carolina, he fought in both the Mexican and the Civil Wars and had been involved in several scrapes with the Apaches and the Comanche's. One time his skull had been fractured by a gun barrel and he was caring a bullet in his left side from another shooting scrape. His old injuries caused a great deal of pain he took morphine and whiskey to dull the pain, and at time became a little crazy. He would die in the Yuma prison in 1878 accused of a crime he didn't commit.

# TEMPE

"Lord" Darrell Duppa looked across the desert and spouting some greasewood and groves of mesquite, it made him think of the Vale of Tempe in Greece. This inspiration was the cause of naming the town site Tempe. In 1870 Charles Hayden was operating a ferry on the Salt River. Hayden had first come to Santa Fe in an ox cart during the late 1840's he became a merchant and later moved to Tucson, arriving on the first Butterfield overland stage in 1858. While he was there he took over the two abandoned flour mills that were damaged by fire during the Civil War. He repaired one of them that wasn't damaged to bad and sold them both to James Lee and W.F. Scott. Then moved to Tempe where he built another flour mill on the south side of the Salt River.

William Hillings built the first flour mill at 30th Street and Fillmore in East Phoenix. He also operated an Inn on Van Buren Blvd. The beginning of the Van Buren Motels.

Hayden took most of Hilling's business from the flour mill and finally William Hillings closed his flour mill down.

Charles Hayden believed that one of frontier Arizona's greatest needs was teachers.

He helped John Armstrong, one of his employees, win election to the territorial house in 1885. Armstrong thought he had a chance to get the insane asylum for Tempe. He took the two day ride in a stage coach trip to Tempe from Prescott to inform his boss. The elder Hayden sent him back to the capital with instructions to get the normal school, and this is what he had done.

The law gave Tempe sixty days to secure a school site of twenty acres. George and Martha Wilson sold their twenty acre cattle pasture for a meager $500.00. This was a personal sacrifice for the Wilson and George was employed as care taker of the buildings and ground at the new college, a job he held until he died twenty five years later.

# ARIZONA STATE UNIVERSITY SCHOOL

1886 the school opened with thirty three student, thirteen men and twenty women. One of the first graduates was James McClintock who later became Captain of the teddy Roosevelt's rough riders during the Spanish American War.

1898 the name changed to Tempe normal Teacher's College
1929 it was a four year Teacher's College
1933 renamed Arizona State Teacher's College
1945 with the enrollment of 533 students the name of the college was changed again to Arizona State College
1958 the last change was Arizona State University

This wasn't with out a fight with the Arizona University student that wanted their identity to remain as the only University.

After the school was built it almost didn't open on time. Two days before the opening date they discovered that there weren't any toilets. The next day the carpenters hurriedly built two out houses one for the girls and one for the boys.

# A COWBOY'S FIRST MOVING PICTURE SHOW

The Babbitts built an opera house and a theater that showed real moving pictures.

The story goes that one of the Babbitts' cowboys came to town (Flagstaff) and saw his first moving picture. In one scene several young ladies were disrobing before taking a dip in a local swimming hole. Just as they were getting down to their undergarments, a freight train went roaring by. When the tracks were clear again, the ladies were safely submerged in water up to their necks. After the film the cowboy went to the ticket window and bought five more tickets. When the sales girl asked why he wanted to see the same movie five more times, the cowboy replied matter-of-Factly, Ma'am I don't know much about moving pictures, but I do know something about trains and I'm betting that out of the next five that goes by, one is bound to be late and I'm going to be there when it happens.

*Opha R. Probasco*

# ALPINE

Alpine is located in northeastern high country and was originally called Bush Valley for Anderson Bush, the first settler. Three years alter in 1879 a party of Mormons arrived and renamed it Frisco for the San Francisco River. Finally someone noticed the Swiss like mountains and the town was then named after Alpine, Utah. Jacob Hablin the greatest Mormon trail blazer is buried there.

# HANNEGAN MEADOWS

So often you hear people talk about the Hannegan Meadows and I'm sure there isn't one out of a hundred that knows how that part of the country got the name.

Bob Hannegan who ran cattle here briefly in the 1890's, a story is told that a reason for his hasty departure came from the way local people collected unpaid debts.

Bob Hannegan owed a couple of ranchers $1200.00 and wouldn't pay up, so they took him out and chained him to a tree until his relatives paid the debt in full. After that Bob Hannegan didn't stay around for very long.

# NUTRIOSO

Some of the most famous fur trappers used to pass through the valley coming from Taos, New Mexico to the White Mountains. In the 1820's nutria means beaver or otter and oso is bear in Spanish. Mormons arrived there in the 1870's and a small fort was built in 1880.

# BILL SMITH'S GANG

The first Mexican settlers arrived in Springerville area prior to 1871 and named the place Valle Redondo (round valley). Horse thieves used round valley as a refuge where they could alter brands of live stock stolen in Northern Arizona and later sold in the southern part of Arizona. On their way back they would rustle a herd that they would sell in Northern Arizona. The Arizona rangers swept through the north in October 1901 in pursuit of Bill Smith and his notorious gang of New Mexico.

The lawmen caught up with the Bill Smith crowd in Graham but lost the fight. Ranger Carlos Tafolla of St. Johns and Apache county deputy sheriff, Will Maxwell was killed. Smith later said he was sorry he had killed Maxwell but was glad he killed the Arizona ranger. Earlier in New Mexico members of the Smith's gang ambushed and killed famed Texas lawman George Scarborough. The gang left Arizona after killing Tafolla and Maxwell. They went to Mexico and were never caught.

*Opha R. Probasco*

# SPRINGERVILLE

Springerville was named for merchant Henry Springer, who extended credit to most of unsavory characters in round valley and eventually went broke. The town site was originally called Omer by the Mormons who settled there. Later they settled in Eagar and the name was changed to Springerville. The two communities are an interesting contrast. Springerville was settled by the Spanish with catholic faith, the Mormons of Anglo ancestry. Springerville's most prominent merchants were Julius and Gustav Becker who arrived in 1876 and opened a freight business, hauling merchandise from Rio Grande by ox trains. Juluis Becker and son of Gustav played a major role in getting U.S. 60 to come through Springerville. The first auto pathfinder passed through here in 1910 on the first transcontinental auto trip. Six years later the ocean to ocean journey brought a caravan of autos through the town.

# GOLD MINES

After the Mormon battalion crossed the Southern Arizona parallel 32nd line in 1846 and left their wagon tracks. The 49ers followed in 1849 to the gold fields in California. Later in 1857 lieutenant Edward Beale made his way across the 35th parallel line with his camel experiment, this opened the northern route across Arizona but most of the immigrants took the southern route due to the cold and snow during the winter.

It wasn't long after this when they had a gold strike in Arizona, this was the first gold strike and it was just north of Yuma in 1858 in Arroyo De Le Tenaja, La Paz.

The miners used two methods to extract the gold, one was by placer, panning it out of a stream when the gold is broken off from the mother lode, in lode mining it's more difficult, the gold has to be separated from the ore. The ore has to be crushed and mercury or quick silver used and it will attach itself to the gold and reject the rock. The gold and mercury creation amalgam and you will use mercury again to separate the two. To reclaim the mercury the mine would use a retort of some kin to evaporate it. When this is done the rich mineral is all that is left.

One way in separating the amalgam was to use tubing similar to distilling whiskey. The amalgam would be placed in a pot and heated. The mercury would evaporate through the tubing leaving the gold. The mercury could be reclaimed when it dripped from the tubing.

One of the more ingenious salvage techniques used by the miners was to take a potato and slice it in half and remove the inside of one of the halves. The miner then would inset his amalgam into the empty half, wire the potato back together, and roast it. When the roasting was finished, the empty half would contain a gold button and vaporized mercury was absorbed into the other half of the potato.

The early American mining techniques used in the far west were learned from the Mexicans or the Spaniards. Mexico had a school for miners seventy five year before the United States did, and graduating some of the top mining engineers. The Mexican gambusino (miner) had a nose for ore. A prospector must process "An eye like an artist" and be able to dig like a gopher. A good prospector had to have knowledge in basic geology. If he didn't, he could be wasting his time. A good prospector had no trouble in finding a grub stake.

After he found a promising area that looks like there were gold, he would stake out two claims one for him and one for the one who grub staked him, and let them take there choice. Gold is approximately nineteen times heavier than water and three to four times heavier than sand.

High-grading is when you shop lift ore form one's employer. A miner might take home a couple of pieces of ore at the end of his shift and set up a small smelter of his own. It has been said that a lot of bow legged men in the west got that way by riding horses, but that's not true, it was carrying lunch pails home full of ore. The mine owners would hold inspection after each shift to try and stop the high-grading. They would have to shed their clothing and stand while various personal and not so personal areas of their bodies were checked. A man caught high-grading was fired and it was hard for him to find a job in the same district. In one case two would be high-graders didn't fare too well. They set up a small smelter in their home and breathing the dangerous fumes of the mercury caused the men to lose their teeth and also their hair. The company felt that justice had been done so they didn't file charges against them.

High-grading has always been a problem, it was estimated that as much as forty percent of the gold from a rich vein was stolen by the miners. It is also said that more than twenty thieves were administered "suspended sentences" by Judge Lynch.

During the first six years of operation, tow and a half million dollars in gold were taken out, and it is estimated a million of it was high-graded. One mine had a hanging tree and this was the Vulture Mine, to try to ward off the high-grading. It is said that Jacob Waltz the lost Dutch man worked at the Vulture Mine and was fired for high-grading. I for one and a lot of others believe that the lost Dutch man mine was myth and the ore he had taken by high-grading from the mines he worked at were taken to the Superstition Mountains.

The largest nugget ever found in the United States was at Calabasas, California, it weighed 195 troy pounds and was worth over $40,000.00. At that time, the world's record holder is Australia, where miners uncovered a nugget of 630 pounds of which 472 pounds were pure gold.

In the days before the mints were turning out coins for currency to purchase anything such as drinks were made by the pinch method. Where the bartender simply reached into a miner's poke sack with his thumb and fore finger and took out as much as he could squeeze between the two. The amount was usually worth about .75 cents and a dollar would depend upon the size of the bartender's fingers.

A story is told by a bartender in California who use to spill a small amount of his pinch on the floor during the process of transferring the dust from the miner's poke sack to the money box. Several times during his shift he would step out side the back door where he had conveniently situated a mud hole. After muddying his boots he would re-enter the bar and walk back and forth over the spilled gold dust. After this was done he would walk over to a bucket and scrape the mud off of his boots. On week-ends alone the bartender would take his bucket home and pan out a hundred dollars worth of gold dust.

A woman who followed the gold strikes brought a touch of class to a male-dominate society. In some of the remote camps the men some times went for month's without seeing a so-called respectable woman.

A group of miners were returning to their cabin after a long days work when they by chance to see a woman's lingerie hanging from a line out the miner's shack. Not used to such fineries, they rushed over to the cabin and demanded to meet the woman who lived there. There were no women and the lingerie hanging on the line was just some one's joke. There was one miner who did pick up some women's underwear while in San Francisco and carried it with him high into the mother lode, where he charged the miners admission to see the lacy garments, for an extra charge he'd let the miners touch them.

The shady ladies who set up business in the mining camps some times came from cities as far as Berlin, Paris, and London. Many of the madams acquired wealth and some becoming the richest and successful business women in their respective states. Many others were doomed to die lonely deaths in the camps form disorders as pneumonia and alcoholism, and some married and started life over again in a new plane. Some of the parlor houses were strict, you had to take a bath and couldn't take your guns in.

# SALTING THE MINES

When P.T. Barnum said "There's a sucker born every minute" he could have easily been talking about the sale of mining claims. Some people would sink their life savings into mining stock. Stock peddlers and swindlers were all over. They could print, issue, sell and be on the next rain out of town all in the same day. Stock certificates on nonexistent mines were sold in the communities where the nonexistent mines didn't exist the list of stock swindlers in the mining west is long and was all part in the financial wheelings and dealings. If a mine is worthless to sell it, the seller would salt the mine in many ways. One is to take some ore from a good productive mine and scatter it around in the worthless mine. Another way was to take a shot gun, load it with gold dust, and blast the walls of the shaft or tunnel. The gold being malleable would imbed itself into the rock. The buyer might ask to have the walls blasted to see what was inside of the rock. The seller still might install salted gold into the head of sticks of his dynamite and when the charge went off, the interior of the rock would be salted. But the buyer would suggest using the stick of dynamite he brought along just for the occasion.

Gold is soluble in aqua regia forming a gold chloride. This gold chloride is soluble in water. Using a syringe, you could inject gold into a crevice or a rock of ore samples. Bi-chloride of gold was used for medicinal purpose during the 1900's for such things as alcoholism and kidney ailments. When taken internally, the bi-chloride of gold will pass through the body, exiting with high assay value. The knowledgeable salter could load himself on the auferous substance and "Salt" any crack, crevice or ore sample a nature or spirit moved him.

The early California gold camps with their board walks and muddy street, false front buildings, and tent houses were vivacious as their names applied. Towns like Whiskey Bar, Hang Town, Devil's Retreat, Flap Jack Canyon, Red Dog, You Bet, Gouge Eye, Gomorrah, and Rough and Ready.

The first gold rush in Arizona was in 1858 some twenty miles up the Gila River from the junction with the Colorado River, when Colonel Jake Snively discovered rich deposits of placer gold. It wasn't long before a town sprang up with a population of 1200 argonauts. Gila Rivert as it was called had everything except a church and a jail.

The gold was there, and a person that didn't have any experience could make $20.00 a day from just a few pans of dirt. In 1861 men were making from $20.00 to $125.00 a day. It was long before the gold played out.

In 1862 another gold town sprung up, it was the river a few miles from Yuma, La Paz out stripped Gila City in people and gold. A population of 5,000 and merchants including Joseph and Mike Goldwater arrived and began supplying the miners. The gold seemed limitless but after eight million dollars were taken out of La Paz folded into oblivion.

Joseph Walker was a mountain man who had led parties in earlier days of the beaver trade. He had first come to Santa Fe, New Mexico in 1821 with the Becknell expedition which opened the Santa Fe Trail.

Joe Walker was looking for gold his whole life had been a serious of adventures. In 1833 he organized an expedition of fur trappers into California, the first white men to cross the Sierra Nevada in the winter time. At that time he was thirty four years old and six feet tall and weighed 200 pounds. He was the best trail blazer of them all. After a year they wound up in Santa Fe, New Mexico. With General Carleton advice they headed for Arizona.

Jack Swilling was a confederate officer during the occupation of Tucson, and recently joined the group. He was elected to serve as captain of a detail of miners to carry out the plans of capture of Mangos Colorado that would cause them trouble. He could be induced to pay a visit then taken prisoner, and held as hostage. That would give them a safe passage through Apacheria.

At that time parties of federal soldiers arrived and were invited to join the party. The Americans then went to Pinos, where a parley with Mangos was arranged. When the Apache entered the camp under a flag truce he was taken a prisoner. Mangos Colorado walked into a trap, he should have known better, for two years before his son-in-law Cochise had done the same things at Apache Pass and was ordered killed.

The miners had planned to release him after they were safely through. However, the army took custody of him and the next day Mangos Colorado was dead. Shot while trying to escape, was the army's report.

However, Conner who was present the night before herd Colonel West tells two soldiers that he wanted that old devil dead. That night Conner saw the soldiers sticking the old man with bayonets that had been heated in the fire, when Mangos protested they shot him. Later they removed his head, boiled the flesh off the bones, and sent the skull east where it was displayed for a time. Several years later, charges were brought against West but he denied them and the matter was dropped.

Mean while the Walker party went on to Tucson and after getting supplies headed toward the Hassayampa River. Within a few miles of Prescott they made their strike. Soon Fort Whipple would be built and become the first territorial capital. From 1863 to the 1870's some $6 million in gold and silver would be taken from the Bradshaw Mountains.

The Weaver Peeples party guided by Paulino Weaver, another old trapper turned Argonaut. August of 1863 they made camp near Antelope Hill, just east of Congress Junction. A Mexican party was also camped near by. Sometime during the night, some mules wandered off causing an early morning search. Climbing to the top of Antelope Hill for a better look see one of the searchers noticed the ground all around him was covered with gold nuggets. It was said that men picked up $4,000.00 each before breakfast. It's doubtful if they even ate.

The Mexicans, exuberant over their find, went back to Mexico, while the Weaver party stayed on. Within three months over a quarter million dollars worth of gold had either been picked up or pried out with a jack knife. On just one acre, over one half million dollars in nuggets were found. It was the richest placer gold discovery in Arizona history. Week-end prospectors still seek gold on the rich hill as of today, but you have to take a number and wait your turn for there are so many.

Henry Wickenburg was so frustrated in not finding any gold, he had missed the Walker party and arrived too late to catch the Peeples Weaver party. He had come from California with Carleton army and like others in the group he was first and always a prospector.

There are different stories in how he had discovered his mine and the stories they use are for the public of today. Henry Wickenburg sold his ore for $15.00 a ton to the local prospectors and let them transport it to Jack Swillings arrastra for milling on the Hassayumpa a few miles to the east. It goes without saying a lot of high grading was going on.

Henry Wickenburg finally sold out for $85,000.00 and one-fifth percent interest. He was swindled out of most of it by the new owners. The Vulture Mine became one of the most productive gold mines in the west before it played out. The buildings at the mine were constructed of stone gathered near by. Some of these buildings were torn down in 1879 yielded $4000 a ton. It was known that one vein was twenty seven to thirty nine feet wide and went down 350 feet into the earth. Before the Vulture played out some twenty million dollars had been extracted. Actual figures are hard to come by due to so much high grading was going on. Henry Wickenburg's luck didn't get any better a flood had wiped out his farm several years later, leaving him penniless.

In 1905 he shot himself to death in the town that was name for him.

*Opha R. Probasco*

# THE SILVER KING MINE

It was during the Apache war fare when Sullivan with other soldiers under General George Stoneman was on a road-building detail. They were stationed at Camp Picket Post three miles west and al little south of the present superior. This was in 1872 when they were building the road leading into the more inaccessible portion of the Pinals.

One evening when Sullivan was returning to camp from the road building detail, he sat down to rest, he examined the rocks around him that were scattered around his feet. He noticed some heavy black fragments that took his interest, especially when he pounded them, they seemed to flatten out and not shatter. Collecting a few he went on into camp, he made no mention of his discovery to anyone. Soon his service expired and Sullivan made his way to the ranch of Charles Mason on the Salt River. Sullivan had displayed the ore on a number of times. One day he disappeared and they thought the Apaches had killed him or he went back to where he had found the ore.

During the next two years Mason and others searched for the spot where Sullivan had found the black nuggets. At different times they were almost on top of the spot without knowing it. One location the Silver Queen, being made only a mile and a half fro the spot where Sullivan had found the samples. In 1874 Mason and his party located the Globe Mine later to be known as the Globe District. The following spring Mason and four of his friends Benjamin W. Regan, WilliamH. Long, Isaac Copeland, and another man whose name has been lost took a train of pack animals to the Globe location with the idea of bringing out a shipment of ore. While returning from the Globe Mine March 21, 1875 this party was attacked by Apaches and its now nameless member was slain. They took his body to General Stonemans original camp site and interred him in one of the abandoned stove ovens that they had used to bake bread in. After simple obsequies the remaining four made camp and Copeland went to get back one of the mules that had strayed after he found the animal he was standing on top of some croppings he examined the ore then rushed back yellowing "I have stuck it" after all of the party examined the ore they said it was the same ore that Sullivan had found three years before. The Silver King location was made the next day. Two weeks later the Arizona Citizen reported the discovery. Mr. Regan brought a ton of ore to town and it assayed $434.00 per ton.

Convinced that it was too good to last Copeland and Long soon sold to Mason and Regan for $80,000.00 each, and in January 1887 Mason sold his half interest to Colonel James M. Barney, of Yuma for a quarter of a million dollars. Despite the predictions the King continued to be good.

Two trains, one drawn by eighteen and the other by twenty mules bringing 36,050 pounds of rich silver ore from the Silver King Mine of Arizona, arrived in town yesterday, reported the San Diego Union. January 19, 1877 and consigned to W.W. Stewart and Company by Colonel Barney and will be forward to San Francisco for reduction.

The two trains put on quite appearance coming into town. The immense wagons are the biggest that ever been seen in town. The rear wheels were seven feet high and looked like they weighed a ton. Benjamin W. Regan the last remaining owner of the four original locators sold his half interest in the mine in May 1877 for $300,000.00.

The Silver King Mining Company was organized in San Francisco that summer of 1877, and was capitalized at $10,000,000.00 and James Barney was named manager. In the vicinity of the King Mine had grown up to a small well behaved mining camp. Five miles from the King Mine was Pinal City, which had a mill where the King had taken their ore.

On October 26, 1926 Perry Wildman one of the merchants of Silver King and Pinal City had written a manuscript for the Arizona Historical Society, recalled many historical and humorous incidents in the lives of the two camps. They were peaceful, contended, and happy people. Every man was a law unto himself and anything unruly wasn't tolerated. They didn't lock their doors and robbery wasn't heard of. Gambling was wide open but always on the square. Water for drinking and cooking was delivered and sold for five cents a gallon. If the wanted to take a bath they either went to the mine and caught the condensed water from the boilers, or waited until it rained then caught enough off of the roof.

In 1883 there was a cloud burst that about washed everything away and almost closed the mine. It was so bad that boulders five feet in diameter were rolling down the hills. One miner got caught in his cabin and before he could get out to higher ground his body was found ten miles away. Perry Wildman's building was flooded and sack of grain, scales, boxes, and barrels of merchandise waiting to be packed to Globe. In the warehouse there were twenty rolls of fencing that was washed out and unrolled tangles up so bad he couldn't save it, it was stretched for miles.

The Sliver King usually paid their men off every month in drafts on the Anglo California bank at San Francisco. In order to keep the money from leaving town as much as possible the store keeper would have cash brought into camp. He had used every method he could think of to accomplish this without it being known. He didn't ship it by express too often due to there were so many hold ups of stages. Between Florence and the mining camps (Pinal and Silver King) he would have his friend Don Carlos Hayden, in Tempe put a bag of silver, mostly dollars inside a sack of grain mixed in a load of the same kind of sacks brought to him by the Mormon freighters. He used this method for a long time and over a period be brought in thousands of dollars.

He never lost one single dollar, some times he would get his coins from Los Angeles by freight packed in boxes with merchandise, and it was still safer than express.

One time he was late in getting ready for pay day so he wrote to Union Hardware and Metal Company in Los Angeles to ship him by express five kegs of nails, each keg to contain about half its weight in silver dollars and the other half in nails. The nails were worth twelve and half cents a pound. It was foolish for him to do this. The express charges were more than that per pound and any-one would think its queer shipping nail by express. The store keeper regretted in doing this but it was too late to do anything about it. The nails came through alright to Florence but when the stage got to Silver King the nails weren't on it. He asked the drive if he had any nails for him. The driver told him there were five kegs on the side walk in front of the office and couldn't bring them on this trip for he was heavy loaded with passengers and bag-gage, but will bring them up on the next trip. They stayed on the side walk all night and came up the next day all in tact. This was the first time and the last time he ever done this.

Pinal was the larger and more livery of the two camps. A year ago Pinal was almost out of hotels, drug stores, assay offices, and professional service reported the Pinal paper July 1881. They have now two large hotels, half dozen restaurants, twelve saloons, tow large blacksmith shops, wagon shops, and drug stores. Grocery stores, watch maker, photo gallery, brickyard, lime kiln, seven assorted stores, lumber yard, two large livery stables, bar-ber shops, lawyers, preachers, large freight teams, bank, Well's Fargo office and a post office. Plus other improve-ments like a church and schools. A lot of houses had been built. Some of the components contributing to Pinals life and energy were an oriental colony.

# SHOOTING AFFRAY IN THE CHINA BLOCK

One shooting affray in "The China Block" was also written up in the Pinal Drill paper.

Qui Gee shot Go Ghu. Dang Fook and Wang Wy shot Sue Gee, all in general row at the Chinese gambling house– Dang Fook and Wang Wy ran away and the police are after them. Sue Gee wash shot in the mouth and shoulder. He can't eat and probably will die. Go Ghu is dead, Qui Gee is under arrest. Dang Fook and Wang Wy will likely be caught. Doctor Bluett says that Sue Gee won't die he is fixing a wire, iron clad, fire proof jaw on him to secure the safety of Sue's chewing.

This is what happened at Go Ghu funeral service in July 1881 as prescribed by Perry Wildman.

The Chinese friends of Go Ghu wanted him buried "Allie same Melican Man". They told them that it would cost $40.00 to have the ceremony preformed to which they agreed. Wildman didn't know who officiated as master of ceremonies, but he dug up a copy of Shakespear some where. When the procession reached the grave Ho opened the book to the play of Romeo and Juliet he read with all the solemnity and reverence he could command and it was a success. The Chinese were satisfied and paid the forty dollar which was distributed over the bars of various saloons.

One of the prominent citizens of Pinals Chinese Colony was Jim Sam, owner of the bank exchange restaurant and chop house. Although he was one of the best known and most highly esteemed Orientals in the territory he refused to acknowledge his ancestry. "I no Chinaman he said I born Hong Cong I Blitish subject".

One day a self asserted bad man known as shoot-em-up-dick wearing fringed buckskin, two guns, and a bowie knife, swaggered into Jim's restaurant and ordered the best meal in the house. After eating he demanded the best cigar started leisurely toward the door, ignoring the cashier's stand. With drawing a big six shooter from under the counter, Jim sang out cheerfully "Hey fliend – you-for-gettum somesing, yes".

"No, you dammed yellow heathern", snarled the departing bad man. I didn't forget nawthing. I was your guest. I'm shoot-em-up-Dick. I'm shoot-em-down-Sam, you pay pletty damn soon, or shoot-em-up-Dick be pletty damn dead. Dick paid.

In hauling ore to the mill in Pinal form the Silver King the drivers had occasions to speak forcibly to the animals rocks were used to throw at the mules and always the best silver specimens that he would use. His friend would be walking by at the right time. It was just another way to high grade the ore.

There appeared in Pinal City an aged man who exhibited great interest in the Silver King Mill where twenty stamps, working around the clock, pounding out the stuff of which millionaire are made. The man was evidently in need of help and soon went to the office of the company and announced himself as Sullivan, the old solider, the original discoverer of the vein and asked for work, reported Harry Brook in the Quijotoa Prospector Paper, February 16, 1884. Long before he had been given up for dead and very few of his-friends survived, he was identified beyond a doubt.

On leaving Mason's shack the man said he crossed the desert to California where he worked as a farm hand trying to save enough so he could go back and file on the claim after finding out that Mason had found the silver ore and his party filed, he knew he was too late for him. Under the mining laws, Sullivan had no right of ownership in the mine. The Silver King Company provided light work for him and took care of him for the rest of his days.

During the fifteen years the Silver King Mine operated there were estimates form $6,500,000.00 to $17,000,000.00 were taken out of the mine. The great mine was closed down February 1, 1891.

*Opha R. Probasco*

# KING OF ARIZONA MINING COMPANY

On the east side of U.S. 95 north of Castle Dome Ranger are the Kofa Mountains. The Kofa Range takes its name from the King of Arizona Mining Company, which use to stamp its K of A brand on any company property, lending its name to the near by Kofa Mountains. The King of Arizona Mine's active years of gold production came from 1896 to 1910. In 1897 a five stamp amalgamation mill was built at Mohawk, thirty five miles south of the mine. A cyanide plant 6to treat the tailings were built a year later. The mine produced $3,500,000.00 in gold before it played out. The old mine, located in the southwest part of the Kofa Mountains, can be reached by taking the dirt road at Stone Cabin.

Although most maps refer to these mountains as the Kofa, old timers around Yuma and La Paz Country call them by their original name, the S.H. Mountains. This name comes from the 1860's when soldiers noted that the physical structure of some of the mountains resembled large houses with small building, better known as out houses in back, with a soldierly touch of bawdy humor, the mountains were dubbed appropriately. Later as women came to the area initials were used in lieu of the full name. The women of course wanted to know what the S.H. meant. They were told "Short Horn" a name that appears on some maps.

In 1896 Charles Eichelberger was prospecting in the south western edge of the S.H. Mountains (now Kofa Mountains) finding he was about out of water, Charlie headed up a canyon in search of a tank (a rock basin containing rain water). After a strenuous climb, he located a tank, filled his canteen and sat down to rest. While idly scanning the canyon, Charlie noticed a shiny object about twenty feet away, so he walked over to investigate it proved to be the gold out cropping that latter developed into the famous King of Arizona mine.

Eichelberger soon joined forces with H.B. Gleason and Epserandolf and organized the King of Arizona Mining Company. The mine was too young to have a town that first summer. So there weren't any accommodations for the workers to sleep or eat. They slept out in the open or a cave if they could find one. The men working the graveyard shift faced a problem of trying to sleep during the day, with no protection from the sun or the heat. Water was also a problem, the closes water was thirty five miles away. For two days their drinking water was sloshed around in an old wine and whiskey barrels as a mule team hauled it from Mohawk. It tasted terrible and many of the miners got ill but it was all they had.

The mine was too rich to let a little inconvenience hinder the development, and before long, everything began to change. A settlement sprang up named Kofa abbreviation for King of Arizona. They had a boarding house, bunk house, company store, saloons, and a school.

After several attempts of drilling, a water supply was struck about five miles away.

There were a hundred twenty five men employed at the mine and most of them were Cornishmen, Mexicans, and Chinese. "The Cousin Jacks" were the miners, the Mexicans chopped and sold wood for running the mill, and the Chinese were the cooks. King of Arizona mine was not a bad place, but occasionally some things do happen. Joaquin Nogales tried to burn down a building at the King of Arizona Mine and got six years for attempt arson. "Pinky Dean" a drunken nigress, slashed up a miner with a knife in her apartment back of a saloon.

# TWO STAGE COACH ROUTES FROM MARICOPA WELL'S STATION THROUGH PHOENIX, ARIZONA TO PRESCOTT, ARIZONA

| #1 ROUTE | #2 ROUTE |
|---|---|
| Maricopa Well's Station | Maricopa Wells Station |
| Morgan's Ferry | Morgan's Ferry |
| Phoenix | Phoenix |
| Whitlow's Crossing | Agua Fria |
| Fort McDowell | Nigger's Well |
| Camp Verde | Lambey |
| Fort Whipple | Wickenburg |
| Prescott | Weaver |
| | Staton |
| | People's Valley |
| | Kirkland |
| | Skull Valley |
| | American Ranch |
| | Prescott |

Prescott was named for William Hickling who worked on the history of Mexico. In the honor of the great historian, McCormick suggested the name of Prescott for the new town, it stuck.

John Goodwin was Arizona territory's first governor. Richard C. McCormick was the second. There were sixteen territory governors in all for Arizona. Arizona was stateless for sixty two years, longer than any other territory.

The state capital was located in Prescott in 1863 to 1867 then it was moved to Tucson until 1877. The capital was then moved back to Prescott until 1889 then the capital was moved to Phoenix where it is today.

History is many times just a rumor we choose to believe, or a myth that we all agree upon.

# STAGE COACH STATION'S MEALS

Not all stage coach station served meals, some of the stations were just a relay station where they changed horses only and if you had to step behind a bush you'd better be on the coach when he was ready to leave for he would go off and leave you, and that would be quiet a wait. All stations did have water and their own wells and they were all hand dug and a few of them going over a hundred feet. Listed below are some of the meals served at different stations:

| | |
|---|---|
| Coffee | Bread |
| Beans | Tea |
| Venison | Fried Steaks of Bacon |
| Mule Meat | Antelope |
| Jerked Beef | Corn Bread |
| Black Coffee | Jars of Chili Peppers |
| Slumgullion | |
| Salt Pork with plenty of mustard | |
| Mustard added Spice | |

The latter tough enough to the meals

The food was never freshly cooked. It was heated, added to, and served over and over. The bread was so

260

hard it had to be soaked before you could eat it. A lot of people got sick from eating the meals. All the stations that served meals always had a lot of mustard, and I think it was to camouflage the taste.

# MORGAN'S FERRY

In Arizona territory two of it's great rivers, The Salt and the Gila (the third being the Colorado) flowed year around from east to west. Near its center they meet the Salt and Gila and they weren't tamed yet with dams up stream. During the dry years they were tamed rivers winding through the mountains and desert but during the flood stage they were wild and fierce. Two pioneer men operated ferries across these rivers, they were Charles Hayden and Henry Morgan.

Hayden had his across the Salt ten miles east of Phoenix in 1870. He brought his bride Sally to his station where she became its charming hostess, and their son was Senator Carl Hayden. Charles Hayden also built a flour mill near his ferry and later the area around him became Tempe which was name by Darrell Duppa an out cast Englishman for London, he also name Phoenix.

Henry operated his ferry across the Gila River fifteen miles south of Phoenix. He built a trading post near his ferry and lived with an Indian woman in common law marriage. They had no sons or daughters so there weren't any heirs.

In the march of progress his ferry as well as the community of Maricopa Wells near it were passed by and completely abandoned, Charles Hayden's name still in the memory of the State of Arizona. His son Carl Hayden had a lot to do with it being a senator for so many years.

The stories of Henry Morgan and Morgan's ferry are still to be found in the archives of Arizona Historical Society and the Arizona Historical foundation. Henry Morgan was born in Wisconsin in 1841 and arrived in Arizona in 1864. He had a contract with White and Noyes of San Francisco to build a steam flour mill at the Pima Indian Village of Casa Blanca, where the Pima's were raising large quantities of a superior strain of Sonoran wheat. After getting the mill erected Morgan stayed for about a year. Though he was only twenty three years old Morgan and the Indians, the first he had every seen had a real close relationship. He was their spokesman with other white men and learned their language, lived with them, treated them kindly and fairly and even fought with them and their neighbor, the Maricopa Indians in their battles with raiding tribe.

Mr. John F. Crampton of Maricopa Wells Station recalled a big battle fought in front of the station between the Pima's and the Maricopa's on one side, and the Yuma's on the other side. The Maricopa's and the Pima's were aided by Henry Morgan, the Yuma's were badly beaten. These battles were fought mostly with clubs and it lasted for days. The battle field was littered with dead bodies on both sides. A young officer from the U.S. Cavalry sent a letter to the Lo Angeles Star in 1872 and it was also published in the journal of the U.S. Cavalry Association which he described the battle field a couple of years later. The Maricopa's were once a large tribe but they nearly were wiped out in the battle with the Yuma's and Cocopah's. The whitened bones of both sides were piled high across the field and it showed how desperate and destructive the struggle had been.

In 1864 Arizona was a wild, savage, unknown wasteland as Charles describes it in this book. It had been a separate territory for only one year and had only two villages. One was a Mexican Pueblo of Tucson and the other was the new state capital, Prescott, being built on Granit Creek. Phoenix wasn't even thought of on any ones mine. Also in 1864 Henry Wickenburg discovered the Vulture Gold Mine. And in 1865 Henry Morgan went there to build a quartz mill for Chase and Company. He stayed two years then returned to the land of the Pima's and Maricopa's and built his ferry which was on the Gila River ten miles west of Casa Blanca and about four miles east of the Maricopa Wells station. All traces of the Morgan's Ferry and station have long ago disappeared. However, it was on the south bank of the river about the location of the bridge on the Phoenix-Maricopa Highway. It was on the road to Fort McDowell from its supply trail terminal at Maricopa Wells. The station at Morgan's Gerry was like all the other buildings in the primitive land, built of adobe bricks with mortared mud, the roof was ocotillo limbs or mesquite limbs cross-laid and covered with arrow weeds with a thick layer of mud on top. The floor was hard-packed caliche clay, watered and swept daily to keep it hard. Morgan worked at his ferrying and treaded with the Indians for twenty five years. He wore out four ferry boats in that length of time. Charlie Clark a telegrapher at Maricopa Wells said that Morgan was a rough and uncouth fellow who had been a pirate in the Gulf of California years before he was rather a good person when he wasn't drunk. Due to some of his fights he has been in, he claimed to have seven bullets in his body, three plainly visible just under the skim one under his right breast and two beneath his shoulder blades.

Morgan described the Pima's whom he had close ties as being sober, honest, upright and fair in all of their dealings. They had one fault and that was an opinion of the commercial integrity of women. When they found Morgan selling goods to their squaws on credit they laughed at him. Morgan always got his money however.

Before 1870 according to a Phoenix Pioneer Madison Loring, Morgan formed a partnership with Daniel Dietrich under the name of H. Morgan and Company, to conduct the trading post at Morgan Ferry. They soon branched out in the new town of Phoenix, putting up a building on Washington Street joining onto a building owned by John George, making it a one long structure. It was reported later that the Morgan Company built another building on Washington Street opposite Meyer's stable. For a time Morgan and Company prospered.

The news papers carried stories of Morgan's combative nature he was fined three hundred dollars for fooling with a six shooter too seriously for the bodily comfort of his adversary. Later he entered Salari's Restaurant drawing his revolver intending to shoot P. Dolan. Bystanders prevented the shooting by wrestling his revolver away and during the melee he was injured enough to spend a day in bed. The news paper also carried a story of Morgan killing a Mexican at his station on the Gila August 21, 1879 Morgan surrendered to the authorities and was charge for the killing of Jesus Figorro. His attorneys were J.T. Alsap and A.C. Baker. The evidence showed Mr. Morgan was fully justified in his act and the justice discharged him at once from custody.

On July 13, 1880 Henry Morgan's partner, Dan Dietrich was shot and killed by Thepima Indians at their station on the Gila River.

Dietrich was alone and had just locked up the store at sundown and was standing about six feet away when he was shot in the back four times. Henry Morgan found his body the next morning. After carrying the body into the station Morgan found tracks coming and returning to the river. Morgan testified that the only one whom he thought might have done this was a long haired Papago whom Dietrich had a quarrel with a year ago. The Papago didn't trade there but he lived below the station as Morgan wouldn't allow him on primises. David Hickey gave this account to what had happened later, Morgan and Tom Rogers arrived from Phoenix and after a little rest he asked Hickey to saddle his horse. He rode over to see the chief of the Indians. He told the chief to get up behind him and they rode back to his house. After arriving Morgan told the chief that he heard that he furnished the Papago a horse to get away on. After hearing this, the chief hollered to his warriors who came a running up. Mr. Morgan told him that he meant them no harm and the warriors soon left. About an hour later a hundred Indians rushed the house and dragged Mr. Morgan outside.

All the Indians had were clubs made of mesquite. He was clubbed three times and the Indians thought him dead. Hickey took off and rode into Phoenix and go t Doctor Conyers and a party of six and returned to the Gila Station. Everything was quiet and Tom Roger was attending Mr. Morgan. They took him back to Phoenix and Doctors Conyers and Jones attended him. He had a severe skull fracture. Later Dr. Conyers did a surgical operation on removing two pieces of his skull. He recovered but from that time on his fortunes declined for the remainder of his life.

June 1881 Henry was back in his station on the Gilas doing business. August 26th a flood had washed his ferry away but four days later he was back in business again first class. On October 31st Morgan placed an ad in the Phoenix Herald "Attention Teamsters" on and after this date I will be prepared to do ferrying in to any extent at my old ferry on the Gila. The reference was to Maricopa and not Maricopa Wells a historical event had taken place. The railroad had been built across Southern Arizona in 1878 and 1879. It bypassed Maricopa Wells Station by eight miles to the south. The new terminal called Maricopa had been established by the railroad and the Maricopa Wells Station was doomed and in short time it was completely abandoned. It was a few years in the future before the railroad built a spur into Phoenix, and when that happened Morgan Gerry was doomed also.

Late in 1881 and 1882 The Moran and Company in Phoenix was taken over by the Sheriff and closed. A. Weil a San Francisco creditor put an attachment on the business for the sum of $5800.08

The Sheriff sold the real estate of Morgan and Company. The store building and lot were bought by Irvine and Company for $2060.00. The house and lots on West Washington Street were bought by E. Thompson for $1210.00. Pierpont Miner and J.L.B. Alexander bought the rest of the property, with his ventures in Phoenix failed and his partner gone, Morgan returned to his trading post and ferry on the Gila.

Reference to Moran and his ferry and trading post through the rest of the 1880's and early 90's were only north and south road through central Arizona and his ferry had a monopoly on all traffic crossing the river. All the ended in 1887 when the railroad built a spur line into the growing Phoenix. The line was built from Maricopa, making a bridge across the Gila necessary. It was torn up and the roadbed leveled again long ago. Piers of the old railroad bridge stood for a hundred years. Morgan's Ferry was doomed but not the trading post.

There's no reference in how long Morgan stayed at his station, but his friendship with the Pimas and the ability to speak their language with their dialect he became an interpreter and expert on Pima Indian affairs with government authorities, receiving up to $20.00 a day for his services.

The Pimas like their hooch they called it "Tiswin" which they made it out of the fruit of the saguaro cactus. The government forbade the making of the brew but the Pimas made it anyway and hiding the knowledge when the tiswin barrel was bubbling. When it was ready the tribe would find a secluded place and put on a party that lasted for several days. There were always fights and some one always got killed. They tried to keep it from the authorities and Henry Morgan was hired by the law to find the killer, In 1891 Morgan noticed the Pimas were absent for a number of day and knew that the tiswin was involved. So Morgan asked one of the Pimas if the party was on, the Indian said that it was a thing in the past. Morgan then asked him how many were killed? The way the Indian answered "No body was murdered" aroused Morgan's suspicious so when he met another member he changed tactics. Quote "Is that Indian that got shot at the feast dead"? He answered no but he can't live long.

During the howling tiswin drunk one Chonah was stabbed by De-Ne-A-Doo. Chonah's soul took flight and so did De-Ne-A-Doc. Armed with a warranty for the murderer's
arrest, Morgan and Marshal De Nure set out for the reservation believing that De-Ne-A-Doc would not stay away very long.

Late the next day Morgan and De Nure returned to town, what they found causing them to abandon the job. After killing De-Ne-A-Doc had fled the reservation, but was so loaded with tiswin that he had to lie down to sleep it off. When Chonah's friends had recovered from the bout with the liquor they set out on De-Ne-A-Doc's trail and found him in his drunken stupor. Chonah's friends lynched his murderer. There were so many Indians involved in the affair that Morgan and De Nure gave up trying to sort all the details out but felt that justice was done.

With the years after the turn of the century Morgan's physical condition began to deteriorate and his mind gave way. At a sanity hearing in December 1905 it was revealed that he had been living in a small shack near the electric plant for a number of years. Mr. Seth Byers who instituted the hearing and others looked after his wants, but now he was hallucinating and the best place for him would be in the asylum.

He was committed and died there on October 15, 1908 at the age of 67 and buried in the pioneer's cemetery in Phoenix.

One of the first residents of Phoenix but by 1900 was living in Scranton, Pennsylvania was Mr. Madison F. Larkin. Mr. Larkin wrote to the Arizona graphic inquiring about several old friends including Henry Morgan, and Count Darrell Duppa, the great epitaph writer one of which I will quote it was not necessary for a man to be dead in those days for Darrell to write his epitaph, which accounts for it's having been written for Henry Morgan.

Weep! Phoenix, weep and well you may great Morgan's soul has passed away. Howl Pimas, howl! Shed tears of blood, and squaws, bedeck you heads with mud. Around his grave career and canter, and grieve the loss of beads and manta. His head so large endowed by fate, no hat could fit but a number eight. He died as leaves of autumn fall, and dying said "I've fooled you all".

# PETE KITCHEN

In the early days of southeast Arizona there was no more feared or respected than Pete Kitchen. He was one of the last few settlers to hang on after 1861 troop withdrawal, due to the Civil War. More men have lost their lives in the stretch from Potrero, Arizona and Magdalena, Mexico during the Kitchen years there than in all the rest of Arizona territory put together and if all the bodies were laid side by side like railroad ties, they would make a track from Nogales to Potrero. To the Apaches, Kitchen was more terrible than an army with banners; to the settlers he was a folk hero.

Pete Kitchen came to Southern Arizona around 1854 with his Mexican wife, Dona Rosa, he stayed to farm the rich bottom land at the junction of the Santa Cruz and Potrero Creeks. Today this area lies about ten miles north of Nogales. His adobe home had a flat roof with a four foot high parapet surrounding it. From this vantage point, a sentinel could stand guard in relative safety. There was always a sentinel on duty. The hacienda commanded a view of the valley in all direction as it sat on a rocky sum-

271

mit. If the Apaches crept up on the house under cover from any direction, the guard would fire his rifle. The shot would bring everyone up from the fields to huddle together in the main house, where Kitchen and Dona Rosa would parcel out the rifles and ammunition. The state of constant vigilance never allowed the Apaches to gain any advantage.

Year after year the Apaches attacked, trying to destroy him or drive him away. They shot his pigs full of arrow, stole his horses and cattle, and drove away all his neighbors, but Kitchen held on. On one occasion his adopted son of twelve years old went with the workers to the field where he fell asleep in hay stack, the workers ran to the house leaving the boy behind. His family could do nothing but watch helplessly as the Indians came upon the youth. The boy made a sign of the cross just before they killed him.

Pete Kitchen was exceptionally Apache smart. While on the trail, no Apache could ever ambush him. He was a cracked shot with his rifle and he never traveled the same route twice. The Apaches lived in fear of him, and it was considered a great coup if one could get close to him. Many tried and many failed. His interpretation on Apache signs or better yet, the complete lack of Apache signs, always kept his senses in over drive. He understood only too well that any mistake would be fatal. His courage quickly became legendary in the region.

On the night that one of his men said that things didn't feel right, Kitchen took his wife to the dugout below the ranch house to stand guard. Hour after hour they kept watch. When the clouds finally passed from the sky, he thought he saw movement. He fired his rifle and heard an awful scream. Although no body was found at the location in the morning, he followed the sign. In an area in a near by field, he found a section of disturbed earth. Digging deep into the ground, he found a body of an Apache.

Out in front of his ranch house, Kitchen had his own private "Boot Hill". He buried everyone, friend and foe alike, with Christian charity. Outlaws he shot and killed lay there, and Dona Rosa followed her Catholic traditions by burning candles at the graves of the men. Two of the men Kitchen buried were bandits he had hung. Several Apaches reposed in the cemetery. The railroad later laid down tracks past the cemetery, and it became some what of a popular tourist attraction.

Among the stories told of Pete Kitchen is the one about the bandits he tracked into Sonora, Mexico, three outlaws had raided his livestock making off with several of his favorite horses. He tracked them for days, finally coming close enough to kill one of the men. Another one fled before he could shoot, but the third one became his prisoner. Taking the man back into Arizona, he camped in exhaustion, before dozing off, he secured the prisoner's hands and feet on his horse leaving a rope around his neck with the other end tied to a tree limb. "You know", quoted Pete as saying "While I was asleep, that damned horse walked off leaving that fellow hanging there".

Kitchen was well known for his Christian hospitality. His place was completely self-sufficient, having its own blacksmith, saddler, wagon makers, and all officials needed to keep the machinery running smoothly. Anyone was welcome and made to feel at ease. Beside Pete and Dona Rosa other family members included eight of his wife's nieces, girls he treated s his own. If food was not already prepared, someone would get busy fixing the traveler a hot meal. He welcomed everyone to stay as long as they wished and to come back as often as they wished. This included all Apaches who came in peace. He believed that Apaches were human beings out to defend away of life which had been theirs for centuries. He became known as champion for their cause, at the same time that he never ceased his vigil against attack. Cochise came to respect him, and since Cochise made war on all whites for more than twelve years, this gesture speaks volumes for Kitchen's reputation with the Indians.

Pete Kitchen lived comfortable at his ranch until the railroad moved in. Competition from goods now much more accessible caused him to sell out and move to Tucson, where he lived out the rest of his life. When he died, he had little in the way of fortune, but he had an unblemished reputation among scores of friends, admirers and Apaches. One old timer gave this epitaph "Muy Valiente! Muy Bueno Con Rifle".

*Opha R. Probasco*

# THE YAQUIS BECOME AMERICAN INDIANS

When the Yaquis began to come into Arizona there were two places in Tucson where they settled, the largest group settled in the northwest part of town near West Grant and Fifteenth Avenue. A smaller group was on South Tenth in the Barrio section of town. Some lived out at Marana.

The men worked for Southern Pacific Railroad section gang. Others worked on farms and anything else just to get food on the table.

With the up rising in Mexico in 1927 and 1929 brought more Yaquis into the area at Old Pascua. When they entered the United States from Mexico they would turn their arms over to the U.S. Army.

Every Easter they put on their ceremonial dances that were told to be wild and eerie. We use to go to their dances in the thirties.

In 1931 when a Sonoran Yaqui named Guadalupe Flores moved to Pascua and assumed the title of Captain General, or Chief and began agitation for the return of all Yaquis to their home land to support the freedom fighters there. He said that he was speaking for all of the Yaquis, the ones in Phoenix and the ones in Tucson. He announced they all wanted to go home and would do so if the Mexican government would give them amnesty. This was welcome news to the Anglos in Tucson.

Another Yaqui voice was raised and it belonged to Cayetano Lopez of Guadalupe Village near Scottsdale who said that he was the chief of all Yaquis and that his people did not want to return to Mexico at all. The Mexicans treated them like dogs and hanged them for a small cause. They were better off in Tucson and wanted to stay. There were a lot of fuss to who was in charge and at one time there was talk of deporting the whole bunch around a thousand in all in the four sites. Because they could not agree on a leader, only the more violent ones were sent back to Mexico including Guadalupe Flores. The rest stayed in Arizona. The Yaquis suffered less than their American neighbors, during the Great Depression. They were use to doing without and living form day to day.

There were other ethnic groups that were in trouble during those years and especially the Chinese who were expelled from Sonora by Governor Francisco Elias on August 25, 1931. All of their property was confiscated, and they headed usually on foot for other Mexican states or the U.S. border. Lots of them crossed at Naco and were picked up by the border patrol as soon as they entered into Arizona.

At Tucson they were brought into court charged for illegal entry and sent to San Francisco for deportation to China.

Anselmo Valencia born in 1918 rose to be a new leader and wanted to move his people out of the city and into the country so they could revive their culture and language and to relieve the over crowding.

1962 and at that time Valencia was working for Morris Udall and asked him for help. The congressman immediately agreed and advised Valencia to form a committee to help the tribe acquire land.

Valencia began by enlisting anthropologist Muriel Thayer a painter and a trusted friend who had written about the Yaquis ceremonial dances and in 1962 along with other Yaquis and Tucson community leaders formed the committee on Pascua community housing. They planned to work toward improved housing at old Pascua and to acquire a new village site. Edward Spicer was also involved. Spicer and his wife Rosamond had lived with the Yaquis in Old Pascua in 1936 and 1937. He had written extensively on the tribe and was the leading authority on their culture and history.

The committee along with some Old Pascua Yaquis solicited business and political leaders of Tucson for support. Because funds were short they looked to either the government or a charitable organization to give them land. Tucsonans such as Gilbert Ronstadt gave their time for Humanitarian reasons, writing letters in support of the Yaquis's goal.

In early 1960 while picking wild tea leaves in the Tucson Mountains southwest of the city near Valencia Road he had a vision the place where he stood would be the next home of his people.

The bureau of land management owned the 202 acres of Pima land next to the San Xavier Indian Reservation. The Yaqui leader believed it was suitable for development and asked Udall for help. The housing committee gave the partition containing letters of support and signatures of over a hundred Pascua Yaquis, to Udall to bolster their case. S. Leonard Scheff an attorney employed by the committee assisted Udall's staff. On May 9th Udall introduced H.R. 6233, a bill to give the land to the Yaquis. On May 13th Valencia formed the Pascau Yaqui association to accept the Grant, shortly after Carl Hayden submitted its companion bills 3015.

Most of the Yaqui Indians in Tucson opposed Valencia's plan and ninety per cent didn't want to move to the new site, saying it was too far from their work. Since some lived in the Old Pascua Village since the 1900s they didn't want to leave their home. A lot of them thought clearing brush and making roads was too much of obstacles to develop a new site.

In 1964 the Yaquis received federal funding on the basis of their poverty and not from their status.

From 1966 to 1969 they made good strides in building some homes. The housing construction continued until 1970 and by 1973 money was drying up and ended altogether.

The housing construction continued until 1970 and by 1973 money was drying up and ended altogether. The average income was about $800.00 a year and unemployed about eighty per cent. So they were ineligible for small loans, they simply couldn't make the small payments. The Yaquis finally applied for full tribal recognition. In 2975 Udall's bill H.R. 8411 passed and made them eligible for all funds. This bill was set aside and a new bill had to be drawn up.

On April 25, 1977 Udall introduced a bill H.R. 6612 to the ninety fifth Congress. Then on June 7, 1977 a bill S 1633 was introduced. These bills finally passed and on September 18, 1978 the public law 95-375 was signed finally recognizing the Yaquis as American Indians. By 1980 there were seven hundred people living in new houses and 4,000 had joined the tribe.

Mark E. Miller did a fine job covering this story.

# YAQUIS IN MEXICO

The Yaquis have been around a long time, for years the tribe without a country.

The original tribe farmed the land along the Yaqui River since early 1500's. The Yaquis defeated the Spanish in the mid 1500's but they did invite the Jesuits to live among them. Gradually the Jesuits persuaded the Yaquis to move from their eighty ranches along the lower Yaqui River to eight towns where churches had been built. These eight Pueblos are the focus of the Yaqui legend that apostles and angels walk and sang the boundaries of the Yaqui country and established Belem, Huiribis, Rahum, Potam, Vicam, Torim, Bacum and Cocorit. Thus, Yaquis claimed their land by devine sanction.

The Yaqui-Mayo prospered for one hundred twenty years except for an epidemic that wiped out half of the population of the Mayos.

In 1740 Spanish settlers pushing north and taking over the rich delta touch off the first Yaqui revolt.

When Mexico won her independence from Spain the Yaquis refused to pay taxes to the new government and from then on it was almost war with the Mexicans. After the French wee driven from Sonora Governor Igancio Pesquiera's commanders massacred Yaqui and Mayo women and children, shot Indian leaders, destroyed their farms and still Pesquiera was unable to control the Yaquis.

Harassed by about four hundred armed Guerrillas raiding from the Bacatete Mountains, Sonora's scientific commission surveyed, divided, and distributed all the land in the Yaqui valley by 1890. Some remained in the Yaqui hands but most went to Mexicans and North Americans.

The railroad was completed through the Yaqui country in 1891. The Yaquis worked in the mines and on ranches to buy supplies and weapons and then joined the band of Guerrillas. Finally in 1897 the Sonoran officials signed a peace treaty with Tetabiate and his follower and were given land, food, seeds and implements. That didn't last but two years, when rebellion flared up again. Gradually the Guerrillas were driven from the mountains but the Yaquis fought where ever and whenever they could.

In 1903 Governor Rafael Izabal began selling 5000 Yaquis (men and women) at sixty pesos a head, for slave labor in the Henequen Plantation of Yucatan and the sugar fields of Oaxaca. Families were shattered and hundreds of Yaquis fled to Arizona.

By 1909 Sonora's mines and hacienda owners were protesting the loss of their best workers, the government respondent by making another peace offering to the Yaquis.

During the revolution Colonel Fructuoso Mendes persuaded many Yaquis to fight for Alvaro Obregon promising without authorization that Obregon would reward them by restoring their country and with drawing troops from it which Obregon rejected.

When Obregon passed through their region again campaigning for his second term as president, Yaqui leaders decided to appeal directly to him of the promises made in his name. On September 11th the Yaquis detained his train at Vicam Station.

William Backer and American Civil Engineer traveling by Motor car from Empalme, Sonora stumbled upon the scene. Born in Nogales, Arizona in 1906, Barker had spent his early childhood in Durango, Mexico where his father was station agent telegrapher for a local railroad.

Because of the Mexican revolution in 1912 the family moved to Crystal City, Texas where Bill graduated from high school in 1923. The following year he went to work in Empalme in civil engineering department of the Southern Pacifica De Mexico, a subsidiary of Southern Pacific Railroad. His projects included rebuilding bridges with steel and concrete, and relining tunnels between Nogales and Guadalajara. He was engaged in his work when he encountered President Obregon's train being detained by the Yaquis in Vicam.

This is his account of the incident. IN 1926 I was employed as a civil engineer for the Southern Pacific Railroad of Mexico and working on a survey for some reconstruction they had planned.

One Sunday morning early Carl Chalk, who was the engineer for the Sonoran Division and based in Empalme, called me and told me that he was coming by where I was living on his way to a place called Carral on the Yaqui River. The railroad proposed to locate a pit to provide ballast, which would be used on the railroad track bed. He was to locate the site for the pit. He asked me if I would like to go with him. He had a nice big motor car and we could do a little dove hunting along the way I said sure so in about an hour he showed up. There were a lot of doves, white wings and we got a plenty. After he finished his business we headed back north toward Empalme about sixty miles away. We had to meet a south bound passenger train on the main line, so we went into a siding about ten miles south of a little town of Vicam. That was the main town and head quarters of the whole tribe of Yaquis Indians. We waited and waited for the train which didn't come. In Vicam there's another siding that we could pull into off the main line and this was done.

This was the year of the Yaqui up rising and we got involved in it right that day. We stopped near the locomotive, hoping to learn why it was there so long.

We were approached by a small band of Yaqui Indians all armed. We asked if they knew why the train was stopped. They said yes they ordered it held. When we asked what was happening they said, "We have a problem with President Obregon", he was then ex-president of Mexico but still very influential, especially in Sonoran state. We further asked if they were holding him. They told us he was on the train and they were not going to let the train leave until the problem is settled. We were told to get out of the motor car and not take our guns. The car was confiscated and we lost our guns, other wise they didn't bother us. We went to the back coach and saw Obregon and everyone wee waiting for the return train to bring the money that was promised to them. It could be troops so we got into the engine and out of line of fire. The Yaquis took us to their head quarters and put us in a room. By next morning the train arrived but the Yaquis with the money had gotten off the train outside of town and every Yaqui there had disappeared.

The Mexican government sent 20,000 troops into the Yaqui country and aerial bombardment. Fighting continued for nearly a year. A lot of the Yaquis escaped into Arizona or fled into the mountains, where they were crushed at Cerro Del Gallo in 1927. In 1936 President Lazaro Cardenas set aside the north bank and a little of the south bank, and the Bacatestes for exclusive Yaqui use. He promised to build a dam to water the north bank and help re-establish the five Pueblos that had been lost to changes in the river or infiltration by outsiders.

The eight Pueblos in the home land defended for four hundred years remain holly to the Yaquis, including those living in Arizona have retained their identity and culture.

In 1935-1936 Bill Barker was involved in building a depot in Nogales, Sonora. When the head quarters for the Sud Pacifico moved form Empalme to Guadalajara, Jalisco he worked there as an assistant to the president until 1950, when the company was sold to the Mexican government. He then moved his family to Douglas, Arizona where he was superintendent of the Southern Pacific's Nacozari Railroad. Which the Phelps Dodge Mining Company built to haul copper ore from its Nacozari Mine to the smelter in Douglas, the Mexican government bought the railroad in 1961 and Barker was reassigned as superintendent of the San Diego, and Arizona Eastern Railroad.

Later he was superintendent of the Tijuana and Tecate Railroad through Baja California, Barker retired form the Southern Pacific Railroad on 1971 after nearly a century's association with the railroad of Arizona, Mexico, and California, now ninety years old he lives in Tucson.

# WILLIAM "BILL" WHITNEY BRAZELTON

David Nemitz was involved in the solution of a series of stage robberies which irritated Tucson law officers for over a year, because they couldn't find a clue to the identity of the Highwayman or men. The Star paper editorialized that if these robberies didn't stop the travel will. Nemitz and other farm workers had their homes south of the flour mills on Silver Lake Road.

South of the flour mill one and half mile was the ranch and home of Guadalupe Sainz. At Sianz Ranch, occurred the capture of William Brazelton that "dead shot and bravest desperado on the road", according to the weekly Star, August 22, 1878.

William Brazelton was an employee of the little giant (Mayor Leatherwood) at Leatherwood's Stable for which he hauled hay, grain and wood. His frequent absence from town could be explained by his occupation and he had the excuse of his target range where he said he was perfecting his marksmanship to protect himself against the

Apaches. He was well liked and seemed above suspicion. There were eight planned and skillfully executed stage coach robberies between 1877 and 1878 in Arizona and New Mexico that began to fall into so similar pattern that the Sheriff Charles Shibell suspected they were the works of one man instead of a band of highwaymen.

He and his deputies kept almost constant virgil on the road, riding all night, trying to apprehend the robber, but were eluded each time. He wore a mask of white sack, coming clear over his shoulders, with holes cut out for his eyes, a puff of cloth for his nose, a piece of red flannel attached where his mouth would come. He always appeared, coolly and sure of himself. Stages not carrying valuables always seemed to go through without any trouble.

In August of 1878 John P. Clum, owner of the Arizona Citizen, Mr. Wheatley, and others wee on the stage coming from Florence to Tucson, where it was robbed by the same masked highwayman. Sheriff Shibell and a posse, which included Pete Kitchen, followed the trail of the robber's horse for several miles on the Eastern out skirts of Tucson but heavy rains washed out the tracks.

Several days later the Indian wife of Nemitz appeared in town to buy groceries. Having ridden in from Silver Lake on a black horse.

Some one recognized the horse's shoe prints. Nemitz was arrested, jailed and questioned. He finally told the officers by telling them that Bob Brazelton had done all the robbing and he was camped on Sainz Ranch near Silver Lake. Nemitz agreed to assist in Bob's capture. After a plan was made he was released to go to Bob's camp.

Bob was furious when he learned of his friend's arrest, and did not suspect of him double dealing. He planned to ride west, take a stage back to Tucson kill Sheriff Shibell and leave the country for good. Bob told Nemitz to bring him a horse, saddle, bridle, pants, overalls, and some grub Monday about 8:00 P.M. We'll meet at the tree that fell over the road down by Sainz. When you see me lay my hat on the log and cough, you give a cough back then I'll know it's you and not those damn bastards.

Nemitz relayed the message to the Sheriff and the next evening Monday, August 19, 1878 Shibell and a few men inched forward, silent to surround the meeting place. There was hardly any light but the men nearest to the log saw Bob place his hat on the tree and give a cough. This is what followed. A gun loaded with buckshot was fired one barrel after another and two other shots followed. After the first shots were fired Bob said you S—O—B— then he turned and fell upon his face exclaiming I'll die brave, my god, I'll pray till I die. A gasp and all was still. He had ten bullets in his body. He was loaded into a wagon and dumped at the court house. He was twenty six years old, six feet tall, and weighed two hundred pounds.

The body was propped up in a corner on a chair so it wouldn't fall over. Pictures were taken and he was left there all day for the citizens to view the body and that evening he was put in a grave. This ended a brief career of one of the most daring, brave, desperados that ever lived.

All of this was remembered by a daughter of Jimmy Lee (who was in partnership with Scott in the flour mills) her name is Mary. She identified the photographs of William "Bob" "Bill" Whitney Brazelton. In 1936, she was seventy four years old at that time.

I, Opha Probasco didn't know Mary, but I did know her children. Charles, her son and I went to Mission View School together and kept in touch with each other for after the W.W. two up to the time of his death. Charles and his siblings' father was killed in an accident between Oracle and Mammoth. Their mother had to take in washing and did odd jobs to put food on the table. During one winter when there was snow on the ground she had taken sick and died with pneumonia. His sister who was the children's aunt was married to Pat Daily who owned a lumber company in Oracle would not take the children in and Pat Daily had them put on the orphanage. This was next to the Mission View School and where I met Charles Moss. There were seven of those children, Charles, Austan, John, Mary, Stanley, Vivian and Rebecca.

# SPANISH AND MEXICAN LAND GRANTS

Jay J. Wagoner's explanation of the Rancheros and land grants are the best that I have come across. Just like his explanation of the working s of the early days of ranching and mining. His book "Early Arizona" should be a must on your reading list of history on Arizona.

There were eight (8) Spanish land grants and two (2) Baco Floats. That were confirmed.

There were seven (7) unconfirmed land grants. There were two (2) fraudulent land grants the El Paso De Los Algodones and the Peralta-Reavis listed as the " Baron of Arizona".

All grants had to be marked with monuments of mortar and stone. IF the grant was abandoned for more than three years then the grant would revert back to the public domain, unless if they were driven off by the Apach4s, then they could come back at a later date to full fill three years of occupation. As it turned out, most of the nineteenth century grants were on lands where the eighteenth century missionaries had established Vistas and Rancherias and just as their predecessors were driven away by the Apaches, so were the later ranchers.

According to the land-grant records, stockmen were still active all along the present international boundary and as far north as the Presidio of Tucson, as late as the 1830's/

In the Santa Cruz Valley, the Ortiz brothers had spreads on the Canoa and Arivaca Ranches. The Tuvera family was farther south on the Buena Vista land, and the Romeros were occupying San Rafael De La Zanja in the Sonoita Valley the Leon Herreras family was grazing large herds.

Along the San Pedro and its tributaries were the vast holdings of the Elias Gonzalez family on the Babocomari, Agia Prieta and other grants and in the extreme southeastern part of Arizona the Perez family controlled the vast San Bernardino holdings which extended across the international boundary.

Most of the claims to the Santa Cruz Valley were filled from 1820 to 1833, and with one exception, the San Pedro titles were issued between 1820 and 1831. The fact that few petitions were presented after that time would indicate that Indian raids discouraged settlements. The San Pedro Valley apparently was deserted completely and remained so until the 1870's and 1880's.

After the Gadsden Purchase in 1854 the United States government recognized the validity of the Mexican and Spanish titles to the land grants provided the land had been located and duly recorded in the archives of Mexico. At the time of the treaty however, most of the Rancherias in the purchase area had been abandoned, some for the second time. Little value was placed upon them until the Apaches were brought under control by the Unite States Cavalry in the 1870's and 1880's. Speculators, mostly from California sough out heirs and purchased the rights for a mere song.

By 1904 fifty years after the Gadsden Purchase, treaty was signed and the work of the court was finished. Titles to 116,540 acres claimed in Arizona were validated out of 837,680 acres and were approved by the court.

It was a long process to search the archives of Mexico and Spain to check the authenticity of the titles; it took time to record the eyewitness testimony of pioneers who were on the Arizona scene in the 18450's. But in doing the work, the surveyor generals and the court accumulated and preserved volumes of invaluable historical data on the Spanish and Mexican periods of Arizona history that might have never been recorded other wise.

In California there were 588 grants totaling over a million acres, of which more than 8,850,000 acres, (nearly 14,000 square miles) we confirmed. These California grants comprised nine per cent of the total land surface of the state and are populated in the most developed areas.

In 1820 in September a year before Mexico gained independence that Tomas and Ignacio Ortiz residents of Tubac petitioned the intendente of Sonora and Sinaloa for four sitios of grass and round La Canoa for the purpose of raising cattle and horses!

In accordance with the Spanish law, the land had to be measured, appraised, and auctioned before a title could be granted the surveying was made under the supervision of Ignacio Elisa Gonzalez, commander of the Tubac Garrison who wrote that the vast domain stretched from Tubac on the south to Saguarita on the north. He describes the vegetation as consisting of mesquite, china tress, tamarisks, Palo versed, giant cactus, and a few cotton woods and willows. The appraisers set the value of the land at only $30.00 per sitio since there was no running water except when the Arroyos and the Santa Cruz River flowed during the rainy season.

A sitio is a square league containing 4,338.464 acres. Four sitios would be equivalent of more than 27 square miles or sections. In 1786 Mexico was divided by Royal Cedula into twelve province called intendancies. This order was put into effect in 1788, Sonora and Sinaloa being one of the twelve units. The man in charge of each was called gobernador intendente, or simple intendente.

A surveyor's chain is 66 feet long and a link is one-hundredth of a chain or 7.92 inches each side of the Baco Float was slightly less than twelve and one half mile.

At the first publicized sale on July 12, 1821, in Tubac, Fray Juan Bano (curate of the San Xavier Mission) bid $210 in behalf of Ygnacio Sanchez and Francisco Flores, resident of the mission. The proceeding were transferred to the capital at Arispe, south of the present United States Mexico border, and the final auction was held on December 13-14-15 interesting people were called by beating of a drum to the office of the intendente, and the auctioneer, Loreto Salido, asked for bids. On the 3rd day the property went to the Ortiz brothers for $250 about nine dollars per section. By the time the Spanish government had been over thrown in Mexico and no titulo (title) to the land was issued. In 1849 however, the brothers presented themselves at Ures, in Sonora, and were given a title for their own protection.

*Opha R. Probasco*

# APACHES ATTACKED THE CANOA RANCH

Late in 1860 a group of twenty-five to thirty Mexicans came to Poston's headquarters at Tubac with information that Apaches has raided their ranches in Sonora and ha stolen some three hundred head of horses and mules. The Mexicans further state that the Apaches were headed for a crossing of the Santa Cruz River between Canoa and Tucson. The Mexicans asked Poston and his men to aid in laying an ambush for the Indians, promising in return to give the Americans half of the animals recovered. When Poston declined, the Mexicans rode to Canoa an encampment of Lumbermen for main, and made them the same offer. They accepted and the ambush was successful. The Apaches were caught in a cross fire and abandoned the stock.

About the next full moon after this event later recalled Poston we had been passing the usual quiet Sunday at Tubac, when a Mexican Vaquero came galloping furiously into the plaza crying out Apaches! Apaches! Apaches! Poston learned from the man that the Apaches had attacked the lumberjacks in retaliation for the participation in the ambush. Poston gathered men and rushed to the lumbermen's camp, to be greeted by a scene of massacre and destruction. Doors and windows had been smashed and the house was a smoking ruin. The former inmates were lying around dead, and three of them had been thrown into the well had first. Buchanan pursued the marauders but the guilty ones were never caught. Despite the incident, the Apaches remained on friendly terms with most of the Americans.

The first Anglo-American to bring cattle to the Canoa was Bill Kirkland, he drove two hundred fro Sonora in 1857 but they were stolen 1860. Another famous pioneer who lived in the ranch was a Kentuckian named Pete Kitchen. Stubbornly defying the Apaches who frequently attacked, he fortified his ranch houses with adobe walls first on the Canoa where he lived form 1855 to 1862 and later at the Potrero, near Nogales. He was about the only settler to hang on after the American troops withdrew during the Civil War. He described the road through the country between the walled Pueblo of Tucson and Sonora with this phrase, "Tucson, Tubac, and to Hell".

The new migrants to Arizona were Frederick Maish and Thomas Driscoll who bought the controlling interest in the Canoa from the Ortiz heirs.

Maish and Driscoll started their ranching about 1870 with some 300 head of Texas long horn battle bought from migrants at $15 a head.

Several years later Maish commented, "It went very slow, the first three years we didn't make our salt", the Indians stole us blind. Afterwards we had smooth sailing, by 1884 the firm was grazing 10,000 head on the Canoa and adjacent public ranges. Twenty miles up and down the Santa Cruz River and about twenty five miles from mountain to mountain.

The firm's capital of $75,000 was invested in live stock including 400 Durham and Devon bulls, steam pumps and about 11% horses, houses, and corrals. Land was no problem until the government forbade all enclosures of the open range in 1885. With fencing of the public domain prohibited the over plus lands seemed more desirable.

IN 1893 a claim for 46,696.2 acres a lot more than the four sitios of 17,333.84 acres in original grant was brought before the court of private land claims. This court confirmed the larger amount, which included over plus lands, but the federal government appealed the case and the United States Supreme court reversed the decision of the lower tribunal in these words we think that the grant should be sustained for the four sitios purchased, petitioned, and paid for, and for no more. After an official survey the title of Maish and Driscoll was confirmed for 17,208.333 acres.

The Canoa Ranch changed hands several times. Just before World War I, it was purchased by an energetic Mississippian named Levi Manning for $165,000 under his management; the Canoa became the nucleus for a sprawling enterprise that grew to encompass thousands of acres of patented and leased lands. Manning sold the north half of the original grant during World War I to the Continental Rubber company which tries to grow Guayule for manufacture of synthetic rubber. About the same time the McGee colony of Baptist were permitted to settle on the Tillable lands. In 1953 approximately 200 sections (128,000 acres) of leased and deeded lands outside of the original Canoa grant were transferred or sold to Kemper Marley by Howell Manning (Levi Manning's son) for $600,000. Other cattlemen, farmers, and real estate promoters including the developers of the town of Green Valley now own a share of the Old San Ignacio De Canoa.

*Opha R. Probasco*

# BUENA VISTA GRANT

The Buena Vista Grant was located east of Nogales on both sides of the International boundary line. It is another Spanish stock ranch that was abandoned in the eighteenth century. The lands on the Arizona side were acquired in 1881 by the enterprising Canoa claimants, Maish and Driscoll. They paid $4,000 for the rights to the grant and were allotted 5,733.41 acres by the court of private land claims. The court traced the grant back to 1826 when Francisco Jose De Tuvera petitioned for the deserted rancho, then called Maria Santisima Del Carmen. He died during the proceedings and the application was then sought in the name of his widow, Dona Jose Fa Morales. A title was not issued until 1831 because there were defects in the original measurements of the four sitios and the land had to be resurveyed. The grant was purchased at the appraisal price of $190 and occupied for stock raised by the Tuveras heirs, until 1851 when it was sold to Hilario Gabilando. In 1872 the tract was transferred to Jose Maria Quiroga for the sum of $500. He in turn sold it nine years later to Maish and Driscoll making an eight fold profit on his investment.

In 1882 the grant was surveyed by George J. Roskruge and the surveyor general of Arizona John Wasson, recommended confirmation of the title for 5,060 acres. But congress took no action and the grant was finally confirmed by the court of private land claims in 1899. The amount of land approved by the surveyor general was increased to 5,733.41 acres undoubtedly the most interesting and novel feature connected with this tribunal was that its proceedings and decisions were governed primarily by Spanish and Mexican laws, even though it was fully constituted in the United States court.

After its confirmation by the court, the Buena Vista changed hands many times, but remained intact until 1934 in that year, Karl and Delbert Peterson ended eleven years of joint ownership, dividing the grant by an east and west line that was surveyed by W.H. Roper, the Santa Cruz county engineer. A month after the partition papers were recorded in the Nogales court house, Delbert sold his share, consisting on the southern portion along the international border, to Thomas F. Griffin. In 1937 Griffin deeded this property to Neilson Brown who in turn transferred it to Victor R. Weiss in 1957. Desert Diet Corporation of Miami, Florida acquired title in 1959 and began subdividing the land to sell in smaller tracts.

The northern portion and larger of the two was eventually purchased by movie actor James Stewart Granger.

In 1969 however, Granger sold all but 119.4 acres of his ranch to Inverurie Realty Inc. which had plans for developing a luxurious residential area similar to the Rio Rico project on the Baco Float No. #3.

Inverurie secured a license to do business in the state from the Arizona Corporation Commission and changed its name to Kino Springs Incorporation.

# SAN RAFAEL DE LA ZANJA LAND GRANT

One of the more controversial land grants was San Rafael De La Zanja. Located east of Nogales in the head waters of the Santa Cruz and between the Patagonia and Huachuca Mountains, it attracted competition for ownership from the beginning. A cattleman named Manuel Bustillo who resided in the Presidio of Santa Cruz, first petitioned for the grant on July19, 1821. Explaining that he possessed considerable live stock and needed more grazing land for their maintenance, he asked the intendente at Arispe to take the necessary legal steps to secure title. The land was measured at the chosen site, under the supervision of Captain Ignacio Elias Gonzalez, commander of the Presido, and appraised. After asking the appraiser to consider that the land was close to the Apache country, Bustillo was satisfied with their evaluation of three sitios with running water at $60 each and the fourth which contained no water at $30 a total of $210 for more than 27 square miles of land. But at the public auction on January 8, 1822 Don Romon Romero in behalf of himself and residence of Santa Cruz bid against Bustillo and bought the land for $1200 plus $97, in fees connected with the sale.

Romero lived well into the American period after the Gadsden Purchase and died in 1873 on his death bed he gave the names of his legal heir to his son Innocencio, but the young Romero misplace his father's papers in 1886 and pressed his claim through courts but was unsuccessful, but six years earlier on June 20, 1880 he had signed a deed assigning his rights to the San Rafael to Rollin Rice Richardson. Richardson owned the Dan Rafael for three years which he spent $40,000 into the improvements of the ranch. He became to be one of the biggest ranchers in Southern Arizona, owning most of the land around the Fort Crittenden and Patagonia a town he founded in 1896. But in 1883 he chose to sell the San Rafael to Colin Cameron who promptly chartered the San Rafael Cattle Company, under the incorporation laws of New Jersey with capital stock of $150,000. He improved the stock raising industries by bringing in pure bred Herefords and fighting for quarantine laws to stop the disease Mexican cattle from coming into Arizona. Right after Cameron received the deed from Richardson he claimed the over plus lands that the Romero's had occupied under the Mexican laws, a grantee could occupy the lands in excess of the stipulated amount, have it surveyed and purchase it at the price prevailing when the original grant was appraised. Cameron paid $1359 to the United States land office at Tucson to acquire a doubtful title to the over plus surrounding the original grant. In 1885 he employed a surveyor named Lewis Wolfley, later a territorial governor of Arizona and a bitter enemy of the Cameron family, to locate the Mexican deeds not yet in hands. Recall that the citizens of the Presidio of Santa Cruz shared the ownership of the San Rafael with Romero. Wolfley bought their part of the title from Cameron for $80 ea. Doctor Green however, claimed to have the original expediente by purchase from the legal heirs of Romero, and never ceased to condemning Cameron for fraudulent possession of the grant. IN 1886 he even wrote to President Cleveland charging Cameron with horrible crimes against settlers in the vicinity of San Rafael. Most of Green's accusations were supported by General Edward M. McCook, a former governor of Colorado and special agent sent to investigate San Rafael by secretary of interior L.Q.C. Lamar.

After hearing witnesses, McCook reported that Cameron employed the worst class of Mexicans to burn down the houses of homesteaders and fill up their wells. Fences had been built to enclose all the watering places and in 1887 Cameron was indicted by the district court grand jury in Tucson and brought to trail for unlawful fencing public domain.

In ordering Cameron to remove all barriers outside of the original four sitios Judge W.H. Barnes explained that all grants were a part of the public domain, even if they were reserved from sale until the claims were adjudicated Barnes was not considering the validity of the claim in his case, but he made reference to the measurements of the San Rafael made by deputy surveyor Solon M. Allis in 1880 and concurred with the recommendation of the former surveyor General John Wasson, that the grant he confirmed for only four square leagues.

John Hise was please he wrote "This is the first gun in Arizona from the bench from a fearless and honest judge in apposition to what is styled" "Land Grabbers" and the people hail the dawning of a brighter and happier period for our young and down rodden territory.

Doctor Green brought suit against the United States and the court made all persons who claimed some interest in the San Rafael Grant "Parties Defendant to the Cause" in addition to Cameron the defendant were Harvey L. Christie, William C. ones, Albert Steinfeld and sixty others.

The San Rafael Cattle Company was claiming 152,889.62 acres approximately 239 square miles. The court's decision was four sitios 17,354 acres.

In 1903 the ranch and stock were sold for $1,500,000 to William C. Green, and Cameron retired from ranching to live in Tucson.

Green wanted a place so he could breed pure Hereford bulls and to improve the low bred Mexican cattle, but as the San Rafael and the adjacent Greene Ranches grew the pure stock also was marketed in the United States. Greene and his heirs used Cameron's 6$^T$ Brand until 1922 when it changed to RO.

Greene was one of the most picturesque characters in Arizona history, a high stake gambler who dreamed big dreams. Born in Wisconsin and came to Arizona in 1877. Born in Wisconsin and came to Arizona in 1877, while he was still in his twenties he built a multi-million dollar legacy.

After searching the Bradshaw Mountains near Prescott he joined the rush to Tombstone during the boom days of that town. Working as a miner and a supplier of wood he married a widow and settled down on a ranch near Hereford. A tragic event occurred after he constructed a dam to water his alfalfa fields, someone dynamited the dam, created a flooded river in which Greene's little daughter and her playmate drowned. He blamed his neighbor Jim Burnett who had been an unpopular justice of peace. Greene angrily looked for Burnett and shot his unarmed victim on the street of Tombstone. The county court house was jammed for his three day murder trail in December 1897. But after B.A. Packard a respected rancher testified that Burnett had earlier threatened the defendant's life, the jury acquitted Greene, taking only ten minutes. Before the end of the century Greene's first wife died and he went prospecting near Cananea in Mexico acquiring an option on the rich Cobre Grande Copper Mine. He established himself at the Waldorf in New York and accumulated working capital to begin operation. Several years later he liquidated his mining interest for six million dollars and began devoting his time to ranching. He became cattle king of the border by the time of his death on August 5, 1911. He died of acute pneumonia from the results of an accident that had broken several ribs after his horses were spooked and ran away in Cananea.

His second wife was Mary Proctor who worked for the Citizen Paper as a typesetter, when she married Greene. Greene also acquired the large Baco Float number 5 northwest of Prescott. They had four sons (William, Frank, Kirk and Charles) and two daughters (Virginia Sturdivant and Florence Sharp).

Mrs. Eva Greene Day, a daughter of Greene's first wife sued for and secured on seventh share in 1961. By that time in 1958 the Mexican government had seized the vast Greene Ranch in Sonora in accordance to a new law passed in 1917 that no foreigners can own land with in 62 miles of the International border. Over 800 Mexican families were destined to be settled on the land. As early as 1970's the Greene's still owned ranches in Arizona.

From 1958 the San Rafael De La Zanja was under operation by the San Rafael Cattle Corporation headed by Mrs. Florence Greene Sharp. Her brother, Charles H. Greene, was president of the Greene Cattle Company that controlled the Hugh Baco Float number 5 from 1937 to 1973.

# SAN JOSE DE SONOITA

The smallest land grant in Arizona was the San Jose De Sonoita which stretches out along both sides of the meandering Sonoita Creek west of the town of Patagonia.

IN 1812 a rancher and resident of Tubac, Leon Herreras petitioned for two sitios of land at a place called San Jose De Sonoita in the jurisdiction of Tubac to pasture his rapidly increasing her of cattle. The surveying was supervised by Ignacio Elias Gonzalez starting at a point within the walls of an old building at the vista the surveyor Zigzagged around rough, rocky country that the claimant did not want included in his grant. Because of the many turn and angles the measurements seemed big enough on paper to enclosed more than two sitios requested. So Herreras consented to the lesser amount. One and three-fourth sitios. After the required public auction he bought the land in November 1821. At the appraisal price of $105 plus fees the grant was valued at $60 per sitio because it had running water. The title was issued in 1825 by Juan Miguel Riesgo a commissary general of the newly combined Mexican state of Sinaloa Sonora called occidente.

The land would revert back to the public domain if abandoned for more than one year unless invaded by the Apaches.

During the 1830's Herreras family was driven away by the Indian depredations. In 1857 the heirs sold out and after several transfers the grant was acquired by Matias Alsua who submitted his claim to the U.S. General Land Office for approval. After investigation the surveyor general in 1880 recommended confirmation of 7,598.07 acres. The court of private land claims rejected the title in 1892, however, on the grounds there was no law authorizing the sale of public lands for several years following the Mexican Declaration of Independence. On March 1, 1821 or the beginning of the provisional Mexican government on September 28, 1821. In other words, the court ruled that the intendente had no power to sell lands to Herreras in November 1821 the court of private land claims also declared that it was impossible to determine the true location of the land because the grant was made for a definite quantity of land with-in a broader area having a specified natural out boundaries. Later the Supreme Court confirmed the grant sale for 5,123.42 acres.

In the 1903's the Sonoita grant became part of the Wilshaw Ranch operated northeast of Nogales by a couple from New York, Frank W. Cowlishaw and his wife. IN 1931 they came to the Circle Z Ranch, adjacent to and south of the Sonoita Grant, for the holidays.

Frank Cowlishaw and his wife made annual trips to Europe to buy antiques for Macy's Corner Shop managed by Mrs. Cowlishaw. They had never been west and didn't know a steer from a cow, but liked what they found and with-in three weeks bought a cattle ranch. By applying the modern merchandising methods to the livestock industry they soon had on of the most efficiently operated spreads in the state. Their ranch house located on the Circle Z southwest of Patagonia on state highway 82 to Nogales was designed by a California architect, with landscaped gardens and eighteenth century antique furniture; it became a show place that has been publicized in national magazines. When Frank Cowlishaw died in 1945 his wife stayed on in the big home and directed the cattle operation. IN 1949 however, she sold the Sonoita Land Grant to Mrs. Leilah. Lewis, the Phoenix Title and Trust Company (now named the Transamerica title Insurance Company), purchased it from Mrs. Lewis in 1960. Today the Hugh Cowlishaw Ranch is no longer intact, though the San Jose De Sonoita itself has not been broken up very much. Some of the land on the east portion has been subdivided and the Patagonia Recreation Association, Inc. Has constructed a dam that holds back a lake on nearly a square mile of land at the western end of the grant.

# SAN IGNACIO DE BABOCOMARI

The Babocomari was one of the most ideally situated grant, stretching out more than twenty miles along a creek by the same name, it is located about 4,000 feet elevation and the rain fall is heavier her than inmost parts of Southern Arizona. The boundary line between Cochise and Santa Cruz counties to day split the grants into almost equal parts for tax purposes, several bunk houses are in the Santa Cruz, but other improvement are on the Cochise tax rolls. The modern headquarters of the ranch is on the site of the Old Pima Indian Village of the Huachuca, after which the fort and mountains south of the grant are named.

In 1827 Don Ignacio Elias Gonzalez and Dona Eulalia Elias Gonzalez asked for a tract of eight sitios of land, known as san Ignacio Del Babocomari for raising large herds of cattle and horses. The land was auctioned and bought by the petitioners the following year. The appraised price was $60 for each of the six sitios that had running water and $10 each for two dry ones, a total of $380 for slightly more than 54 square miles of some of the best grazing land in Arizona. The title which was issued at Arispe on Christmas Day in 1832, it contained a three year abandoned clause and required the purchasers to mark the boundaries with monuments. For practical purposes, however, the usable area extended from the Santa Rita Mountains on the west to the San Pedro River on the east. For nearly twenty years the Elisa livestock grazed the lush well watered grass lands of the valley. By the end of the 1840's the family, like the Pimas before them, left their hacienda to the Apaches who had already killed two of the Elias brothers.

In September 1851 Boundary Commissioner John R. Bartlett camped near the ruins of the Elias Ranch House and recorded the following description of the deserted Mexican land grant.

The valley of Babocomari is covered with luxuriant growth of grass. The stream which is about twenty feet wide and two feet deep winds through this valley with willows, cottonwoods trees, growing along the banks of the stream. This hacienda was one of the largest cattle ranches in the state of Sonora. When it was abandoned there were no less than 40,000 heads of cattle and a large number of Arizona's first pioneer Indian fighters Captain James H. Tevis camped at the ranch headquarters wrote that the old Mexican fort at Babocomari consisted of adobe buildings covering about an acre of ground. The fifteen foot wall that encircled the entire fort had a look-out post at each corner. The only entrance was large enough to drive a wagon through, but later asked the court of private land claims for about three and one half times that amount. Including the over plus lands. This claim was rejected in a split decision the court confirmed title to approximately eight sitios, but ten years later he bought one sixth interest which he gave up in 1917.

In 1936 the Frank Brophy family acquired a deed to the Babocomari's Ranch from Perrin Properties Inc. an undivided 2500 acres of the garn had been sold to Byron Waters in May 1898 and transferred to Walter Vail a month later.

Fifty years of over grazing and several period of drought help to diminish the grass cover. The rains washed a lot of the top soil away. Frank Brophy worked with check dams to divert the water and finally it paid off. Pastures were reseeded and new wells were dug. In the mid 1960's after 30 years of conservation warfare peace had come to the San Ignacio Del Babocomari. I knew Frank Brophy when he had the dealership in Lowell Arizona, and had been on the Babocomari a number of times. My under standing now is that there is some family disputes over the Babocomari Grant. Some want to sell and some don't.

# SAN JAUN DE LAS BOQUILLAS Y NOGALES GRANT

The Boquillasa Grant is located along both banks of the San Pedro River. Extending about an equal distance from the north and south juncture of the Babocomari Creek. Boquillas (little mouth in Spanish) is an appropriate name. Because of the little streams that run into Babocomari near its confluence with the San Pedro. This area was controlled by the Apaches in the last half of the eighteenth century. In 1827 Captain Ignacio Elias Gonzalez an active military commander on the Arizona frontier, and Nepomucino Felix applied for an elongated grant of four sitios. Approximately three-fourth of a league wide and one half leagues long. The grantee paid $240 for the four sitios they were issued a title I 1833 and complied with the customary provisions for occupying the lands until the Apaches drove them away.

The initial point of survey was about a half mile south of the present railroad station Fairbanks. Above the northern boundary is the town of St. David which was located in 1877 on the southern end the wild town of Charlestown with rustlers, miner, and soldiers during the 1880's.

The original Mexican owners each left numerous children and heirs to the Boquillas Grant. The rights of the descendants who could be found were bought by George Hill Howard. Since some of the Mexican families had the same name, it caused a lot of confusion in the transaction. Legal question also clouded the Howard Claim. One of Nepomucino's sons Francisco Maria Felix was never heard from after he left home to join the California Gold Rush. His interest and those children he might have had remained out standing. Another legal technicality developed with the death of Concepcion Bustamonte whose mother, daughter of the original grantee Felix was also deceased. Concepcion's husband, Jesus Lopez Leon, sold the rights of her three children.

By 1880 Hoard had established a claim to the Boquillas, he transferred half of it to his wife, Janet G. and the other half to George Hearst. These two claimants petitioned Surveyor General John Wasson for recognition of their title. John Wasson had the grant surveyed and recommended approval of the claim in 1881 for 17,355.86 acres.

Hearst a newspaperman, mine owner and a U.S. senator from California in 1886 and again from 1887 until his death in 1891 purchased Mrs. Howard's half interest in 1889 then his widow, Phoebe and their famous son William Randolph Hearst, petitioned the court of private land claims for confirmation of 30,728 acres including the over plus lands, and finally of February 14, 1899 Chief Justice Joseph R. Reed informed the plaintiffs that their title was valid but only for the four square leagues auctioned by the Mexican authorities in 1827 cold be confirmed. No appeal was made to the Supreme Court and John A. Rockfellow made the official survey 17,355.86 acres by measurements for surveyor General George Christ in 1889.

President William McKinley's name was affixed to a patent issued January 18, 1901. In July of the same year, the Hearst family sold the property to the Boqullas Land and Cattle Company operating out of Bakersfield, California. This company faced the same problem that the Brophys had on the Babocomari of erosion and deterioration caused by over grazing during the 1880's. The flat land, originally covered by high sacaton grass and groves of trees, was changed into a forest of mesquite. The Boquillas Land and Cattle Company became a subsidiary of the Kern County Land and Cattle Company which recorded a deed in its name to the Rancho San Juan De Las Boquillas Y Nogales in 1958, The Kern Company was one of the largest ranching, farming, and land owning operations in the U.S. with holdings in Oregon, California, and New Mexico, as well as Arizona. In addition to the Boquillas Grant the Kern Company acquired ownership of the San Rafael Del Valle, and the two grants became known as little Boquillas Ranch. In 1967 the Kern Company consolidated with Tenneco Inc. and did business in Arizona as Tenneco West Inc. since 1971.

# SAN RAFAEL DEL VALLE GRANT

There were two Arizona Land Grants in the San Pedro Valley south of the Boquillas, the San Pedro and the San Rafael Del Valle. Each was a grant of four sitios given to Rafael Elias Gonzalez who also had a share of the Agua Prieta. The Sam Ragaeldel Valle which stretches out over rolling hills on both sides of the river, north of the present day Hereford, was acquired by the grantee in 1827 for $240, he received the title five years later. Following the same pattern of a large herd of cattle and cultivation and the Apache raids and desertion of the land grant. When Rafael Elisa died he left a widow, Guadalupe Perez De Elias and three sons (Jose, Manuel, and Jose Maria) in possession of his land grants.

In 1862 the Elias brothers and their mother gave a $12,000 mortgage on thirty-two leagues of their inheritance including the San Rafael Del Valle, in favor of the Camou brothers (Joseph, Pierre, and Pascual) of Hermosillo, Sonora.

When the three year mortgage was up in July 1865 the French army was occupying Mexico and the two parties to the loan were not in communication. Jose Juan Alias was killed fighting in the army of General Pesqueira, the governor of Sonora. The Camou brothers being French citizens sided with the invaders. The Camous never foreclosed their mortgage since the real objective was to acquire the property not to collect the money. On March 23, 1869 the Elias lands were deeded to them by the surviving mortgagers, Bernadino the widow of Jose Juan and mother of his seven children also signed the deed.

Valid and recommended confirmation of a title for the Camous, Congress took no action and twenty years were to lapse before the Camou family had a clear title. In 1905 the San Rafael De Valle was purchased from the Camou family by Cornell Greene then of Bisbee.

In 1912 after Greene's death the San Rafael Del Valle was sold by the Greene Cattle Company to the Boquillas Land and Cattle Company, which also owned the San Juan De Las Boquillas Y Nogales down stream. During World War II the U.S. government bought 2000 acres on the south end of the San Rafael for $11,000. The larger remaining part of the San Rafael Del Valle has under gone the same changes in ownership as has the Boquillas Grant. After 1958 the title was in the name of Kern Country Land and Cattle Company, a huge California corporation that merged with Tenneco, Inc. in 1967.

*Opha R. Probasco*

# SAN BERNARDINO LAND GRANT

The San Bernardino Land Grant was located seventeen miles east of Douglas, in the midst of a desert valley in southeastern Arizona. The water flows from natural springs, from the late 1600's to the days of the California Gold Rush days.

From a high mesa near the present ranch house one can see sixty miles north to the Chirichua Mountains and almost as far south into the Bavispe Valley of Old Mexico. The high ground called "Mesa De La Avanzada" or mesa of the advance guard, because it is believed that an advance detachment of soldiers from the Presidio of Fronteras was once stationed there.

In 1820 Lieutenant Ignacio De Perez proposed to establish a buffer state against the Apaches at San Bernardino. Petitioning for a grant he offered to induce the Indians to settle down to peaceful life of farming. Four sitios of land were surveyed in 1821 and witnesses testified that Perez had enough live stock to start a ranch. The land was advertised at Fronteras and auction held at Arispe in May

1822. Perez had to bid a total of $90 to get the property though the land had been appraised for only $60 one sitio with the springs at $30 and three dry sitios at $10 each. A record of the grant was filed but no titulo (title) was ever issued to Perez by the Spanish king whose authority in Mexico ended in 1821. The ranch was occupied with thousands of cattle, horses, and mule until the 1830's when the Apaches were again on the war path.

The Spaniards departed hastily abandoning a large number of cattle that revert to being wild. Some of the animals were encountered by Philp St. George Cooke and the Mormon Battalion during the Mexico was in 1846.

Boundary commissioner John R. Bartlett visited the deserted old hacienda of San Bernardino in May 1851 and described it in his diary.

San Bernardino's buildings are in a ruined state with nothing but the walls standing all the old building covered about tow acres with a high wall of adobe being elevated some twenty to thirty feet above the valley. This place was abandoned about twenty years ago. No attempt was made to reoccupy it.

IN August 1852 Bartlett was back at San Bernardino and met Colonel Gilanin Garcia with troops from Tucson Garrison at the springs. After the Gadsden Purchase another boundary commissioner, William H. Emory stopped at the deserted ranch. His survey of the new international boundary put most of the ranch in Mexico, of approximately 70,000 acres, including over plus, only 2383 acres were found to be on the American side.

The owner of the ranch after 1884 on both sides of the border was John slaughter who came from Texas with a large herd of long horns during the boom days of Tombstone. When slaughter spotted the San Bernardino Grant with its plentiful supply of water, he arranged to buy it from G. Andrade Fo Guaymas Mexico. His claim before the court of private land claims was for 13,746 acres north of the border but only slightly more than a half sitio was confirmed and no appeal was made to the Supreme Court.

He was able to build up one or of the largest spreads in Arizona. Until 1890 Slaughter had a partner, George W. Lang who helped him to accumulate up to 50,000 head of cattle. His brand A"Z" on the right shoulder was the first to be registered in Cochise County.

From 1887 to 1890 the county seat was at Tombstone and the whole Cochise County was infested with cattle rustlers, border bandits, gamblers, and other lawless men. When an offense occurred while Sheriff Slaughter was in office he took to the trail and seldom returned with a prisoner. After cleaning up the county, he concentrated on his ranch.

Slaughter built a rambling ranch mansion of adobe, a village for the cowboys, barns, granaries, and eventually even a school house. Wells were drilled and a concrete dam was constructed to back up a lake. John Slaughter was a prominent cattle king in Arizona until his death in 1922. Two years later his wife Viola, turned the ranch over to John H. Slaughter Ranch Inc. in 1937 the San Bernardino was sold to Marion L. Williams who transferred a 60 foot wide strip stretching for three miles along the border, totaling 21.81 acres to the United States government the following year. In the late 1906's the ranch was purchased by Mr. and Mrs. Paul a Ramsower formerly the operators of super market in Tucson.

I knew the Ramsowers when they had the market on North Dodge at Ft. Lowell and across from the market Mr. Ramsower had a garage and worked on cars. She would take are of the market and Mr. Paul Ramsower took care of the garage.

# BACA FLOAT NO. 3

Don Luis Maria Baca had been grazing several hundred horses, and mules and a flock of sheep and goats, near San Miguel Del Bado. They were having trouble finding grass and water for their stock. They had heard stories form sheep herders about the lush pastures of the Las Vegas Grande and the Rio Gallenas that ran through it. Baca formally applied for a Spanish Land Grant that was confirmed by the proper officials at Durango on May 29th with the title in his pocket Don Luis moved his large family, servants, and live stock to the new ranch. Establishing his headquarters on the site of the present city of Las Vegas, about sixty miles east of Santa Fe, he had been given a grant by Metes and bunds and had no idea how big the grant was. Later years the American surveyor found it contained 496,446.95 acres.

The Baca family prospered on the Las Vegas Grande despite the theft of live stock and the harassment of the field hands by the Navajo raiders. Finally the Navajos burned down most of the buildings on the ranch and drove off all the horses causing Don Luis to fear for the lives of his family. He returned to San Miguel and later settled at Pena Blanca. Don Luis was killed in 1827 by a Mexican soldier who had been refused entrance to the Baca home to search for furs. Some of the American trappers had been trapping without legal papers and they stored them in Baca's home.

After Don Luis's death, the affairs of the huge Baca's clan were taken over by his son Juan Antonio Baca. Later Juan was killed by the Apaches and from there the family seemed to disintegrate and none of them made an attempt to return to Las Vegas. The land was abandoned until 1835 when Mexican citizens interested in colonizing the region successfully, petition Governor Francisco Sarracino at Santa Fe for a grant having identical boundaries as the one given to Baca. The reason for the governor's issuance of conflicting title is not clear.

The conjecture, however, is that he wither found no record in Santa Fe to corroborate the previous Baca ownership because Don Luis petition had been filed with Spanish officials in Durango, or he believed that the grant had been abandoned too long and thus legally had been forfeited by the Baca heirs. At any rate, the new owners moved on the land and began building the town of Las Vegas around a large plaza. By 1839 the town was a favorite stopping place for wagon trains rumbling over the Santa Fe Trail.

The Baca heirs finally protested, arguing that the Colonist was squatting on the Las Vegas grant, but their plea was ignored by the Mexican authorities. Mexican was surveyor General William Pelham acting in accordance with the terms of the treaty of Guadalupe Hildalgo where by legitimate Spanish and Mexican title was to be recognized by the United States. Reported to congress that both the Baca heirs and the citizens of Las Vegas had valid claims.

In 1860 congress gave the five heirs of the Baca's grant each 100,000 acres to pick from the public domain of non mineral land. At this time New Mexico included all the present Arizona and a portion of southeastern Colorado, between the 37th and 38th parallels of latitude. In 1861 all of the territory of New Mexico north of the 37th parallel was transferred to the new territory of Colorado, than in 1863 Arizona was created as a territory separate from New Mexico. So Baca float number one is in New Mexico west of Los Alamos, number 2 is north of Tucumcari. Baca float number 4 is located in the northern part of the San Luis Valley in Sagachi County, Colorado number 3 Baca float is in the south central of Arizona with the northern boundary near Tubac and the south boundary is just north of Guevavi Vistas, and number 5 is west of Prescott. These Baca float measured 12 miles, 36 chains, and 44 links on each side. A surveyor's chain is 66 feet long and a link is one hundredth of a chain or 7.92 inches were slightly less than 12 and on half miles.

The settlement of Tubac, Tumacaori, and Calabasas were within the boundaries to be surveyed. An attempt to survey the Baca float was postponed when the Apaches went on a rampage. Two well known Arizona pioneers Gilbert W. Hopkins and William Wrightson were killed in the vicinity of the Baca Float and now have two peaks named after them. The highest is Wrightson and the next on the west side is Hopkins.

In the 1880's John C. Robinson became the owner of Baca Float number 3 by purchasing the deed from the

Santa Rita Land and Mining Company. Since that time the Baca Float has been divided in many different and complex ways. Today it has many owners, both individuals and corporate. The most famous investor in the grant was Ex-Senator Joseph W. Bailey of Texas. IN 1924 he and a Dallas bank bought 40,000 acres for $250,000 at a sheriff's foreclosed on the holdings of the Baca Float land and Cattle Company. In 1929 the Bouldin family and Wallace Branford deeded a large tract which they had acquired to Tol T. Pendleton and F.M. Daughterty. Most of their land was in the west part of the grant, along the Santa Cruz River and the Tucson Nogales Highway.

In 932 Pendleton and Daughtery formed the Baca Float Ranch Corporation in which others including the Merry Weather family of Nogales have share ownership. Pendleton who had been in the oil business in Texas introduced the cherry red Santa Gertrudes breed of cattle to the Baca Corporation of Baltimore and Florida in 1966. Gulf American which changed its name in 1969 to G.A.C. Properties of Arizona bought the land to subdivide for its multi-million dollar Rio Rico Real Estate Development. There are still large grazing tracts in the eastern part of the grant and several dozen smaller parcels of land along the highway and river south of Tubac which were once a part of Baca Float number 3.

*Opha R. Probasco*

# BACA FLOAT NO. 5

The only land in northern Arizona that can be traced back to Spanish or Mexican Land Grant is Baca Float No. 5 the last of the five float is located in Yavapai Country about fifty miles northwest of Prescott. Most of the land is covered with pine, oak, juniper, and native deciduous trees in addition to miles and miles of pasture and grazing lands. The grant drains into a number of streams that have their sources high upon its wooded slopes which are Burro Creek, flowing to the south Trout Creek to the west, Muddy Creek to the north, and Walnut Creek to the east across the present day Prescott National Forest.

The original deed on this property was recorded in Santa Ana County, territory of New Mexico on June 1, 1871 given to John S. Watts at that time and recorded I the Yavapai County recorder's office a year later by recorder Edmund W. Wells, it indicates that Baca was the progenitor of a large family. Some of eighty six of his heirs signed the document conveying their rights to Baca Float no. 5 then measured as being 99,289.39 acres in area.

Watts who paid $6,800 for Baca Float No.5 didn't hold onto the grant very long. IN 1872 he sold it to William V.B. Wardwell for $30,000 other owners of the grant during the 1870's were Atwater M. Wardwell.

The Yavapai Country records show that the title to Baca Float no. 5 was transferred several times during the last decades of the nineteenth century. Interestingly enough the grant was sometimes sold at a sheriff sale for delinquent taxes. Under the territory law, the highest bidder was given only a tax collectors deed and the owner had six months to redeem his property by paying the taxes due.

Dr. Edward b. Perrin was the owner who started subdividing the grant and letting it go for taxes. He was also the man who bought up the smaller shares. Consolidated the grant, and combined it with thousands of acres of railroad checker board sections, private patented lands in the vicinity of Williams with the forest leases to create on of the largest ranches in the northwest.

A story in the weekly, Arizona Miner, April 6, 1880 tells about Perrin's first arrival at Prescott by stage from California with Dr. George Thornton. A few weeks earlier Perrin had visited the offices of the Atchison Topeka and the Santa Fe Railroad was soon to be built across the northern Arizona. Perrin was willing to speculate that the railroad would increase the Baca Float's value. With George Ruffner, Perrin took a buckboard to look at the grant, which was in the hands of the Merchant's Exchange Bank of San Francisco. Thorton bought it for the amount of $27,500 mortgage on May 6, 1880 and transferred it to Perrin a week later for the same amount. To help defray the cost Perrin sold an undivided five nineteenths share of the grant on May 17th to Burwell B. Lewis of Tuscaloosa, Alabama for $14,000.

It was some time before Perrin turned the ranch into a profitable investment. Baca Float No. 5 was kept intact by the Greene's except for a small parcel of 1,227 acres on the southern edge that was sold in 1940 and became a part of the seven up ranch.

Perrin's holdings and now comprise the Greenway, Bar Cross, Poquette, and Copper Ranches as well as homesteads and subdivisions.

# UNCONFIRMED LAND GRANTS – ARIVACA

Arivaca located thirty miles northwest of Tubac, is another Arizona Ranch like the Canoa, that was owned by Tomas and Ignacio Ortiz. "La Aribac" was at one time a vista of the mission at Guevavi. Abandoned after the Pima uprising in 1751. In 1833 the Ortiz brothers petitioned the Alcalde at Tubac for two sitios at Arivaca to be used for stock raising. They claimed to be legal owners on the basis of an 1812 grant to their father, Augustin Ortiz. Don Augustin had paid $747 and three reales into the treasury at Arispe, after the public auction he was the highest bidder. There was an entry in the treasure's book for that amount. There were no title or expediente containing a record of a survey, appraisements and auctions could be found. The Ortiz brothers asked their ownership of the ranch which had been granted to their deceased father. The official took the testimony of witnesses who swore that the Oribac Ranch had been occupied by the Ortiz family since 1812. The boundaries given for the land were vague. There were four land marks, one towards the north on the high pointed hill that rises on this side of the Tagito

Mine and borders on the Sierra De Buena Vista. The one towards the south standing on this side of the Longorena Mine on a low hill next to the canon covered with trees. The one toward the east standing up the valley from the spring on a mesquite tree that has across cut in it and borders on the Sierra De Las Calaberas and the one towards the west standing at the Punta De Agua on a pointed hill opposite the sierra Del Baboquivari. Despite the lack of a definite location by survey, Sonoran officials approved the Ortiz petition of 1833 and directed that a title to two sitios of land for raising cattle and horses which comprise the place called Aribac be issued, but twenty years later Arivaca was made part of the United States by the Gadsden Treaty and in 1902 the Supreme Court denied confirmation of the grant because of its uncertain location.

# UNCONIFRMED LAND GRANT – EL SOPORI

An old corral and loading shute on the Sopori Ranch

Sopori has been around for a long, long time, its one of the oldest ranches in the Southern Arizona. The first school in Arizona was at the Sopori Ranch which didn't have windows just port holes to shoot at the Apaches.

The word Sopori could be a corruption of Sobaipuri, the name applied to the Pima Indian group in Southern Arizona by Father Kino. For years the Pimas had a Rancheria at Sopori but the place was abandoned in 1751 during the Pima up rising. The Jesuits author of the Rudo

Ensayo described it in 1762 as a depopulated ranch more than two leagues north of Tubac.

There is some evidence that the Sopori Ranch had people living there during he Spanish and Mexican periods but it wasn't the wealthy Joaquin Astiazaran of Sonora who was deeded 31 and 718th sitios and a Caballeria of unoccupied grazing lands stretching from Tubac to San Xavier Mission in 1838. Joaquin supposedly paid $919 for the large tract of land. He never occupied the land but his heirs sold their rights of the unconfirmed grant to American interest after the Gadsden Purchase. The principal negotiator with Theastiazaran family was Sylvester Mowry, a big stock holder in the Sopori Land and Mining Company and the Arizona Land and Mining Company. In 1858 he purchased part of the Mexican claims. Two years later he and the heirs of Astiazaran sold all their interest to the Arizona Company. Most of the people in the territory were surprised to learn of the existence of the grant including Charles Poston who was acquainted with both parties, the American and the Mexican in the transaction.

Mean while the Sopori Land and Mining Company bought out the Americans who occupied the land during the 1850's. Among the latter was Colonel James W. Douglas a colorful Virginian who had served in the Mexican army and C.C. Dodson. As early as 1854 these pioneers were erecting buildings grazing cattle on the nutritious wild grasses and farming the rich bottom lands in the Sopori Valley. Charles Poston, who established Tubac as the headquarters of his mining enterprises in 1856 entertained Douglas at a Christmas feast that year. The Colonel road over from Sopori, Poston explained, with a motley retinue, including a harper and fiddlers three. Another occupant of the Sopori Land was Federick Ronstadt one of about twenty men in the Poston party that rushed in to the Gadsden Purchase region in 1854 to develop mines. With Poston acting as his agent for 114th commission, Ronstadt sold his doubtful claim of four square leagues of land to the Sopori Land and Mining Company for $4000.

The mining company took control of the Sopori Ranch in the late 1850's, under the guidance of a superintendent, the employees occupied the old houses at the Sopori Spring, made a survey, cultivated the land raised cattle, and worked a gold mine. In June 1861 several hundred Apaches swept through the Santa Cruz Valley and killed Richmond Jones Jr. the man in charge, and drove off all the live stock, forcing the company to close down operations. It was in the 1870's before the Apaches let up enough for the Sopori Ranch could be occupied again.

In 1866 the Sopori Land and Mining Company repurchased the interest of the Arizona Company, and began the long struggle for confirmation of a title. Their hope were thwarted in 1881 when surveyor General John Wasson advised rejection of the claim, "On grounds that the original title papers are forged", ante-dated and other wise invalid, while attempting to adjudicate the claim. Wasson heard the testimony of numerous witnesses, including Poston and Pete Kitchen. Poston reacted in his usually forward fashion when advised of the boundaries claimed for the Sopori Grant with the San Xavier Mission Lands on the north Tubac on the south, the Santa Rita's on the east and the Baboquivari Sierra on the west.

After completing his investigation of the Sopori claim, surveyor General John Wasson made his negative report. The secretary of the interior in turn submitted it to congress where it was studied by the Senate Committee on private land claims and ordered printed but no action was taken as usual. Since the status of its title was indefinite, the Sopori Company held on to the grant without having to pay taxes on it. But its claim in 1895 and the United States Supreme Court refused to hear an appeal.

Today the Sopori Ranch is about half the size of the amount rejected. It sprawls out over some 124 sections of desert ranges, including both privately owned patented and leased lands. The country side has changed very little, except the winding road forms the Nogales Highway about forty miles south of Tucson borders fields of cotton and forage crops. The main house is till at the head of the valley. The old adobe ruin which had walls two feet thick and no windows was reconstructed in 1924. Mr. and Mrs. Handman took over the ranch in 1950 have completely modernized the place.

El Sopori Ranch as of today has changed ownership again. It was owned by John Brissot Croll who died June 29, 1999 at a very young as of 59. His son Steve Croll took over the ranch and sold it in 2004, he kept several acres and the headquarters for his home which also has the pioneer cemetery located on the east side of the property. Steve buried his father, John in this same cemetery with a beautiful head stone.

My guess would be that there are between 30 and 40 old pioneers buried in the cemetery, and all of the wooden markers have deteriorated and none is left.

As you enter the old cemetery through a wire gate there is an inscription on a granite stone which reads

"Tread softly here, these stony mounds shelter the bones of Arizona's oldest pioneers".

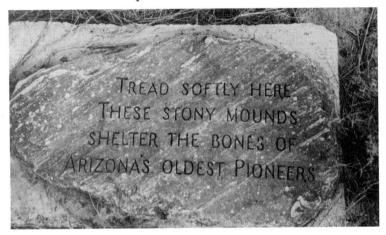

A sign carved in granite as you enter the Old Pioneer's Cemetery on the Sopori Ranch owned by Steve Croll

John Brissot Croll is buried in the north east part of the cemetery with a very nice head stone and well kept.

John Brissot Croll's headstone in the pioneer's Cemetery. He was the owner of the Sopori Ranch.

Ann's headstone in the Pioneer's Cemetery

Ann Pennington died form Malaria; there was an epidemic of Malaria along the Santa Cruz Valley at that time. She was the first of the Pennington's to be buried at this cemetery. In 1868 James Pennington was killed by the Apaches and John had James buried at the pioneer cemetery next to Ann so she wouldn't be there by herself. In

James Pennington's headstone

1869 Elias and Green Pennington were killed by the Apaches were also buried there. Ellen Pennington died with pneumonia in 1869 and the last of the Pennington to be buried at the pioneer cemetery she was 34 years old and her infant son died shortly there after.

Headstone of Elias Green and Ellen Pennington
(Green was the father of the other ones)

Larena and John with the rest of the family decided to return to Texas but at the last minute married John Hemstead Page December 24, 1859. A year later Larcena was captured by the Apaches, she was ill and couldn't keep up so the Apaches lanced her and threw her over a cliff and left her to die. After days of crawling and eating greens of some kind along with what snow she could find she finally made it back to her husband camp. A year later her husband was killed by the Apaches. July 27, 1870 Larcena married Fisher Scott. Scott Street in Tucson was named after him.

Larcena died March 31, 1913 at the age of 76 of unrecorded causes. She was laid to rest in the Tucson Cemetery.

Assorted headstones and grave mounds in the cemetery

Also buried at the pioneer cemetery is Diego Valenzuela, who is the grandfather of "Al" Diego Valenzuela who had a Mexican restaurant he called Gordo's on East Broadway. He used to advertise on the T.V. "Do you like Chimichongas, if you really like Chimichongas, go to Gordo's" on 7701 East Broadway. He died in 2003 and the restaurant closed up.

Diego Valenzuela's headstone also in the Pioneer's Cemetery. His grandson, Al Diego Valenzuela, owned the Gordo's restaurant.

*Opha R. Probasco*

# UNCLAIMED LAND GRANTS – TUMACACORI AND CALABASAS

The history goes back to the Jesuits but it wasn't until 1784 that it became a head mission. Guevavi and Calabasas were vistas but were abandoned near the end of the century, while the Tumacacori continued to prosper. As the herds of cattle and horses increased at the mission under Fray Narciso Gutierrez, the lands became insufficient plus the title had been lost some time before 1806. In the same year Juan Ligarra, governor of Pueblo of Tumacacori, petition the intendente of the province, Don Alejo Garcia Conde, for an adjudication and survey of the land for farming and grazing purposes to replace the old title. Complying with this request Conde issued a royal patent to the Indians of the Pueblo of Tumacacori and instructed Manuel De Leon the commander of the Presidio at Tubac to measure mark off the four square leagues to which each Pueblo was entitle plus two sitios of grazing land which each Pueblo was entitled plus two sitios of grazing land which was occupied by the Pueblo of Calabasas.

In the new title the stipulation was in event the land should be abandoned for a period of three years, any person could claim them.

341

As fate would have it Tumacacori declined during the 1830's and 1840's as did other missions.

The Mexicans abolished the Peace Policy previously used by the Spaniards. As a result the Apaches returned to plunder trail and many of the missions on the northern frontier wee deserted. In 1842 the Mexican government under Santa Anna began selling abandoned church lands valued at $500 or less. By that time Tumacacori though not completely abandoned had declined and was sold in 1844 along with the stock farm of Calabasas and adjacent land to Francisco Aguilar for $500 at a public sale. Actually Aguilar was a stand-in for his brother-in-law Manuel Maria Gandara who got the ranch in operation for a short time during the 1850's.

Gandara was governor of Sonora off and on for two decades, beginning with his appointment by the Mexican President Anatasio Bustamente, in November 1837. At that time Gandara supported strong central government in Mexico City at the expense of states rights. He was opposed on this issue by Jose Cosme Urrea, a Tucson born military hero of the Texas war who was also to serve as governor of Sonora in the 1840's. The centralism versus federalism controversy divided the Sonorans into two factions which waged bloody Civil War until 1846.

Through out this conflict the Apaches stepped up their depredations showing contempt for an ineffective military defense line that was weakened even more by the participation of many Presidio troops in La Guerra Gandara-Urrea.

With the Apache warriors in control of the Sonoran frontier it was 1853 before Gandara could capitalize on the land investment which he held in Aguilar's name. On December 9, 1852 he entered into a partnership with a German named Federico Hulsemann, to develop a hacienda with livestock which he supplied, Luis P. Chambon, Clemente A Payeken, and Carlos Hundhausen, representing the firm of Payeken, Hundausen and Company. Gandara agreed to give up half ownership of the Hacienda and furnish 5,000 sheep, 1000 goats, 100 cows with calves, 100 brood mare, 10 yokes of oxen, 6 pack mules, and 10 horses for use.

The old Calabasas church was converted into a ranch house and Mexican herdsman were soon watching over thousands head of stock. The ranch was an established operation by April 1854 when a large band of Apaches struck only to meet with one of their rare reverses. An Apache squaw had revealed the Indian plan of attack to Gilanin Garcia, the Mexican Commander at Tucson. On the day of the attack Garcia was waiting in readiness at the ranch with sixty Mexican dragoons and forty friendly Apache mansos form Tucson. When the Apaches made their attack, the Mexican Cavalry charged taking the attacker by surprise.

Pete Brady an early Arizona pioneer who was camped near by with Andrew B. gray a railroad survey crew saw the battle.

No cry for mercy was given. The carnage was awful. They killed and butchered as long as there was an Apache in sight. There were only three or four shots fired during the massacre. They were all killed by the Mexican dragoon lances and their brave allies. Don Gilanin and Don Federico invited us over to another part of the courtyard to show us more evidence of the slaughter. It first looked like a string of apples two to three feet long but close inspection they were the ears off of the dead foes.

Later on the Apaches were more successful and forced the abandonment Gandara's operation several months before the arrival of the United States troops in 1856. By 1859 the lands around Tumacacori and Calabasas were full of American squatters. There were enough people to organize a government. But Civil War broke out and the troops were sent to New Mexico. Once again Southern Arizona was paralyzed by the Apaches attacks and the country was soon deserted.

After the Civil War the Americans began to populate the Gadsden Purchase country and the land value increased. IN 1869 Aquilar sold the Tumacacori and Calabasas Grants to Gandara for $499 Charles P. Sykes of San Francisco paid $12,500 in gold coin for the lands in 1878 and sold a 3/16 interest the same year to John Currey, for $9,000. In 1879 Sykes and Currey transferred their interest to some Boston men for $75.000 the new owners organized the Calabasas Land and Mining Company, later the Santa Rita Land and Cattle Company. Sykes remained as director of the company and attempt to attract capital to Calabasas with exaggerated advertisements including one picture of a line of steamers on a river. Sykes built a two story brick hotel he called Santa Rita, and supplied it with walnut furniture through out with Brussell carpet.

Excellent cuisine was served to gala parties from Tucson who came on the railroad via Benson and the distinguished visitors from as far away as England. The hotel was a beehive of activity until 1893 when business fell apart. The Tombstone epitaph gave the place the name of

"Pumpkinville". They did sell all of the lots but no one ever build any houses.

The Sykes heirs lived at Calabasas until 1915 then they moved to Nogales. The Santa Rita hotel deteriorated badly and the ranchers were using it as storage for hay. Then in 1927 the hotel burned down.

The company sought confirmation of its claim to what it was called, Tumacacori, Calabasas, and Guevavi Grants. The surveyor general recommended that congress approve the title for 52,007.95 acres, 17,363.55 acres of arable land and 34,644.40 acres of grass land. The claimants asked the court of private land claims to confirm 81,350 acres. The court refused to recognize the validity of the title issued to Aquilar in 1844. In the opinion of the judges only the national government of Mexico could sell lands form the public domain in 1844. The United States Supreme court heard an appeal of the case in 1898 and upheld the decree of the lower court and there was a fatal want of power to make the sale but most of the Tumacacori lands and a large part of the Calabasas grant including Calabasas itself were part of the Baca Float number 3 grant that the Supreme Court validated in 1914.

# UNCLAIMED LAND GRANTS – LOS NOGALES DE ELIAS

By the decision of the Supreme Court of the United States in the case of Ainsa vs United States, the right of the claimants of the Los Nogales De Elias private land claims was denied and their claims disallowed and the lands included in said claim have been restored to the public domain. So wrote the surveyor general of Arizona George J. Roskruge in 1897 the grant he was referring to was located on the border between the Calabasas Grant in the United States and the Sonoran Ranch. They wanted all the vacant land between the two ranches. The Los Nogales De Elias Grant was for 7-1/2 sitios and 2 caballerias, or 32,763 acres.

On January 7, 1843 a title was issued to Don Jose Elias and his parent Francisco Elias Gonzalez and Balvanera Redondo the owners of the casita and residents of the Pueblo of Imuris. All at he land was classified as desert since there were no running water and was bought for $15 per sitio a total of $113.121-1/2 cents.

The Camou brothers of Sonora secured ownership of one undivided half of Los Nogales De Elias and submitted a claim to surveyor General John Wasson. IN 1881 after having Roskruge survey the grant, Wasson said the title was properly recorded in Sonora and valid and recommended confirmation for the part of the land lying in Arizona territory. That is to say 10,638.68 acres, half which belonged to the Camou brothers and the other undivided half to the legal representative of the original grantees. Congress did not act upon the claim and it came before the court of private land claims in Tucson in 1894.

Separate claims were filed by Juan Pedro Camou, George Hill Howard and Santiago Ainsa. Administrator of Frank Ely, the claimants had acquired the rights to the grant and admitted to owning the lands in common and each pleaded his own case.

On March 30, 1894 the court rejected the claim, explaining that the grant was specific as to quantity but not location. The only effect of the proceedings prior to the issuing of a title was to designate certain out boundaries within which the lands granted could be located but the grantees took no subsequent action prior to the Gadsden treaty to have the limits of their grant surveyed and properly identified. The United States was therefore not bound according to the court to recognize the grant.

# UNCLAIMED LAND GRANT –
# SAN PEDRO

Don Jose De Jesus Perez put in a petition on 1821 to the governor intendente for four sitios of land on to which to raise live stock. Perez asked for the grant, south of the present international line, in the depopulated area near the house of San Pedro, the ancestral home of the Elias family, this house was two or three miles northeast of the abandoned place named Las Nutreas. Perez wanted the survey to be made up stream so the marshy lands and better pastures would be included in the grant. One Antunes of near by Terrenate objected since he claimed part of the area. There was a compromise and the land was divided. After the survey, appraisal, and sale Perez paid $190 ($60 for three and $10 for the fourth) plus tax of $18. The title to the land which lay entirely in the present day Sonora was issued in 1833 not to Perez but to Rafael Elias Gonzalez the owner of San Rafael Del Valle who had bought that land from the petitioner during the interim.

The sons and heirs of Rafael secured over plus lands in addition to the grant of four sitios. Manuel Elias petitioned for the over plus that maybe in the ranch of San Pedro. The Mexican department of public works denied the claim in 1887 because surveyor Pedro Molera could find no monuments that would determine the limits of the ranch.

Over plus lands could not be measured unless the boundaries of the original grant were first located, but the President Porfirio Diaz ordered a title to be given to the Elias family in 1888 for 17,350 acres (four sitios) and an over plus of about 37,150 acres.

While Manuel Elias was working successfully south of the border, his brother Jose Maria Elias was active in the Gadsden Purchase area. Elias was making arrangement for again putting stock on the vast San Pedro Ranch.

The grant is claimed by Don M. Elias, of Sonora and its 36 square miles of territory in the valley of the San Pedro River. The title to this land has never been passed upon under the United States laws. The Reloj Cattle Company had been purchasing quit claim deeds from the Elias heirs for two years. In a case before the court of private land claim sin 1899 the company asked for confirmation for 38,622.06 acres, more than 60 square miles. It's a whopping demand since the Elias deed of doubt validity themselves were for only about 18,000 acres of over plus land. The court reminded the claimants that the officials in Mexico had decided in 1880 the San Pedro had no boundaries and thus no demasias or over plus. Therefore the claim was turned down.

# UNCLAIMED LAND GRANT – AGUA PRIETA

The Agua Prieta Grant was located in Mexico south of the international boundary. But there was an attempt to extend to over plus land into the United States.

On July 21, 1831 Juan Rafael and Ignacio Elias Gonzalez petitioned for more land. The public domain from which the Elias clan wanted to select three tracts which their cattle were already grazing extended as far north as the Chiricahua Mountains. The out boundaries that were listed became important in claims for over plus lands before the American courts.

After the survey and appraisal, the dates for the auctions to be held in Hermosillo were September 15-16-17, 1836.

The Elias petitioners bought the three tracts for the total of $432.50 plus $142.50 for the Agua Prieta. This grant was so named because the center of the survey was a lagoon in the Agua Prieta Valley, south and east of the border town of Douglas.

The American courts later held that the grant was one of quantity of 6 and _ sitios and it was located by the original owners to be entirely south of the international boundary line.

The Camou brothers acquired the rights to the Agua Prieta from the Elias Grantee in 1862.

Then in 1880 the Camou went before the district judge in Guaymas and asked for the over plus in addition. The Elias family contested the claim arguing that they had transferred the cabida legal to the Camous but not the demasias. The final result was an issuance of a title to the over plus to the Hermanos Camou.

Santiago Ainsa administrator for counter claimants to Agua Prieta land, filed a petition of February 28, 1893 with the court of private land claims in Tucson.

He argued that no resurvey of the grant had been made prior to the Gadsden Treaty and that neither the original grantees nor their successors in interest had any knowledge of their legal entitlement under the laws of Mexico and Sonora, to surplus lands with in the outer boundaries described in the papers. Ainsa paid in gold for the over plus and costs for the land as originally surveyed tract. The area delineated on Ainsa's Maps as included in the grant claimed was 163,797.48 acres on nearly 256 square miles of land. Of this claim 68,530.05 acres were in the United States. The claim came before the court in 1899 and was rejected. It was appealed to the United States Supreme Court and on March 17, 1902 their reply was that all the land was entirely south of the International Boundary Line.

# UNCLAIMED LAND GRANTS – TRES ALAMOS

Two attempts were made during the Mexican period to colonize the lands along the San Pedro River north of the Boquillas Grant. In 1831 Lenardo Escalante in the name of eight different empresarios (promoters) was authorized by the congress of Sonora to occupy 58 sitios. The following are limits to the tract. On the north it has the River Gila and the mountains of Pinal, on the south it adjoins the land taken upon the San Pedro River. To the east it extends to a long distant to the Cobre Grande, and on the west it will have the common lands of Tucson. With the Apache up rising it made any attempt to occupy lands impossible.

After the end of the Mexican War in 1848, and before the Gadsden Purchase in 1854 the government of Mexico attempt to colonize the unoccupied frontier with Mexican citizens, hoping to prevent settlements by Americans who might be attempted to seize the lands.

In September 1852 Don Jose Antonio Crespo requested ten square leagues of vacant land for purpose of raising stock and farming at a place on the San Pedro known as Tres Alamos (meaning three cottonwoods). The grant was made by Governor Fernando Cubillas. The recipient was given eight years to take possession and to settle a hundred or more catholic families in the area north of Benson. The terms of the grant were never fulfilled. In 1883 George Hill Howard sought confirmation of the grant after working out an arrangement with Crespo's widow and her family. A clause was included in the agreement where by the Crespo's would be compensated in the event Howard succeeded in getting the title.

Surveyor General J.W. Robbins recommended on September 12, 1883 that Howard's claim be approved for ten square leagues (over 43,000 acres), but Robbins' successor, John Hise revoked this decision and was hailed as a hero by the press and the American settlers in the San Pedro Valley.

Hise's report on the Tres Alamos investigation was printed in the Arizona Daily Star on July 18, 1886 under the heading "Tres Alamos", a great fraud exploded-settler saved!" actually the surveyor general didn't go so far as to call the claim a fraud. He just said that the grant was too indefinite and vague to permit intelligent survey and that the grantee never entered into possession of the alleged tract of "Tres Alamos: nor in any way fulfilled the requirements of the grant. The Tombstone epitaph praised the Hise reported and called him the most fearless surveyor general Arizona ever had.

Howard filed a claim with the court of private land claims in 1893 for 4,384.64 acres of land stretching north from the Boquillas Grant. A co-plaintiff was Francis E. Spencer to who Howard had sold and deeded a share of 18,500 acres in 1883. The court rejected the claim because the grant was made originally on the condition the grantee should settle one hundred families from Spain or South

America on the land upon several other conditions which had not been met at the time of the Gadsden Cesson the United Supreme court refused to review the case.

*Opha R. Probasco*

# FRAUDULENT LAND GRANTS –
# EL PASO DE LOS ALGODONES FRAUD

"The truth is that, with any my personal knowledge and many others the grant was manufactured by the Mexicans subsequent to the treaty, is antedate, fraudulent and forgery". So wrote Charles D. Poston in 1893 after the court of private land claims, Poston went on to accuse the new court of bribery or stupidity. He said the people of Arizona had endured the Apaches, famine, and thirst. Some pioneers had waited nearly forty years in the wilderness for the government to organize tribunel to settle land titles and their first act is to confirm a forgery.

The government appealed the Algodones case to the Supreme Court where the decision of the land court was revered in 1898. In a rehearing a year later the higher court stayed with its decision.

The grant was for five sitios along the Colorado River between the Gila on the north and the Algodones pass on the south. The petitioner, Fernando Rodriguez of Hermosillo said the lands applied for were situated in a desert country which the Indians had made uninhabitable. The appraisers valued the land at $400 because it could be irrigated with the water from the Gila River.

It was as unusual for citizens of Mexico to petition for grants of land which could not be occupied as it was for Mexico authorities to grant lands with no condition to inhabit them.

Poston recalled that no settlement had been attempted as of 1854 when he had the original town site of present day Yuma surveyed, and there wasn't anyone in the vicinity.

According to the records in Sonora, the rights to the grant was sold in 1845 to Juan A. Robinson of Guaymas and transferred in 1873 to the Colorado Commercial and Land Company. To satisfy the company government withdrew the lands from entry on January 9, 1875 and agreed to study the claim. The investigation of surveyor General John Wasson in 1879 showed that the original title papers recorded in the Toma De Razon had been antedated and forged. Spanish documents expert R.C. Hopkins discovered that the signature of one Jose Justo Milla an auditor in Treasure General Jose Mendoza's office was not genuine in one place Milla's given names were written Jose Jose instead of Jose Justo a very unlikely mistake on a document of such importance.

The secretary of interior continually urged congress to place the lands in the public domain and open them to settlements. Finally a motion made by Arizona's delegate in congress Marcus A. Smith to reject the Lagoons Grant as fraudulent was passed by the house committee on private land claims.

The new claimant Earl B. Coe presented his case before the court of private land claims and mentioned above, secured confirmation for 21,692 acres not with standing some irregularities in the title papers. The Southern Pacific Railroad was given a quit claim deed to its right of way through the Lagoons, and the Yuma territorial penitentiary was left in public hands despite being on the grant. After this decision the owners of the grant began selling deeds to settlers. They in turn thought they had secured Bona Fide titles to their lands and started improvements and permanent homes. The effect of the Supreme Court 1898 and 1899 decisions reversing the Londoners claim was to restore the lands to the public domain. Congress passed an act on January 14, 1901 to relieve the occupants. By this law all the lands in the grant were opened to entry on March 18 of that same year. Congress gave prior rights to Bona Fide settlers who were on the land before the Supreme Court's decision of May 25, 1898. Each person was limited to 40 acres and required to pay $1.25 per acre, after proving possession. Additional land could be homesteaded for 160 acres.

# PERALTA REAVIS FRAUD

Of more than eleven million acres of land claimed in Arizona under Spanish or Mexico title, only about 120,000 acres, exclusive of the Baca Float, were confirmed. Most of the rejected acreage was in the fraudulent claim of James Addison Reaves, a master crook who first came to Arizona about 1880 as a subscription agent for the San Francisco examiner. With a vivid imagination and a developed talent for forgery, Reaves nearly succeeded in pulling off one of the most gigantic swindles in history.

He spent years in altering, adding, and replacing records in the depositories of Spain and Mexico. He was an ex-confederate soldier and a Missouri street car conductor. He went to Tucson in March, 1883 to file a sheaf of documents with surveyor General J.W. Robbins to prove his claim to the Peralta Grant.

Reaves invented a family lineage starting with Don Nemesis Silva De Peralta De La Cordoba. With the fictitious data Reaves had accumulate, Peralta was given the title of Baron De Los Colorado by King Ferdinand Vi of

Spain in 1748 and also an extensive grant of land in the northern province to go with it. Reaves said he had acquired title to the Peralta Grant from George willing a mine developer from the east. Willing supposedly had purchased the deed from a descendant of the original Baron De Los Colorado's, a poverty stricken Mexican named Miguel Peralta. Miguel only existed as a character in the forged deeds and transfers. George Willing couldn't testify since he died in Prescott the next day after Reaves recorded the deed in March 1874. Reavis found a Mexican orphan girl and had her educated and later made her his wife giving her the title of Baroness of Arizona. He changed the church birth records in California making his bride the last surviving descendant of the Peralta family.

In September 1887 Reavis applied for a survey of the fictitious Peralta-Reavis claim. It was a large rectangle of land, stretching from northwest of Phoenix to the south of Silver city, New Mexico, including the cities of Phoenix, Tempe, Mesa, Globe, Clifton, Solomonville, Casa Grande, and Florence. The Southern Pacific Railroad paid Reavis $50,000 even through the claim was never validated in any court and others paid him for quit claim deed to their homes, farms, mines, businesses, and even schools. Even a couple of famous lawyers, Rosco Conkling and Robert Ingersoll checked out the fraudulent documents and found them to be good in law and unassailable in court plus millionaires Charles Crocker and Collis P. Huntington said the claim in search of historical evidence. With this income Reavis maintained homes in St. Louis, Washington D.C., Madrid, and Chihuahua City and traveled in royalty.

Mean while the investigation of the Peralta claim being conducted by the surveyor General Robbins died of tuberculosis and was succeeded by Royal A. Johnson the chief clerk, and a well trained lawyer and his interest in the claim was indicated by the advice which he gave to his father, a New York attorney to refuse a retaining fee offered by Reavis.

The newspapers and the citizens criticized Johnson for dallying around but they became his admirers when he released his carefully prepared expose of the fraudulent Peralta Grant in 1889 his analysis of the documents disclosed several forgeries and historical inaccuracies which led him to the conclusion that the Reavis claim was spurious and should be rejected.

This is some of Johnson's observations, one noticeable feature is that no will is produced, he didn't even own a watch, had no money, heir looms or even books, carriages, or that inseparable companion of the average Mexican, a horse. In the will of the grantee in 1783 and the codicil of 1788 not a thing is devised but the Peralta Grant. Are we to be asked to credit a showing that a grantee of Spain a man under the immediate patronage of a great king, a friend of the viceroy and a captain of dragoons possessed nothing in the world that he could leave his child except this very land claim, which is so essential, should be trace din these wills.

Reavis was placed under arrest and after a year of legal maneuvering was convicted of conspiracy to defraud the government. He was fined $5,000 and sentenced to two years in prison as a convict no. 964 in the penitentiary at Santa Fe, New Mexico.

# EARLY MORMON MISSIONS

The first Moron Mission entered into Arizona around 1854 but the Navajos were on the war path and by 1855 the Mormons were driven out. Sometime between 1858 and the early 1870's Jacob Hamblin the Mormon's trail blazer made several missions into Arizona locating river crossings, water holes, and trails to travel on. By this time the Navajos were at peace.

The primary mission of the church was expansion. With the leader ship of Brigham Young, the Mormons wanted to establish an empire form Utah to California and south to the Salt River Valley and eventually to Sonora, Mexico. The settlements at Kanab (Utah) Pipe Springs, and Lee's Ferry would serve as bases to launch new settlements in Arizona. The first expedition into Arizona was on the Little Colorado River Valley. The scouts reported it was unsuitable and no fit place for humans to live.

In spite of the bad reports from the scouts by late May 1873 there were hundred colonists that arrived on the Little Colorado after a miserable journey from Meonkopi,

Washington. One journal referred to the Little Colorado as a loathsome and disgusting a stream as there is on the continent. The dispirited colonist soon packed their gear and returned to Utah. But Brigham Young was still determined to establish a colony in the valley of the Little Colorado River and after three years he succeeded.

The major figure in the Mormon colonization along the Colorado River was a red-headed frontiersman named Lot Smith which was remembered for his attacks on the United States army supply trains during the Mormon War in 1857 and 1876. A mission was established at the Hopi community at Moencopi. Over the next two years Smith and their church leaders William A. Allen, George Lake, and Jesse O. Ballinger led parties of colonists to the lower Colorado River Valley near today's Joseph city, Sunset crossing (Winslow) and Holbrook. Town sites were marked, irrigation ditches dug, dams erected, and crops planted. The Mormons had finally taken a permanent root in Arizona.

There were four colonizing parties with about fifty in each. They established camps and named them after their captains. Later, Lake Camp became Obed, Smith's camp changed to Sunset, Ballinger's Camp became Brigham City, and Allen's Camp became St. Joseph and later Joseph City. Sunset and Brigham City were located on opposite side of the Little Colorado River near the site of present day Winslow. The four communities constructed forts of cottonwood logs and sandstone. The forts were self contained units including mess halls and housing. The average size was about tow hundred feet square with walls reaching seven to nine feet. Guard houses at each corner and each community had shops, cellars, store houses, and wells in case of prolonged siege. St. Joseph was the only one of the four communities to survive and is considered the oldest Mormon Colony in Arizona. In 1880's the other three succumbed to the rampaging Little Colorado River. In 1939 the river was tamed by constructing a durable dam.

The Little Colorado or Rio Chiquito was known by the Navajo as Tol-Chuco meaning red or bloody. Coronado named it Rio De Lino, or Flax River due to the wild flax growing on the banks of the river. In 1604 explorer Don Onate named it Rio Colorado or Red River. The head waters are near the 11,470 foot elevation and empties into the Grand Canyon after cutting a two hundred fifty mile gorge south across the Colorado plateau. Although the Little Colorado isn't known as some of the others but the ones who know the Little Colorado River had become to love it, feared it and respect it.

# LEE'S FERRY

A few miles north of Marble Canyon is Lee's Ferry the noted river crossing on the Hamblin Road to Utah. In 1864 Jacob Hamblin made his crossing at the confluence of the Paria and Colorado Rivers.

John Doyle Lee arrived here in 1871. He was a fugitive from justice and he figured that this place was as good as any to hide out. John Wesley Powell passed through on his second Grand Canyon expedition with an extra boat which he gave to Lee and he converted it into a ferry boat.

John Lee was an early convert to the Mormon Church, joining in 1838. During the Mexican War Brigham Young sent him to collect on behalf of the church wages due members of the Mormon Battalion. A few years later Lee was living in Southern Utah near one of the immigrant trails to California. Some of the travelers were old adversaries from Missouri where a lot of blob shed had taken place a few years earlier. On September 11, 1857 Lee and some more Mormons organized a Paiute Indian attack on a wagon train. The battle lasted four days before the Mormons offered the immigrants refuge if they give up their arms. As soon as the immigrants had placed themselves in their custody the Mormons killed all of the adults 140 of them leaving only seventeen children to young to witness any of the Mormons.

When the word got out of the killing there was an up roar against the Mormons and they wanted the guilty ones brought to justice. The church decided that John Lee should be the one who was responsible. Lee claimed he had orders from Salt Lake City then he headed for the hills as a fugitive. The United States Marshall caught with him at Lee's Ferry in 1874. At his trail Lee said he was being made a firing squad at Mountain Meadows where the massacre took place. On March 2, 1877 Lee sat in his coffin while the Marshall read his death warrant. Several of his sons were there but wee kept at a safe distance, because the lawmen were afraid they may attempt to rescue him.

Lee stood in his coffin and faced the five riflemen and told them that he was ready to die. Five shots were fired and a dark chapter in the Moron history was thought to have ended. For seventy three years the church denied they had any involvement. IN 1950 Juanita Brooks a Mormon wrote a controversial book about the incident called "The Mountain Meadow's Massacre", because of her book and pressure from Lee's many descendant (he had nineteen wives) the church in 1961 reinstated him to full membership. Lee's old ferry operation continued until 1928 when a bridge was built over the Colorado River.

# WHO NAMED ARIZONA?

William A. Douglass director of the Basque studies program at the University of Nevada in Reno had a theory that the name of Arizona had originated from the Basque immigrants to New Spain. Some doubters tried to discredit Douglass's theory and that it may have applied the name to an area south of the International Border between the United States and Mexico. The problem the critics had was the understanding of the Basque language and her arguments. In her 1978 article on "The Silver of El Real De Arzonac", Historian Patricia Roche Herring said the second problem was the fascination of the bolas y planchas, the romance of silver and man's imagination. In other words virtually every published account of the 1736 discovery of the bolas y planchas (or balls and chunks of silver) had been composed of ninety percent romance and tem percent historical fact. A deeper look into primary materials points strongly to the Basque origins of "Arizona". Douglass put forth two possibilities for the Basque origins of meaning of "Arizona". First the existence of a royal mining camp or district named "Arizonac" the name might come from the Basque words arri (rock) ona (good) with the letter C added makes it plural.

As second possibilities that Arizonac may derive from the plural combination of the basque word ortiz (oak) and ona (good). Any basque speaker anywhere would recognize aritz onak as "The good oak trees". Before getting into a discussion of how the name possibly came about and whether it was "Arizona or Arizonac". Both made sense in the basque language.

The story begins in October of 1736 when the largest Spanish settlement in northwestern Sonora was the newly established Real De Minas of Nuestra Senora De La Limpia Concepcion Del Agua Caliente lies ten air miles south of the Arizona Sonora border and eighteen air miles southwest of Nogales, Sonora.

A tiny settlement of few ranch houses in the narrow Planchas De Plata Canyon. Now as in 1736 there is what modern English speaking cowboys would all a line camp in La Cienega Canyon near its confluence with the Poanchas De Plata a stone through away from Agua Caliente. It was known as Arizona, several people were living in Arizona in 1736 and two or three times as many at Agua Caliente. They were mostly prospectors who searched the mountains to the north for mineral deposits. It's not clear where Agua Caliente ended and Arizona began.

A little over twenty air miles northeast of the Agua Caliente and Arizona settlements (four miles east of Nogales) across the mountain terrain was an older and larger Spanish settlement. Located in the San Luis and upper Santa Cruz River Valleys which today straddles the

International border where two missions Guevavi and Suamca, a number of ranches and Pima Rancherias. Although in 1736 the majority of the ranches were in the San Luis Valley. On a hill between the San Luis Valley settlements and Agua Caliente a Yaqui Indian (Antonia Siraumea) a prospector stumbled upon some large chunks of almost pure silver. From his home in Agua Caliente he returned t the site with some of his children to help look for more pieces of the silver. News of the discovery spread like wild fire and Francisco De Longoria of Agua Caliente filed the first claim at the site Jose Fermin De Almazan who discovered a large slab weighing about 2500 pounds chipped off some pieces and rode over the mountain to Diego Romero's Ranch in San Luis where he traded the silver for trade goods.

Justicia Mayor (Chief Justice) of Sonora Juan Bautista De Anza heard of the discovery while he was conducting court at the village of Bacanuchi 90 miles away, on Tuesday November 13, 1736 Anza was also Capitan Vitalicio (Captain for life) Antonio Sirawmea, who found the silver asked Captain Anza to make all the late comers pay him so much of their silver. But Captain Anza thought the silver was some one's buried treasure instead of a natural vein. If that's the case than all the metal belongs to the king, but if it is a vein then all the miners would have to file claims and the king would get a five percent of the total ore extracted. Three Jesuit priest, Captain Anza, and some soldier escorts set out to the discovery site. Stopping on his way to the Guevavi Ranch to pick up his foreman and cousin by marriage Manuel Jose De Sosa Anza. After arriving at the site which he named after his patron saint, San Antonio De Padua on November 20 and began taking depositions. There were 400 people there digging in the ground for more of the Bolas Y Planchas. Anza quickly put a stop to the illegal prospecting. He first put an embargo on the silver until it could be determined how much belonged to the king. He then rode twelve miles down the canyon to Benardo De Urrea's house the place called Arizona. Anza stayed at his house from November 20th to November 3rd dictating orders that impounded all the silver that had been found. In doing so he seems to have brought Arizona to the fore ground and left San Antonia Padua in obscurity.

In all sixteen important documents dictated to Manuel Jose De Sosa ad signed by Anza wee written and dated at Benardo De Urrea's house in El Puesto De Arizona. Anza also took statements from individuals who filed a petition for the return of the impounded silver. In the next several years in other areas of Sonora and as far away as Mexico City the place called Arizona became confused with the place called San Antonio Anza appointed several miners to take samples and assay the silver. Just as Anza was about to mount his horse, he was presented with a petition form fifteen residents of the Real De Agua Caliente asking him to lift the embargo as soon as possible so they cold get their silver back. Instead Anza tightened security at the site of the discovery.

In January of 1737 after all the silver had been impounded Anza sent Sosa to Mexico City with copies of all the letters, orders, dispatches, and petitions pertaining to the silver discovery.

Two court cases emerged Ruiz De Ael petitioned the high court through appointed lawyers in Mexico City to order Anza to return the silver that Ael had accepted in trade and Anza had impounded. Investigation of the Plancas De Plata shifted to Mexico City in his report to the royal tribunal. The state attorney Ambrosio Melgarejo argued that the silver was a treasure, hidden by some ancient people therefore all the silver belongs to the king. Five of the six members of the Real Acuerdo believed the same way but felt farther investigation was necessary. The sixth member's opinion was that it was a natural vein. Viceroy Juan Antonio De Vizarron Y Equiarreta the Archbishop of Mexico followed the majority and ordered further assays and studies.

One June 8, 1737 Vizarron instructed Anza to immediately with the most expert miners of those regions to survey the make up and quality of the land in the canyon where the silver was found and find out how the silver chunks had been produced. Anza estimated that it would take him three weeks to gather a group of expert miners at the site from 150 miles away. On August 8th Anza and his miners convened at San Antonio De Padua where the authorities unanimously agreed that the silver had come from several natural veins.

Satisfied he had resolved the issue Anza went to Agua Caliente where he lifted the embargo and returned everyone's silver minus the king's fifth and the deductions for expenses during the investigation going back to the discovery site he surveyed a 140 0square foot claim and registered it to Antonio Siraumea. He also had a 300 pound piece chiseled from Almazan's one ton Plancha and ordered it to be sent to Mexico City for further study and since Almazan's claim had been confirmed he would be paid for the sample. Melgarejo wasn't satisfied with the decision of Anza's and wanted true experts be sent to further study the site of discovery of the silver. The controversy raged on and off for a decade, even after several of the principals had passed on Anza was killed by the

Apaches may 9, 1740 and Archbishop Vizarron left office as Viceroy in August of the same year. On orders form the king Viceroy Pedro Cebrain of Agustin Count of Fuenclara reopened the investigation on May 20, 1743. In a report a year later facts were starting to become garbled, instead of identifying the site of the silver discovery as the Cerro (Hill) of San Antonio De La Arizona. They even dropped San Antonia entirely and referred to it as the Cerro De La Arizona. The name Arizona quickly replaced San Antonio in eighteenth century documents. But contrary to popular belief it was not until the twentieth century that Arizonac replaced Arizona as the name of the discovery site.

In the 185 Folios of original documents beginning on November 15, 1736 and ending July 8, 1738 in the Archive General de La Nacion, Arizona is mentioned thirty five times. Arizonac is not mentioned once. Although there are numerous references to Arizona in other documents between 1738 and the end of the eighteenth century not one calls it Arizonac.

# GEORGE W.P. HUNT – ARIZONA'S FIRST STATE GOVERNOR

George W.P. Hunt was born in 1859 at Huntsville, Missouri a town his grandfather founded. His family's wealth in land and slaves was largely lost due to the Civil War. George as boy had very little schooling he always had a problem with grammar.

At the age of eighteen George, left home to seek his fortune in the Colorado gold fields. HE wasn't any good in prospecting so he drifted across New Mexico into the White Mountains of Arizona. In October of 1881 he walked into the town of Globe wearing overalls and leading a burro. He took a job as a writer in Pasco's Restaurant and later he quit and just took assorted jobs around town. One job he had he worked his way up from a delivery boy to being the President of the Old Dominion Commercial Company. This company operated a large general store and bank in Globe. By 1900 Hunt was one of the most prosperous men in the country.

George W.P. Hunt's political career began with his election to the territorial legislature in 1892. Among the laws he authored was a bill offering a $5,000 reward for the capture of the Apache kid. Hunt go the first compulsory school attendance law passed in 1899 and an antigambling bill in 1907. He grew in stature during seven terms in the legislature. In 1910 George Hunt was chosen president of the constitutional convention. His efforts to get the constitution Ratified by the voters launched him into state wide politicking and into the governor's chair. Hunt identified himself with the organized labor and the people understood his manner of speaking, being it simple and direct and they weren't bothered about his unpolished English. He maintained his power in politics by listening to the voters and their needs. He traveled over the state in the back seat of an automobile studying the people in different towns he's going to go through, than he would bring his files up to date on his return trip back to Phoenix.

Hunt always had trouble with the legislature even though they were Democrats, there was no party loyalty. Hunt said that they were a do nothing group. The law makers passed a penal code over his veto which was later approved by the voters in 1914. This code was provided for capitol punishment and also set up a board of pardons and paroles.

The governor could not grant a pardon, reprieve, or commutation with out the approval of the board that the legislature had set up.

A test had come up on 1915; Hunt gave an unconditional pardon without the board approval, to a convicted murderer. Hunt's friend, Warden Robert B. Sims refused to release the convict from the State Prison. The Arizona Supreme Court upheld the penal code and the board's power over pardons.

By the end of Hunt's first term the conflict between the governor and the legislature continued during most of the states history. In the 1914 election Hunt defeated republican Ralph Cameron by 8,000 votes, and was inaugurated on January 4, 1915 and still had his troubles with the state legislature.

During the world one era 1914-1918 Arizona had labor problems especially in the copper mines. Governor Hunt was in sympathy with the miners particularly the Mexicans who were paid at a lower wage. Hunt worked with both sides to try and settle the strikes. He sent the National Guards to Clifton and Morenci to prevent violence. He also issued a public call for relief contributions to help families of strikers. The strike was finally settled.

Hunt was elected governor in 1911, 1914, 1916, 1922, 1924 and 1930. His close call was in 1916, the republican candidate Thomas E. Campbell appeared to be the winner by 30 votes 27,976 to 27,946. Campbell was inaugurated on New Years Day 1917; Hunt refused to leave his office and demanded a recount. When Judge R.C. Stanford ruled against him, he appealed to the Supreme Court which ruled in his favor. The higher court threw the ballots of voters who marked an X beside the name of Campbell in the Republican column and another X for a straight Democratic ticket. It was clear that these voters had intended to vote for all Democrats except Hunt. But they did not use the correct procedure to vote a split ticket.

Campbell gracefully moved out of the capitol. He had served one year without pay.

Hunt did not run in 1918 for he was appointed minister to Siam by President Woodrow Wilson. After his wife and daughter had returned to Arizona Hunt got bored and later returned to Arizona also and ran for governor again. He was elected in 1922, 1924, and 1926.

George W.P. Hunt never did like capitol punishment and always fought for the abolition. He said it was legalized killing and compared it to the burning of witches. Hunt also worked for better prisons, minimum wage laws, improved highways and a bigger share of the Colorado River for Arizona.

In 1924 Governor Hunt put an embargo on cattle from California due to the hoof and mouth disease which he tired to stop the spread of. He also ordered motorist and trains form California stopped at the Colorado River. All travelers had to pass through a corrugated iron disinfecting station. While they took showers, their cloths were sprayed. Their autos and baggage were steamed. Railroad cars were fumigated. No passenger could get off the train in Arizona without a certificate from the board of health. Hunt stationed the Arizona National Guard at the disinfection stations to enforce the embargo. California newspapers called it "Hunt's Folly". After four months Governor Hunt lifted the embargo.

Hunt was defeated by Republican John C. Phillips in 1928. Restless in retirement he took a trip around the world and returned to Phoenix in time to win his last term in 1930.

Two years after he was defeated in the Democratic Primary by Benjamin B. Moeur, a Tempe doctor in 1934. Hunt did the unforgivable by his code, he supported the Republican candidate.

He was completely bald and was called "Old Roman", he died on December 24, 1934 and was buried beside his wife on a hill in Papago Park in East Phoenix.

Governor George W. P. Hunt used convicts on roads and other public projects. It was the convicts that built the Tempe bridge across the Salt River in 1913.

## About the author

Coming to Tucson, Arizona in 1925 as a six year-old child was a dramatic change in my life after living on a farm thirty two miles from Sterling, Colorado. Our farm was southeast from Sterling on the prairie, where our closest neighbor was one half mile away and the Lone Star School we went to was five miles south of us.

When we arrived in Tucson the population was 25,000 and coming out of the horse and buggy stage. The Indians on the reservation were still using horses and buggies for transportation. There wasn't an automobile on the reservation that belonged to the Papago tribe. Mr. Nelson who was the agent for the Indians did have an automobile.

By the time I was sixteen years-old I was working along side of grown men and collecting the same pay, which was $5.00 a ten hour day. I was one of an eight man crew. We were using Allis Chalmers Semi Diesel Cats, building dirt reservoirs for all of the ranchers on both sides of the Sasabe Road southwest of Tucson. I was with them for a year and half, sleeping in a tent on the ground. We had one gas lantern and the cook had it. We didn't have a cooler or any kind of a heater. It was sure hot-t-t in the summer with plenty of flies and cold-d-d in the winter.

I saw Tucson grow up through the eyes of a child, teenager, a young man and as an adult. I listened to a lot of stories told by the old timers, some good and some bad. The history of Tucson and Arizona kind of grew on me and the more I heard, the more I was fascinated by it. It was after I had gotten out of school and watched the change coming to our town that I wanted to know more about it's history. It was after the World War Two when the big change came. People from all over were entering our state in droves and are still coming.

I fell in love with Arizona and Tucson a long time ago so much that I wanted to write about some of the history on both.

The stories you hear now only go back as far as some people remember. That's only forty or fifty years, and some of that is only hearsay. This book is history. I am sure you will enjoy the reading of *KEEPING OUR HISTORY ALIVE.*